WHEN GOD BECOMES MY ENEMY

WHEN GOD BECOMES MY ENEMY

The Theology of the

Complaint Psalms

by

Ingvar Fløysvik

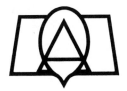

Concordia Academic Press
A Division of
Concordia Publishing House
Saint Louis, Missouri

BS
1445
,L3
F56
1997

Unless otherwise noted, Scripture quotations are translations by the author.

The LaserHEBREW™ and LaserGREEK™ fonts used in this publication are available from Linguist's Software, Inc., P.O. Box 580, Edmonds, WA 98020-0580, telephone (206) 775-1130. E-Mail 75507.1157@compuserve.com

Library of Congress Cataloging-in-Publication Data

Fløysvik, Ingvar, 1959-
    When God becomes your enemy: the theology of the complaint psalms / by Ingvar
    Fløysvik.
        p.   cm.
    Includes bibliographical references.
    ISBN 0-570-04263-1
    1. Bible. O. T. Psalms—Criticism, interpretation, etc. 2. Laments in the Bible
I. Title
BS1445.L3F56   1997
223 '. 206—dc21   97–34972

Library of Congress Cataloguing-in-Publication Data

To

Helga,

Hanna, Pål, and Marion

Acknowledgments

This study is a slight revision of my dissertation submitted to Concordia Seminary, St. Louis, in 1994. I want to thank my advisor Dr. Paul R. Raabe for many useful suggestions along the way and for quick and thorough responses to materials submitted to him. He has been most helpful throughout this project. Also, I would like to thank the readers, Dr. Jacob A. O. Preus III, who spent much time correcting my poor English, and Dr. Arthur D. Bacon.

The Director of Graduate Studies at Concordia Seminary, Dr. Wayne E. Schmidt, has been very supportive, making sure that every practical matter during my stay here would run as smoothly as possible. Very much to his credit, it has been a pleasure to be an overseas student at the Graduate School of Concordia Seminary.

I want to thank Norwegian Lutheran Mission, which has given full financial support during my studies.

In a work on the Old Testament, where one is so dependent on the Hebrew language, it is also appropriate to thank Dr. Ebbe E. Knudsen, Director to the Semitic Institute at the University of Oslo, who taught me Hebrew.

Finally, much of the credit for this work goes to my wife, Helga, who has had to bear more than her share of the responsibilities for home and family and has done so with a loving attitude and an excellent manner.

Contents

List of Abbreviations 10

Part One: Introduction 11
1. Introduction 13
   Translation.. 16
   Terminology 17
   The Subgenre of the "Complaint Psalms"........................... 18
   Structure and Interpretation.. 21
   Theological Questions... 23

Part Two: The Texts... 25
2. Psalm 6 27
   Translation.. 27
   Translation Notes 32
   Structure 38
   Strophes 38
   Stanzas.. 39
   Progression in Content and Mood 40
   The Problem 45
   The Prayer 45
   The Appeal 45
3. Psalm 44 47
   Translation.. 47
   Translation Notes 49
   Structure 59
   Strophes 59
   Stanzas.. 59
   Progression in Content and Mood 60
   The Problem 66
   The Prayer 66
   The Appeal 67

4. Psalm 74 68
   Translation.. 68
   Translation Notes 69
   Structure 83
   Stanzas.. 83
   Progression in Content and Mood............................... 85
   The Problem 91
   The Prayer 91
   The Appeal 92
5. Psalm 88 93
   Translation.. 93
   Translation Notes 94
   Structure 106
   Stanzas.. 106
   Progression in Content and Mood............................... 107
   The Problem 111
   The Prayer 111
   The Appeal 112
6. Psalm 90 113
   Translation.. 113
   Translation Notes 114
   Structure 124
   Strophes 124
   Stanzas.. 126
   Progression in Content and Mood............................... 126
   The Problem 131
   The Prayer 131
   The Appeal 132

Part Three: Theological Assumptions and Implications.................... 133
7. Theological Assumptions and Inplications—Introduction 135
   Structure and the Progression in Content and Mood 135
   The Problem 138
   Disasters Interpreted as Caused by God's Wrath.................... 138
   God's Wrath as the Heart of the Problem 140
   The Character of God's Wrath.................................... 142
   General 142
   Terminology for God's Wrath.................................... 144

God as Absent and Indifferent 146
God as Actively Hostile 149
The Absence and Hostility of God Viewed Together 151
Why is God Angry?..152
The Prayer 155
Presuppositions for the Prayer...155
The Contents of the Prayer..159
The Appeal 162
Appeal to Yahweh's Abiding Character 162
Appeal to Yahweh's Relation to His People 169
Appeal to Yahweh's Reputation...173
Other Appeals..174
Conclusion... 175
Selected Bibliography... 177

Abbreviations

BDB	F. Brown, S. R. Driver, and C. A. Briggs, *A Hebrew and English Lexicon of the Old Testament*
BHS	*Biblia Hebraica Stuttgartensia*
CBQ	*Catholic Biblical Quarterly*
CJ	*Concordia Journal*
Even-Shoshan	*A New Concordance to the Old Testament*
GKC	*Gesenius' Hebrew Grammar*
JBL	*Journal of Biblical Literature*
Jastrow	*A Dictionary of the Targumim, the Talmud Babli and Yerushalmi, and the Midrashic Literature*
Joüon - Muraoka	*A Grammar of Biblical Hebrew*
JSOT	*Journal for the Study of the Old Testament*
KB	L. Koehler and W. Baumgartner, *Hebräisches und Aramäisches Lexikon zum Alten Testament* (3rd. edition)
KTU	*Die keilalphabetischen Texte aus Ugarit*
TWAT	*Theologisches Wörterbuch zum Alten Testament*
Waltke - O'Connor	*An Introduction to Biblical Hebrew Syntax*
ZAW	*Zeitschrift für die alttestamentliche Wissenschaft*
ZTK	*Zeitschrift für Theologie und Kirche*
§	Paragraph (The grammars are referred to by paragraph rather than by page)

PART ONE

INTRODUCTION

Chapter One

Introduction

The experience of being forgotten, rejected, or even attacked by God has been very real for people of all times. An untimely death in the family, prolonged sickness, unfair treatment in the community or in court, or, on the larger scale, natural disasters, war and persecution; these and other catastrophes may make individuals or whole communities perceive God as being an enemy. Readers of the Hebrew Bible recognize that in some psalms the psalmists shared these perceptions. They complained to God that he had abandoned them or had become angry with them. The present study is an investigation into the theology of these psalms. We will approach them with the question: What did the faithful in ancient Israel do when their experiences led them to perceive God as being an enemy? What theological assumptions underlie these psalms?

This aim also puts some limitations on the scope and focus of this study. It is first of all a study of the theology in a particular group of psalms within the Hebrew Psalter. We do not claim to write a theology of the book of Psalms. Nor do we presume to cover all the literature in the Hebrew Bible where God is viewed as being hostile. The relationship between the book of Job, the book of Lamentations, and several complaints in the book of Jeremiah to the complaint psalms would certainly be a valuable study, but it would exceed the limits of what is possible to do in this study. Therefore this study is limited to the complaint psalms. This is a study of Hebrew psalms and not a comparative study. Mesopotamia has a very ancient and rich lament literature, some items of which show distinct similarities to the body investigated here.[1] Also, Egypt has handed down to us some lament

---

[1] A good example and a fine piece of literature is "Prayer of Lamentation to Ishtar," J. B. Pritchard, ed., Ancient Near Eastern Texts Relating to the Old Testament, 3rd. edition with supplement (Princeton, NJ: Princeton University Press, 1969), 383-385.

psalms.[2] It is our conviction, however, that we first have to work with the psalms in their own context and evaluate their precise function in their own religious system before a meaningful comparison across ethnic and religious borders can be made. This has not always been observed in comparative studies, with the result that superficial parallels have been highlighted while possible differences in function have been ignored. Our aim is to study the theological assumptions of ancient Israelite believers. Therefore we will not deal with the use of these psalms in the New Testament,[3] by the church fathers, or by the reformers.[4] We will work merely within an Old Testament framework and aim to answer the question mentioned above. Though the books on Psalms are legion, as far as we know no one has approached the complaint psalms specifically to investigate how the believers of ancient Israel handled God's anger.

Five psalms have been selected for in-depth study: Psalms 6, 44, 74, 88, and 90. These psalms are representative of the body of psalms in which the psalmist expresses his experience of God as an enemy. Psalms 6 and 88 are individual psalms where a near-death experience, probably associated with severe sickness, is central. Examples of similar psalms are Psalms 13, 22, and, to some extent, Psalm 42-43. Psalm 44 is occasioned by military defeat, as are Psalms 60, 80, and 89. Psalm 74 looks back on the destruction of Jerusalem and the temple. This feature is shared by Psalm 79. Finally Psalm 90 is a psalm where no external disaster is described but where the problem is life under God's wrath. Psalm 39 has some similarity with this psalm. Psalm 90 further shows a certain "wisdom" character, as does Psalm 9-10.[5]

---

[2]As far as we know, the excavations in Ugarit or any other Northwest Semitic remains have so far not brought us any piece of lament literature.

[3]For example, Psalm 22 was quoted by Jesus on the cross. This raises interesting hermeneutical questions for a Christian reading of these psalms. As we look for the theology of the psalms in their Old Testament context, these questions would be outside the scope of this study.

[4]For example, the importance of these psalms for Martin Luther's distinction between Deus revelatus and Deus absconditus would be worth exploring.

[5]See G. Castellino, *Libro dei Salmi* (Rome: Marietti, 1955), 772-784. Castellino groups Psalm 9-10 under "Salmi sapienziali," wisdom psalms.

This study consists of three parts. In the first we present the issues, explain our method, and survey some of the background in contemporary scholarship. The second part presents our translation of each text, translation notes, structure, and progression in content and mood of each psalm. In this part we will further study the problems, the content of the prayers, and the appeals presented in the five psalms investigated here. In Part Three we will look for the theological assumptions in these psalms, particularly with reference to the description of the problems, the nature and content of the prayers, and the appeals employed in order to persuade Yahweh to change his course of action. We will also make use of evidence from the complaint psalms which were not included in Part Two. From this we will try to answer the question: What did the faithful in ancient Israel do when they experienced God as an enemy against them?

It is our hope that this investigation also may be of some help for those who struggle with these kinds of questions themselves in their lives. May the psalmists' prayer become their prayer.

We have not tried to ascertain the particular occasion that led to the writing of the individual psalms, except for Psalm 74, where the destruction of the temple in 586/7 seems clearly to form part of the background. We have also not looked for a cultic setting for the psalms. No doubt there was a particular situation that caused a particular psalm to be composed, and we are convinced that the psalms functioned in the worship life of the individual and the community; if not, they would hardly have been handed down to us. But precisely because they were intended for use in worship, they usually exhibit a generalized language that is applicable to different situations. Thus it is not necessary to define, for example, the particular disease from which the psalmist in Psalm 88 suffers in order to appreciate the mood and the theological assumptions of the psalm. Similarly, we need not know the specific war mentioned in Psalm 44 in order to understand how the psalmist interpreted this defeat and what this interpretation assumes about God.

The psalms in the Hebrew Psalter were written by different people over a period of several hundred years. It may thus appear a bit hazardous to approach them with a synchronic method. However, a diachronic approach would face almost insurmountable difficulties.

There is at present no consensus as to the dating of the psalms. A psalm that is assumed to date from the earlier years of the divided monarchy by one scholar may well be regarded as late post-exilic by another.[6] However, since the psalms chosen for this study all share the features of protesting God's treatment of his people and of addressing this protest to God while still claiming him as their God, we think the corpus is homogeneous enough to make a synchronic method adequate.

Translation

The translations are based on the Masoretic Text as printed in *Biblica Hebraica Stuttgartensia* (BHS). We take a very cautious attitude to emendations, sensing that though quite a few can claim to make a smoother reading, the probability of ever having been part of the text is slight for the vast majority. Recent commentaries are also generally more reluctant to emend than those written in the earlier part of this century. The third edition of *Hebräisches und Aramäisches Lexicon zum Alten Testament* (KB) is also more restrictive than the first and second, and BHS is more careful than Kittel's editions of the Hebrew Bible. We do not emend *metri causa* since one now often speaks of a prevailing pattern rather than a consistent meter in Hebrew poetry. The few emendations advocated here are put in brackets.

How to understand and translate the Hebrew verbs as to *tempus* is not an easy question for poetry. We have tried to make use of the insights from the grammars, but in the end it is probably fair to say with H. Ringgren: "What follows from all this is that one ... is left to

---

[6]Unfortunately the superscriptions of the psalms give us little help in ascertaining a date for the psalms that can be generally accepted by the scholarly community. These titles are usually regarded as late and not reliable as to authorship and date of the individual psalms. The practice of adding a colophon to a poem or another piece of literature as it is written down is well known from Mesopotamian and Ugaritic sources well before the time when the Biblical psalms were written. There is accordingly no reason why, for example, David, provided he wrote psalms, could not have had them recorded with colophons. However, with our present knowledge there is also no evidence that he did. The titles then may well be reliable but may as well be late and of less historical value. We simply do not know.

try to ascertain the most likely progression and choose Swedish [in our case English] tempus accordingly. In many cases the result is uncertain."[7]

Bible references give verse numbers according to the Hebrew Bible. The verse numbering in most English translations varies slightly from this. The translations in this study are our own unless otherwise indicated.

Terminology

The *complaint psalms* are psalms in which God is partly or totally blamed for the distress the people or the individual are currently experiencing. These psalms are further subdivided into "complaints of the community" and "complaints of the individual."

We have retained the term *lament psalms* in the sense in which it is traditionally used in Old Testament scholarship. This is done out of convenience; the term is inadequate. C. C. Broyles' suggestion "Psalms of appeal" is much better,[8] but since experimentation with technical terms makes a work more difficult to read, and since promotion of new terminology is not an aim of this study, we think it wise to stick to the familiar.

When the word p*salmist* is used in this study, it refers to the "I," or the person who speaks in the psalm. It is not, thereby, meant that this "I" is necessarily identical with the composer of the psalm. S. Mowinckel is probably right when he says that many psalms, for example some of the psalms that describe the "I" as suffering from severe sickness, are written *for* the person who was to use it rather than by that person.[9]

---

[7]"Följden av allt detta blir att man . . . måste försöka finna ut det sannolika händelseförloppet och välja svenskt tempus därefter. I många fall blir resultatet osäkert." H. Ringgren, Psaltaren 1-41, Kommentar till Gamla Testamentet (Uppsala: EFS-förlaget, 1987), 185.

[8]C. C. Broyles, *The Conflict of Faith and Experience in the Psalms: A Form-Critical and Theological Study*, JSOT Supplement Series 52 (Sheffield: JSOT Press, 1989), 52.

[9]S. Mowinckel, *The Psalms in Israel's Worship*, 2 vols. translated by D. R. Ap-Thomas (Oxford: Basil Blackwell, 1962; reprint Sheffield: JSOT Press, 1992), 2:133-141.

A *colon* is a unit of text, usually a clause, with two, three or four stresses.

A b*icolon* is a combination of two cola, a *tricolon* a combination of three cola, and a *tetracolon* a combination of four cola.

In two parallel cola the first colon may be called the *A-colon* and the second the *B-colon*. Similarly, if two words are parallel, the first may be called the *A-word*, the second the *B-word*.

A *strophe* is sometimes a bicolon, tricolon, or tetracolon but, usually a combination of two or more of these that exhibits a semantic and/or syntactic unity.

A *stanza* is a major subdivision of a poem which comprises one or more strophes.[10] P. R. Raabe has shown that the stanzaic structure in the Biblical psalms tends to be symmetrical. The psalmists generally work with stanzas of equal size, counted in cola, or some combination of full-stanzas and half-stanzas. There is, however, also freedom for variation.[11]

The Subgenre of the "Complaint Psalms"

According to H. Gunkel, the main types or genres to which the psalms of the Hebrew Psalter belong are "hymns," "laments of the community," "thanksgivings of the individual," and "laments of the individual."[12] In addition there are smaller genres (for example "royal psalms"), mixed forms, and later developments. This division is by and large also followed by Mowinckel. However, his stress on a cultic setting makes him group together psalms which strictly speaking do not belong to the same genre. Thus the royal psalms "comprise nearly

---

[10]This terminology follows that of P. R. Raabe, *Psalm Structures: A Study of Psalms with Refrains*, JSOT Supplement Series 104 (Sheffield: JSOT Press, 1990), 11-12, "verse" and "section" are used in a non-technical way in our paper. When the word "verse" is used, it refers to the Masoretic verse division as found in BHS.

[11]Ibid., 175. Raabe mentions as an example of stanza-length variation Psalm 42-43, where the middle stanza is three cola longer than the other two.

[12]H. Gunkel and J. Begrich, *Einleitung in die Psalmen: Die Gattungen der religiösen Lyrik Israels*, Göttinger Handkommentar zum Alten Testament (Göttingen: Vandenhoeck & Ruprecht, 1933), 27.

all kinds of psalms,"[13] whereas for psalms connected with the so-called Enthronement Festival of Yahweh, "we are at once forced outside the narrow circle of the enthronement hymns proper."[14] Whereas Gunkel regarded nearly all "I" psalms as individual,[15] Mowinckel, taking a middle course between Gunkel and extreme advocates of a collective interpretation, maintains that in some psalms the king or another leader speaks on behalf of the whole people.[16] C. Westermann builds on Gunkel, but subsumes Gunkel's "hymns" and "thanksgivings of the individual" under "psalms of praise," and "laments" under "psalms of petition."[17] He maintains that all the "smaller categories" are to be included in these two categories or derived from them.[18]

It is a bit puzzling that the so-called lament psalms are called "lament psalms," for they are not laments. With this observation we come to E. S. Gerstenberger. A mourning song for the dead is a dirge and a mourning song for a fallen city is a lamentation,[19] but "*a complaint*," either individual or collective, was articulated when the final blow had not yet fallen and there still was time to argue a case before Yahweh."[20] He thus calls the lament psalms "complaint psalms."

C. C. Broyles finds that the most characteristic of the so-called lament psalms is that they are *appeals*.[21] Looking at the "God-laments," the laments where the psalmist laments not the situation in and of itself, nor the enemies, but the way God deals with the psalmist, Broyles finds that some psalms contain statements showing that God is

---

[13]S. Mowinckel, *The Psalms in Israel's Worship*, 2 vols. (Oxford: Basil Blackwell, 1962; reprint Sheffield: JSOT Press, 1992), 1:47.

[14]Ibid., 1:107.

[15]See e.g. *Einleitung in die Psalmen*, 123.

[16]Mowinckel, *The Psalms in Israel's Worship*, 1:226.

[17]C. Westermann, *Praise and Lament in the Psalms*, translated by K. R. Crim and R. N. Soulen (Atlanta: John Knox Press, 1981), 33.

[18]Ibid., 35.

[19]E. S. Gerstenberger, *Psalms, part 1, with an Introduction to Cultic Poetry*, The Forms of the Old Testament Literature XIV (Grand Rapids: Eerdmans, 1988), 10.

[20]Ibid., 11.

[21]Broyles, *The Conflict of Faith*, 14.

just in his severe treatment. In other psalms, however, there is no justification given for God's course of action. These unexplained God-laments are what Broyles describes as "complaints," and he calls the psalms in which they appear "complaint psalms."[22] He surveys the different elements of the lament psalms and shows that these are somewhat different from the rest of the lament psalms. For example, the element "God's actions in the past" is found only in the complaint psalms.[23] He further compares the description of the distress and finds that in the complaint psalms God is regarded as partly responsible for the misery, whereas in the other lament psalms the blame for the trouble is laid on the enemies, on one's own sin, or on other causes, but not on God.[24] He concludes that, whereas the other lament psalms argue with God and plead with him, the complaint psalms argue against God. He thus subdivides the genre of "psalms of appeal" into subgenres of "psalms of plea" and "psalms of complaint."[25] To the complaint psalms he assigns eleven communal psalms, Psalms 9-10 (regarded as one psalm), 44, 60, 74, 77, 79, 80, 85, 89, 90, and 108,[26]

---

[22]Ibid., 37-40.

[23]Ibid., 42-43, see also pages 51-53.

[24]Ibid., 111-131.

[25]Ibid., 52. He defines "genre" in this way: "a shared pattern of communication, usually shaped in a particular social context, that signals certain expectations on how a text/speech is to be understood" (pages 25-26).

[26]I cannot see that Psalm 108 should be included in this category. The psalm is formed by removing the complaint-section from Psalm 60 and replacing it with praise from Psalm 57. What remains from Psalm 60 is an oracle of salvation and a section which Castellino rightly calls "la rinata speranza," the revived hope (*Libro dei Salmi*, 335). I think Bentzen has understood these verses correctly: V. 11 is a question of doubt concerning the oracle in the preceding verses. This is followed up with a new question in v. 12. These two verses thus express doubt, not complaint. V. 13 is then a prayer for victory. Finally, in v. 14 the faith breaks through and trusts in God's help. A. Bentzen, *Fortolkning til de Gammeltestamentlige Salmer* (Copenhagen: Gad, 1939), 348. A. Maillot and A. Lelièvre, *Les Psaumes*, 3 vols. (Geneva: Labor et Fides, 1972, 1966, and 1969), 3:63, say about Psalme 108: "La double omission de la supplication individuelle au début du Ps. 57, et de la lamentation collective au début du Ps. 60, font du Ps. 108 un magnifique chant d'actions de grâces en l'honneur de YHWH, le vainqueur des nations."

and eight individual psalms, Psalms 6, 13, 22, 35, 39, 42-43 (regarded as one psalm), 88, and 102.[27]

Broyles has provided us with a limited corpus of psalms that share the key characteristic of protesting against what the psalmists experience as unjust or unintelligible treatment by God. Since we want to investigate how the ancient Israelite believers dealt with a situation where God was experienced as an enemy, this corpus serves well as a basis for our study.[28]

Structure and Interpretation

Against those who feel that the traditional language and phraseology of the psalms together with their cultic and often collective/communal use make them impersonal and ritualistic, Mowinckel has argued that the psalms are personal creations and reflect personal convictions, personal feelings, personal experiences, and the poet's own imagination.[29] Each psalm, to a large degree made up of traditional material, is nevertheless a new and unique poem. If we take a look at Westermann's tables over the structural elements in public and individual laments, we at once notice that the different typical parts found in psalms of these genres do not necessarily follow each other in a fixed sequence.[30] This observation underlines the same truth: If we will interpret a poem properly, the task is not merely to find and examine the different elements typical for the genre.

---

[27]Broyles, *The Conflict of Faith*, 135-211.

[28]We have seen above that the term *complaint psalms* is used with different meanings by Gerstenberger and Broyles. In this paper the term refers to the corpus of psalms which Broyles has included in his subgenre of "complaint psalms" (omitting Psalm 108).

[29]Mowinckel, *Psalms in Israel's Worship*, 2:126-143.

[30]Westermann, *Praise and Lament*, 53-54 and 66-69. In Psalm 74 the "vow of praise," "let the poor and needy praise thy name," does not end the psalm, and would hardly have been called so at all if the schema had not required so. In Psalm 6 he will also be seen bouncing back and forth to fill in the blanks. See M. Weiss' criticism in "Die Methode der "Total-Interpretation," *Supplement to Vetus Testamentum* 22 (1971): 97-98, and *The Bible from Within* (Jerusalem: Magnes Press, 1984), 281-285.

M. Weiss has advanced what he calls the method of "total interpretation." He stresses that structure and content of a poem constitute a unity:

> Da die Aufgabe des dichterischen Werkes Gedanken, Lehren, Gefühle usw., nicht mitzuteilen, sondern zu gestalten ist, spricht es seine Wahrheit nicht in den einzelnen Aussagen, sondern ausschliesslich in der Einheit des Gestaltung, als Ganzes aus. D[as].h[eißt]., die Dichtung macht ihren Sinngehalt nur in dieser ihrer konkreten, einmaligen Gestalt offenbar, in dieser Wortprägung, in diesem Satzbau, in diesem Rhytmus und allein in diesem besonderen Verhältnis der Teile untereinander und der Teile zum Ganzen - kurz: in dieser Struktur.[31]

Weiss tries to follow the thoughts and moods throughout the poem, paying close attention to the relation between the different elements, contrasts, intensification, use of recurring theme words, *Leitwörter*, and other devices that create the exact mood and thoughts which the poet wanted to express. In short, he wants to read each psalm as a whole and as poetry.

R. Alter has a fine discussion of the "narrativity" of Biblical poetry.[32] He shows that even though true narrative poems (epics) hardly exist in the Hebrew Bible, there is a "narrativity" that draws the metaphors forward. The two cola in parallelism are usually not exactly synonymous. The point is not just to state the same in another way:

> If, however, one recognizes that the semantic orientating of the system of apparent repetitions—let us say, cautiously, in two-thirds of the cases—is toward a focusing, a heightening, a concretization, a development of meaning, it is possible to see that movement generated between versets [in our terminology: cola] is then carried on from line to line into the structure of the poem.[33]

---

[31]Weiss, "Total-Interpretation," 92.

[32]R. Alter, *The Art of Biblical Poetry* (New York: Basic Books, 1985), 27-61.

[33]Ibid., 29. Good treatments of parallelism are found in J. Kugel, *The Idea of Biblical Poetry: Parallelism and its History* (New Haven: Yale University Press, 1981), 1-58, and A. Berlin, *The Dynamics of Biblical Parallelism*, Bloomington: Indiana University Press, 1985.

Finally, Raabe has made clear the importance of the stanzaic structure of a psalm for the understanding of the flow of thought in the psalm. He makes the observation that the major turning points of a psalm occur between stanzas.[34] The movement from start to finish in a psalm is "in stages corresponding to their sections [in psalms with no refrain: corresponding to their stanzas]." Thus he argues: "First the reader should focus on each stanza with its own integrity and then investigate the relationship between the stanzas."[35]

Taking the cue from these insights, after having provided a translation and translation notes, we will try to ascertain the structure of each psalm. Some of the psalms exhibit both strophes and stanzas, while in others there is no subdivision between the stanza and the individual bicola or tricola. This investigation of the stanzaic structure will then form the basis for our study of the progression in content and mood. We will try to trace the movement from colon to colon within the stanza, and the way the stanzas relate to each other. We will pay attention to the place and function of different elements in the poem, as well as to recurring words and phrases. In short, we will approach each of the five psalms which are selected for in-depth study as a unique creation. Yet these five are also typical of the general category "psalms of complaint."

Theological Questions

The psalms are not a series of dogmatic statements. Those which form the subject for the present investigation, the complaint psalms, are not even composed primarily to say something about God. They are, rather, prayers addressed to God. But that does not mean that they have no theology. Often this theology is seen on the level of assumptions underlying what is said rather than explicit formulations.

We have seen above that in these psalms the psalmists come before God with problems to which they want him to attend. If so, the first question to ask is how they present their problems. Let us say a person suffered from a certain disease. This disease could, with

---

[34]Raabe, *Psalm Structures*, 183-186.
[35]Ibid., 187.

different assumptions, be depicted as caused by a viral infection, as evidence of an attack by evil spirits, as a result of a curse by an enemy, as a consequence of former sins either by the sufferer or by his ancestors, or as a punishment from God. The reason that it was bad could be that it stopped the person's career plans, that it prevented him from leisure activities, or that it stigmatized him in society. The way the problem is presented discloses the composer's "value system," his "world view," and also his assumptions about God.[36]

Second, in these psalms the psalmists want something from God. For one thing, the very fact that they can address God and expect him to respond assumes something about God. For example, it would make little sense to pray to a mere cosmic force.[37] Not only that they pray, but also what they pray for, is important. What do they want from God? Is it primarily health, food, victory over enemies, and a life in wealth and fame, or are other matters more crucial for them? Has God any role in their wishes, or is he simply the source from which they can have their wishes fulfilled?

Third, what do they say to God to cause him to change his course of action and grant them what they want? What kind of arguments are thought to move him? This will tell us much about what kind of God they regard their God to be and what kind of relationship exists between them and God. What do they expect from God and why should he do it?

Thus investigation of the problem, the prayer, and the appeal will give us a good picture of the theological assumptions operative in the complaint psalms, and so reveal how the faithful in ancient Israel responded when they experienced God as an enemy.

---

[36]Even if God was left totally out of the problem, that would still betray what was thought about God: It would depict a God that either was assigned to a special religious sphere or did not exist at all.

[37]It is interesting to note that religions throughout the world tend to personify crucial or potentially dangerous natural forces. There is (was at least) no way to influence the sea, the weather or the fertility of women. A sea god, a storm god, or a fertility goddess can be given sacrifices and approached in prayer.

PART TWO

THE TEXTS

Chapter Two

Psalm 6

1.   For the musical director. With stringed instruments, on the eighth, a psalm of David.

2a.   O Yahweh, do not in your anger reproach me,
b.   and do not in your wrath correct me!
3a.   Be gracious to me, O Yahweh, for I am feeble.
b.   Heal me, O Yahweh, for my bones are terrified,
4a.   and my soul is very terrified—
b.   but you, O Yahweh, how long?
5a.   Turn around, O Yahweh;
b.   deliver my life!
c.   Save me for the sake of your steadfast love!
6a.   For in Death there is no remembrance of you;
b.   in Sheol, who praises you?

7a.   I am weary of my sighing.
b.   I flood my bed all night;
c.   with my tears I drench my couch.
8a.   My eye has become dim from distress;
b.   it has grown old because of all my enemies.
9a.   Turn aside from me all you who do injustice,
b.   for Yahweh has heard the sound of my weeping.
10a.   Yahweh has heard my supplication;
b.   Yahweh receives my prayer.
11a.   All my foes will be put to shame and will be very terrified;
b.   they will turn back, they will be put to shame suddenly.

Translation Notes

v. 1.   בִּנְגִינוֹת – "with stringed instruments"

The phrase, found in Psalm superscriptions in Pss. 4:1; 54:1; 55:1; 67:1 and 76:1 (and Ps. 61:1), is used as a technical musical term also in Hab. 3:19. It means string music in Isa. 38:20 and Lam. 5:14, and apparently "taunt song" in Ps. 69:13; Job 30:9; and Lam. 3:14. In Ps. 77:7 it appears to mean plain "song" or to need emendation.[1]

v. 1.   עַל־הַשְּׁמִינִית – "on the eighth"

The term is found also Ps. 12:1 and 1 Chron. 15:21. Several suggestions have been given. H. J. Kraus, A. Maillot, and A. Lelièvre think the title means "on eight-stringed instrument." J. Calès, L. Jacquet, and F. Delitzsch, among others, suggest "on the octave." S. Mowinckel takes it to refer to the conclusive eighth ritual act of the New Year Festival, immediately preceding the announcement of Yahweh's answer and promise.[2] None of the suggestions is conclusive. Thus we translate the Hebrew and refrain from filling in any explanatory glosses.

v. 1.   לְדָוִד – "of David"

The preposition can have several meanings. Mowinckel argues that the natural translation of the phrase is "for David." He finds support for this in the heading of Psalm 102: "a prayer of the afflicted," that is, for the use of someone in a such situation. Thus these psalms were

---

[1]See, e.g., Mowinckel, *The Psalms in Israel's Worship*, 2:210.

[2]H. J. Kraus, *Psalms 1-59*, translated by H. C. Oswald. (Minneapolis: Augsburg Publishing House, 1988), 31; A. Maillot and A. Lelièvre, *Les Psaumes, Traduction, notes et commentaires* (Geneva: Labor et Fides, 1972), première partie, 39; J. Calès, *Le livre des Psaumes*, 2 vols. (Paris: Gabriel Beauchesne et ses fils, 1936), 1:128; L. Jacquet, *Les Psaumes et le coeur de l'homme*, 3 vols. (Gembloux: Duculot, 1975-1977), 1:274; F. Delitzsch, *Psalms*, 3 vols. Commentary on the Old Testament. translated by F. Bolton. (Grand Rapids: Eerdmans, 1871; reprint, 1975), 1:131; Mowinckel, *The Psalms in Israel's Worship*, 2:215-216. See further KB, 1445.

used by David or by a king of the house of David. He says, "such information was a good recommendation for the psalm; a psalm which helped . . . David, must needs be pleasing to God and effective, useful prayer."[3] Mowinckel thinks the expression later was misunderstood to refer to the author. This in turn produced the description of the situation found in the headings of several psalms.[4] However, since such a change in understanding cannot be traced, and because the description of the situation found in some psalms (for example Pss. 3:1 and 7:1) makes it clear what is meant there, it appears more natural to translate "of David," implying authorship, even in such psalms where there is no description of the situation.[5] David further is said to have composed poems (2 Sam. 1:17-27; 3:33-34). On the other hand, we find it by no means implausible that many of these psalms would be used at the court of the royal house he founded.[6]

v. 2. אַל־בְּאַפְּךָ תוֹכִיחֵנִי וְאַל־בַּחֲמָתְךָ תְיַסְּרֵנִי – "do not in your anger reproach me, and do not in your wrath correct me"

יכה is sometimes used with reference to the court. If the subject is the judge (or the king as judge), the verb overlaps with שׁפט, "judge" (Isa. 2:4; 11:4; and Micah 4:3).[7] When it applies to one of the parties,

---

[3]*The Psalms in Israel's Worship*, 1:77; cf. *Psalmenstudien* 6:72-81. It should be noted that Mowinckel held this view independent of the "evidence" from Mari once thought supporting it. He advances the theory before the reference to Mari was brought forward. In the above quoted work p. 77, note 110, he says the "evidence" from Mari is refuted by Tadmor.

[4]Ibid., 78.

[5]Cf. Kraus, *Psalms 1-59*, 22-23.

[6]A related, though not identical, question is when the psalm was written. For different views see M. Buttenwieser, *The Psalms* (Chicago: The University of Chicago Press, 1938), 555-559; Kraus, *Psalms 1-59*, 161; Jacquet, *Les Psaumes*, 1:277, and J. F. Brug, *Psalms*, 2 vols., The People's Bible (Milwaukee, Wisconsin: Northwestern Publishing House, 1989), 1:58. Different answers to the question of whether the psalm is dependent on Jeremiah is given by Calès, *Le livre des Psaumes*, 1: 133 and J. Coppens, "Les Psaumes 6 et 41 Dèpendent-ils du livre de Jérémie?" *Hebrew Union College Annual* 32 (1961): 217-226.

[7]A. Even-Shoshan, *A New Concordance of the Old Testament*, 2nd. edition, (Jerusalem: "Kiryat Sefer" Publishing House, 1993, distributed by Baker Book House) (below referred as "Even-Shoshan"), 466, assigns this meaning to the verb even in our verse, as well as in Pss. 38:2 and 94:10.

it connotes "putting forward a complaint" or "argue the case" (see Gen. 21:25 and Job 13:3). Outside the court, the verb often means "reproach" (Job. 13:10; Prov. 3:12 and 15:12). יסר is often used of the teaching and disciplining of a child with the goal that the child shall be a God-fearing and useful member of the society (Prov. 19:18 and 29:17). Often it connotes correcting (Deut. 21:18). The two verbs are used together in Pss. 38:2; 94:10; Jer. 2:19, all with God as subject, and Prov. 9:7. Ps. 38:2 is almost identical with Ps. 6:2. There the psalmist confesses that the reproach and correction is required by sin. Also here the choice of verbs probably is intended to imply some kind of sin or unfaithfulness as the reason why God became angry.[8]

Note that the prepositional phrase is placed between אל and the verb for emphasis in both colons.[9] This construction is also found in Ps. 38:2 and Isa. 64:8, where it is a prayer against God's wrath, and Jer. 15:15. See also Jer. 10:24: "Correct me, Yahweh, but only with justice, not in your anger, lest you reduce me to nothing."

v. 3a.   חָנֵּנִי – "be gracious to me"

The root חנן, when it is used on the interpersonal level, is used in situations where one party is, or is asked to be, "favorably disposed" toward the other party. It may refer to the particular situation in which a favorable disposition was needed (Gen. 30:27; 47:29). In other cases it connotes a party's continuous disposition toward another (Ruth 2:2, 10 and 13; Esther 2:17 and 5:2). In Exod. 34:6 Yahweh reveals himself to Moses as a "compassionate and gracious [וְחַנּוּן] God." The imperative with suffix for first person singular is used 18[10] times in the Psalms (for example 4:2; 31:10; and 41:5, 11) and nowhere else in the Old Testament. The certainty that Yahweh has heard the psalmist's

---

[8]See further G. Mayer, "יכח," TWAT, 3:620-628, and R. D. Branson, "יסר," TWAT, 3:688-697.

[9]Cf. GKC, § 152h, though Briggs thinks the purpose is to make the suffixes of the verbs end the colons so as to create rhyme. C. A. and E. G. Briggs, A Critical and Exegetical Commentary on the Book of Psalms, 2 vols. International Critical Commentary. (Edinburgh: T &T. Clark, 1906-1907), 1:49.

[10]If we include the peculiar form חנני found only in Ps. 9:14.

תחנה, "supplication," indicates that we should understand the verb in v. 3 not as referring only to the following prayer for restoration of health. It is rather a prayer that the psalmist may once again be allowed to experience God's gracious disposition toward him as his lasting relation to God. Unlike what is said of God's חסד, it is never said that God should do something because of his "grace" or because he is "gracious." Ps. 51:3 asks God to "be gracious" because of his "steadfast love."[11]

v. 3a.   אָמְלַל:–"feeble"

Technically the adjective is a hapax, but it is clearly related to the pulal of אמל, "be or grow feeble, languish." The verb is mostly used with inanimate subjects, such as geographical areas (Nah. 1:4), walls (Lam. 2:8), the earth (Isa. 33:9), but also with personal subjects (1 Sam. 2:5 and Hos. 4:3).

v. 3b.   נִבְהֲלוּ – "are terrified"

BHS apparatus mentions two proposals for emendations, נבלו, "wither and fall" (cf. Exod. 18:18; Ps. 18:46) and בלו, "are worn out" (cf. Ps. 32:3). Both would fit the context well. In either case perhaps the scribe was influenced by v. 4a and thus miscopied the word. However, בהל may be regarded as a key word in this Psalm, since it occurs again in v. 11. The Septuagint (LXX) and the other ancient versions attest to the Masoretic Text (MT), and the text as it stands makes perfect sense. We therefore retain MT.

v. 5a. שׁוּבָה – "turn around"

W. L. Holladay places this verse, Isa. 63:17, and Ps. 90:13 together in his group 7e: imperative with God as subject and without qualification or immediate context. "Here the faithful ask God to

---

[11]See further D. N. Freedmann and J. Lundblom, "חנן, חן, חנון, חנינה, חנה, תחנון," *TWAT*, 3:23-40.

change the total direction of his activity, that they may be saved"[12] The imperative is sometimes taken to mean "return (to me)," implying that God has been absent.[13] The clause שׁוּב מֵחֲרוֹן אַף, which is used with God as subject in Exod. 32:12; 2 Kings 23:26; and Jonah 3:9, makes Gunkel's rendition more probable: "vom Zorn ablassen." In Ps. 90:13 שׁוּב is parallel to נחם, "repent," which seems to support the understanding that God is asked to turn away from his wrath.[14]

v. 5c. לְמַעַן חַסְדֶּךָ – "for the sake of your steadfast love"

Although one sees חסד translated in various ways, the traditional translation "steadfast love" still conveys the sense as well as any.[15]

v. 6a. אֵין בַּמָּוֶת זִכְרֶךָ – "in Death there is no remembrance of you"

Note that the prepositional phrase is placed between אֵין and its *nomen rectum*. Though this is more common than between אַל and the jussive,[16] it still puts the stress on the prepositional phrase (cf. Pss. 5:10 and 32:2).

"Death" is capitalized since it has the article and is parallel to Sheol, and thus connotes the nether world. For this meaning, see Job 28:22; 30:23; Prov. 5:5; and 7:27. "Death" and "Sheol" are found together in 2 Sam. 22:6; Pss. 18:6; and 49:15.[17]

---

[12]W. L. A. Holladay, *The Root šûbh in the Old Testament* (Leiden: E. J. Brill, 1958), 77. His group 7 covers emotions, attitudes, vows, oaths, deeds as the expression of a person. On p. 117 he notes that these passages might be interpreted as a "covenant usage," but "are better considered within the pattern of the total encounter in prayer than within the discursive framework of the covenantal idea."

[13]For example Delitzsch, *Psalms*, 1:134 and Kraus, *Psalms 1-59*, 162.

[14]H. Gunkel, *Die Psalmen übersetzt und erklärt*, Göttinger Handkommentar zum Alten Testament. (Göttingen: Vandenhoeck & Ruprecht, 1926), 23. See our discussion of the repentance of God in chapter 3.

[15]See our discussion in chapter 3.

[16]See v. 2 above.

[17]All these and several others are indefinite. For a use with the article (and כ), see Hab. 2:5; Cant. 8:6.

v. 6a.   זִכְרֶךָ – "remembrance of you"

The noun is derived from זכר, "think of, be mindful of, remember." This verb in the qal is used with God as subject 68 times. In 23 of these God thinks of/remembers humans, in another 12 he is mindful of the covenant. Of the 100 times the qal is used with a human subject, the object in 69 cases is God, his salvific deeds, etc.[18] Of 23 occurrences the noun is used 12 times with a human antecedent, nine of which speak of the memory of the ungodly or the enemies of God's people being forgotten or blotted out (Isa. 26:14 and Ps. 34:17). Two occurrences speak of the memory of the righteous, and one of Ephraim in the future when Yahweh has restored him. With one exception,[19] the remaining occurrences refer to God. It is closely related to God's name (Exod. 3:15 and Hos. 12:6). It is related to God's self-revelation (Psalm 97) and his actions in the past (Ps. 135:1-14). It is the object of praise (Pss. 30:5 and 145:7).

The divine זכר in the cultus is the revelation of Yahweh's name: his active presence, his character, and his saving deeds (cf. also Ps. 111:4). Israel's response to the זכר, by which Yahweh makes himself and his deeds to be remembered in the present, is one of confession, praise, and thanksgiving.[20]

In our verse where אֵין זִכְרֶךָ is parallel to מִי יוֹדֶה־לָּךְ, "who praises you," the focus seems to be on the human response. We have therefore taken the suffix as objective. However, the whole picture is entailed: The dead are not the object of Yahweh's self-revelation. They are never reminded of his gracious works in the past. The mutual relation experienced in worship by the living does not exist in Sheol.[21]

---

[18]H. Eising, "אזכרה, זכרון, זכר, זכר," *TWAT*, 2:575.

[19]Esther 9:28 speaks of the remembrance of the events which underlie the purim festival.

[20]A. G. Ludwig, "Remembrance and Re-Presentation in Israel's Worship" (Master of Sacred Theology Thesis, Concordia Seminary, St. Louis, 1991), 55. See further his discussion of the remembrance of the name of Yahweh, ibid., 51-60.

[21]Cf. Gunkel, *Psalmen*, 23: "das Gedenken Gottes im Hymnus" and the translation given by Maillot and Lelièvre: "Car on ne te rend pas de culte dans la mort" (*Les Psaumes*, 1:39).

v. 7a.   יָגַעְתִּי בְּאַנְחָתִי – "I am weary of my sighing"

We understand the preposition here as giving the cause for the verbal action.[22] The same phrase is found also in Jer. 45:3 (cf. Ps. 69:4).
BHS thinks several words are missing after "my sighing." But there is no textual evidence for this. In Jer. 45:3 the parallel colon is "and I find no rest," but there is no way to tell whether that or any other clause originally stood in Psalm 6.

v. 8a.   עָשְׁשָׁה – "has become dim"

The meaning of this word (compare Ps. 31:10,11) is uncertain. "Grow dark," "grow weak, waste away,"[23] and "swell"[24] have all been suggested as possible meanings. "Swell" is the remotest parallel to עתקה of the three. The other two are both nice parallels, but the first is difficult in Psalm 31. Thus we follow BDB and understand it as "waste away," but because an eye wastes away by not seeing clearly any more, we translate, "has become dim."

v. 8b.   עָתְקָה – "it has grown old"

The qal is used three other times in the Bible, all in Job. In 21:7 it simply means grow old of years and become an old man (and thus attain a long life). In 14:18 and 18:4 the subject is a mountain which *erodes*. Thus we shall probably think of the eye as in some way withering away.
The conjecture suggested by Fenton,[25] to read עֵקָתִי, "my eyeball," from Ugaritic 'q, is unnecessary, because the colons are already parallel. The meaning of the Ugaritic word is also uncertain.[26]

---

[22]KB, 101. This sense is number 19 in his list over different meanings for the preposition.

[23]BDB, 799.

[24]L. Delekat, "Zum hebräischen Wörterbuch", *Vetus Testamentum* 14 (1964): 52-55.

[25]T. L. Fenton, "Ugaritica-Biblica", *Ugarit-Forschungen* 1 (1969): 66-67.

v. 8b. בְּכָל־צוֹרְרָי – "because of all my enemies"

The preposition is taken in the same sense as in 7a (see note). There is no need to change to מכל, as LXX also witnesses to MT. Gunkel proposes to emend צוררי and read צרתי to make the two colons parallel.[27] This conjecture lacks textual evidence, and the psalmist seems to have put "all my enemies" at the end of this line to prepare for the following where the enemies figure very prominently. These arguments can also be applied to M. Dahood's suggestion "my heart . . . for pining," from Ugaritic *ṣrrt* and Akkadian *ṣurru*.[28] We are not told who the enemies are.[29]

---

[26]Cf. J. C. L. Gibson, *Canaanite Myths and Legends* (Edinburgh: T & T. Clark, 1977), 86, note 3.

[27]Gunkel, *Psalmen*, 21, 23. So also e.g. Jacquet, *Les Psaumes*, 1:274 and BHS apparatus.

[28]Dahood, *Psalmen*, 1:38. It has further been pointed out that the alleged Ugaritic evidence does not support the hypothesis, see P. C. Craigie, *Psalms 1-50*, Word Biblical Commentary (Waco, TX: Word Books, 1983), 90, note 8b.

[29]The identity of the enemies in the individual lament psalms has been hotly debated for a long time. Early in this century it was fashionable to look to the conflicting parties of (late) post-exilic Judah. A different approach was proposed by Mowinckel in *Psalmenstudien 1*. He argued that the enemies were sorcerers which were thought to have caused the sickness (esp. pp. 76-81). H. Birkeland, on the other hand, thought that most, or all of the so-called individual laments, were in fact royal psalms (arguing from psalms that are undoubtedly royal and finding similarities to them in the rest). Thus the enemies were national enemies, and the "sickness" was the distress caused by defeat or by an advancing powerful enemy (*Die Feinde des Individuums in der Israelitischen Psalmenliteratur*. Oslo: Grøndahl & Søns forlag, 1933). See, e.g., his treatment of Psalm 22, pp. 216-228. Psalm 6 is treated briefly on p. 311. This work caused Mowinckel to moderate his view, while maintaining that Birkeland went too far by pressing *all* psalms into his royal interpretation (*Psalms in Israels Worship* 2:250, Note XXVIII). H. Schmidt (*Das Gebet der Angeklagten im Alten Testament*. Giessen: Alfred Töpelmann, 1928) takes his cue from the attitude found, for example, among Job's friends, that sickness is caused by sin, and from 1 Kings 8:31-32: The accused can take an oath before Yahweh and then Yahweh will judge in the case. He argues that neighbors and townspeople will use sickness as evidence for the sick being guilty of crimes which have never been solved and thus bring this sick person to court. The lament psalm is then the sick person's appeal to Yahweh. O. Keel (*Feinde und Gottesleugner*. Stuttgarter Biblische Monographien 7. Stuttgart: Verlag Katholisches Bibelwerk, 1969) uses xenophobia as an explanation. One's own fear is projected on the enemies. Thus the enemies, whoever they were and however they were, are always painted as the רשע—the ungodly, which means that

v. 9a.   כָּל־פֹּעֲלֵי אָוֶן – "all you who do injustice"

The expression is found, for example, in Pss. 5:6; 14:4 and 28:3. In the 1920s Mowinckel advanced the theory that this phrase means, "doers of sorcery."[30] He thought they were looked upon as those who caused the sickness. It is not said in our psalm that the enemies/doers of אָוֶן caused the sickness, and it has proved very difficult to substantiate the claim anywhere. The theory apparently has not gained many followers. Later Mowinckel also moderated his thesis by allowing for a more general meaning of the word as a secondary development.[31] Our translation is in line with the traditional, and at present prevailing, understanding of the phrase and the one that seems to fit the texts best.

v. 11a. יֵבֹשׁוּ וְיִבָּהֲלוּ מְאֹד – "will be put to shame and will be very terrified"

בּוֹשׁ is not so much "to feel ashamed" (though see Ezek. 16:63) as it is to be put to shame. The worshippers of idols are put to shame when it becomes evident that the idols are unable to help them (Isa. 1:29), and those who trusted foreign powers are put to shame when these powers do not help them (Isa. 20:5). In the psalms an individual or the people often pray to Yahweh that he may not let them down (Pss. 22:6; 25:20; and 31:2). On the other hand, the enemies must fail in their scheme and thus be put to shame (Pss. 31:18; 129:5 and in our psalm).[32]

BHS apparatus suggests that יֵבֹשׁוּ ו be deleted. Gunkel, on the other hand, keeps this phrase but deletes the second יֵבֹשׁ in this

---

there is no way to ascertain who the enemies are in each case. Finally, we should mention G. W. Anderson ("Enemies and Evildoers in the Book of Psalms," *Bulletin of the John Rylands Library* 48 (1965-66):18-29) who, after surveying different views, concludes: "We must . . . allow for a wide range of interpretation, taking the assaults of national enemies, the bane of illness in national leader or private individual, the potent words of slander or derision, and a variety of cultic acts and situations"(p. 29).

[30]Mowinckel, *Psalmenstudien* 1 (the whole volume).

[31]Mowinckel, *The Psalms in Israel's Worship*, 2:7.

[32]See H. Seebaß, "בושׁ, בושׁה, בשׁת, מבושׁים," *TWAT*, 1:568-580.

verse.[33] It seems to us, however, that there may be a deliberate structure of the verse. The two verbs in the middle both reflect verbs used earlier in the psalm. In vv. 3-4 the psalmist was terrified, but now the enemies will be terrified. In v. 5 Yahweh was asked to turn around from his wrath and deliver the psalmist. Now that he has done so, the enemies will have to turn around and leave the psalmist. These two verbs are then framed by "they will be put to shame." There seems also to be a play on consonants: יבשׁו, ישׁבו . . . יבשׁו. A further argument for keeping the word is that it is difficult to account for how it accidentally became added. Finally, MT is also supported here by the versions.

In view of the preceding verses we take the verbs in this verse as imperfects, not as jussives. The Psalmist is sure these things will happen.[34]

v. 11b. רָגַע – "suddenly"

We understand the word as a temporal accusative.[35] Dahood, on the other hand, takes רגע as a name for the underworld. He gives Pss. 9:18 and 31:18 as examples of the thought that the enemies shall be sent down to Sheol. For the meaning of the word he gives Num. 16:21; Ps. 73:19 and Job 21:13. In all these cases the traditional translation of רגע is both possible and natural. In our opinion Dahood's conjectured meaning remains, at best, doubtful. This is even more true about N. Airoldi's[36] understanding of the verse. He makes Dahood's understanding of רגע his starting point and tries to find a translation of מאד that can make it parallel to this. Thus he repoints מֵ(י)אֹד, "from ruin," so also in v. 4a. Thus, as Dahood's translation can not be substantiated, Airoldi's loses its very foundation.

---

[33]Gunkel, *Psalmen*, 21, 23.

[34]So e.g. Craigie, *Psalms 1-50*, 90; Briggs, *Book of Psalms*, 1:46, and the Norwegian translations of the Bible. Contra Dahood, *Psalms*, 1:37.

[35]Cf. GKC, § 118i-k. See Isa. 47:9; Jer. 4:20 and Job 34:20.

[36]Dahood, *Psalms*, 1:38. N. Airoldi, "Note critiche al Salmo 6," *Rivista Biblica* 16 (1968): 285-289.

Structure

Strophes

The psalm has four strophes: vv. 2-4, 5-6, 7-8, 9-11. C. A. and E. G. Briggs notice the rhyme created by the personal suffixes throughout the psalm.[37]

Vv. 2-4 opens with a vocative followed by negative jussives and imperatives addressing Yahweh. They are followed by כִּ clauses. V. 3 has an ABA'B' structure.[38] V. 4a further stands chiastically to v. 3b.[39] Knitting vv. 3-4a so closely together singles out v. 4b. The psalmist sort of pauses after v. 4a, gathers his breath, and then shouts: But you, O Yahweh, how long?[40]

---

[37]*Book of Psalms*, 1:46-47, though admittedly he makes the rhyme even better than it is.

[38]For this see J. T. Willis, "Alternating (ABA'B') Parallelism in the Old Testament Psalms and Prophetic Literature," in *Directions in Biblical Hebrew Poetry*, ed. E. R. Follis, JSOT Supplement Series 40. (Sheffield: JSOT Press, 1987), 49-76, though he does not count this verse among his 199 instances of alternating structure.

[39]Cf. N. W. Lund, *Chiasmus in the New Testament* (Chapel Hill: The University of North Carolina press, 1942), 39. Lund extends the chiasmus from v. 3b to 4b (and Smit Sibinga argues from this that 4b belongs to Strophe 1 (J. Smit Sibinga, "Gedicht en getal. Over de compositie van Psalm 6, *Nederlands Theologisch Tijdschrift* 42 (1988):185-207, see page 190)), but that seems forced. For the effect of this chiasm, see further A. Mirsky, "Stylistic Device for Conclusion in Hebrew," *Semitics* 5 (1977): 9-23.

[40]That v. 4b. is not interwoven into the structure of either the preceding or the following has caused much uncertainty whether it should be taken with v. 4a or with v. 5. V. 4b. is taken with Strophe 2, e.g., by T. P. Wahl (*Strophic Structure of Individual Laments in Psalms Books I and II* (Dissertation, Union Theological Seminary in the City of New York, 1976. Ann Arbor, Michigan: University Microfilms International, 1984), 78-79), Calès (*Le livre des Psaumes*, 1:128), and Briggs (*Book of Psalms*, 1:46-47). Wahl argues as follows: A close relationship between עַד מָתַי and שׁוּבָה is suggested by Ps. 90:13a; Jer. 31:21; Prov. 1:22-23 and Neh. 2:6. Further, there is a coherence of topic between v. 4b and v. 6. H. Gunkel (*Psalmen*, 21), Smit Sibinga ("Gedicht en getal," 185-207), Craigie (*Psalms 1-50*, 92), and BHS put the division after verse 4. We feel v. 4b belongs together with the preceding, making a contrast to the miserable state of "I" (my bones, my soul) with the emphatic "but *you*." Further, D. N. Freedmann voices the "impression" that conjunction is not used at the beginning of the first colon in Standard Hebrew poetry ("Another Look at Biblical Hebrew poetry,"

Vv. 5-6: Three imperatives addressed to Yahweh are followed by a double motivation: first by a prepositional phrase, then by כִּי.

Vv. 7-8 contain a perfect and two imperfect verbal clauses with "I" as subject and two perfects with "my eye" as subject, all describing the psalmist's distress.[41]

Vv. 9-11: Those "who do injustice" are addressed by an imperative. Again the reason for stating the imperative is introduced by כִּי. תְּחִנָּתִי, "my supplication," picks up v. 3 חָנֵּנִי, "be gracious to me." With the psalmist's attention focused on this reason, he "forgets" those he was addressing and meditates on the result of what he just stated. The result is given by 4 imperfects, one of which (יֵבֹשׁוּ) picks up vv. 3-4.[42]

Stanzas

The first two strophes clearly belong together in one stanza, both because of the similarity of structure (imperatives + כִּי clauses), and because of the second taking the first a bit further (sickness to death,

---

in *Directions in Biblical Hebrew Poetry*, ed. E. R. Follis. JSOT Supplement Series 40. (Sheffield: JSOT Press, 1987), 24), though see Ps. 74:12.

M. Girard (*Les Psaumes: Analyse structurelle et interprétation 1-50* (Montréal: Bellarmin, 1984), 83) takes vv. 2-5 together, suggesting an ABA'B'A''-structure. However, in view of the clear ABA'B' structure of v. 3, it seems strange to take vv. 2-3a as A and let 3b, which syntactically is closely connected to 3a, count as B.

[41]BHS, Delitzsch (*Psalms*, 1:133) and Craigie (*Psalms 1-50*, 93) (and Smit Sibinga, but see below) take vv. 5-8 as one single strophe. But whereas v. 6 took the "terrified bones" to its climax by indicating death as imminent, with v. 7 we are back to a picture of the distress, though now comparable to being dead. V. 7-8 thus connect both to vv. 3-4 and to v. 6. Smit Sibinga singles out v. 8 as not belonging to any strophe, being characterized by the subject "my eye"("Gedicht en Getal," 200-202). But we saw the variation from "I" to "my bones" to "my soul" in vv. 3-4—which no one doubts belong to the same strophe—so a variation from "I" to "my eye" is not surprising. Looking at the content, vv. 7 and 8 clearly belong together.

[42]Wahl, *Strophic Structure*, 74, singles out v. 11 by itself, but in view of the sliding movement through v. 10 it is best to take v. 11 together with vv. 9-10. So BHS, and e.g. Briggs, *Book of Psalms*, 1:48; Gunkel, *Psalmen*, 21; and J. Ridderbos (*De Psalmen*, 2 vols., Commentaar op het Oude Testament (Kampen: N. V. Uitgeversmaatschappij J. H. Kok, 1955), 1:51.

which is then used for a new argument). Likewise the last two make one stanza, the reasons for which are given below in our treatment of the progression in content and mood.

The psalm thus has a very symmetrical structure. The first and the fourth strophe contain 6 cola each. The second and the third strophe have 5 cola each. The two stanzas are, accordingly, of equal length, 11 cola each.

Progression in Content and Mood

The Psalm is generally regarded as an individual lament,[43] more precisely a psalm of sickness.[44] Broyles assigns it to the subgenre of the complaints of the individual.[45] The psalm contains most of the elements of the genre of lament: address to God, complaint, petition, and expression of trust. However, every individual psalm is "special," and we thus have to pay attention to the progression in content and mood in this particular psalm.

In the first stanza there are only two actors, Yahweh and "I." "I" is the speaker. The whole stanza is addressed to Yahweh. The psalm opens with two negative petitions, "do not *in your anger* reproach me and do not *in your wrath* correct me!" The italicized words are stressed by being put between the negation-marker and the verb. The psalmist knows he is a sinner deserving Yahweh's chastisement. His choice of verbs tells as much. We are not allowed to take the fact that no specific sins are numbered as revealing a shallow conscience or lack of penitence. The problem for him, however, is that Yahweh deals with him in his wrath rather than in his mercy.[46] The two negative petitions

---

[43]Different: Buttenwieser, *The Psalms*, 560; Briggs, *Book of Psalms*, 1:46. Birkeland, *Die Feinde des Individuums*, 311-312, thinks the "individual" here is the king.

[44]J. Ridderbos, *De Psalmen*, 1:52 + 55, and Birkeland (previous note) think of distress brought about by the enemies rather than bodily sickness. But it is doubtful whether the verb "heal" would be used if the main problem were the enemies.

[45]C. C. Broyles, *The Conflict of Faith and Experience in the Psalms*, 179.

[46]So Gunkel, *Psalmen*, 22, and H. C. Leupold, *Exposition of the Psalms* (Wartburg Press, 1959; Reprint, Grand Rapids: Baker Book House, 1969), 84; *pace* Calès, *Le livre des Psaumes*, 1:130; L. Sabourin, *The Psalms, Their Origin and Meaning*, 2 vols. (Staten Island: Alba House, 1974), 2:8-9. In Jer. 10:24 the meaning is clearly: It is right that you punish me, but do it not in wrath. Here the prayer for grace

are followed by two positive ones, each followed by a 'כ clause. The imperatives ask Yahweh to be gracious and to heal, the latter functioning as a specifying of the former, and the 'כ clauses give the reason why the psalmist needs this:[47] because he is feeble and because his bones are terrified. The latter verb has often been emended (see translation notes above) or assigned a special meaning that was thought more suitable for bones.[48] We think the psalmist means to say he is terrified. He is feeble, sick, and understands his state as being under God's wrath. V. 6 further shows death approaching. He is scared, and the fear takes hold of his very body. Thus we see "for my bones are terrified" intensifies "for I am feeble" in v. 3a, just as "Heal me" (v. 3b) specified "be gracious to me" (v. 3a). The verb is then repeated and strengthened in v. 4a: "and my soul ("my very self") is *very* terrified." With his own distress thus laid bare, the psalmist takes a breath and turns his eyes to God: "but you, O Yahweh." The key to the whole situation lies in Yahweh. Therefore the name "Yahweh" is repeated four times in these few lines. The psalmist is totally helpless. His future lies with Yahweh. "How long" lets a beam of hope come through; the psalmist does not think that Yahweh's wrath will last forever, but he is concerned for how long. On the other hand, it also points forward to the end of the second strophe; will his life end in death? Finally, this phrase makes it crystal clear that the negative petitions in v. 2 do not portray some hypothetical situation to be prevented but the present situation which the psalmist wants to end.

The second strophe of the stanza begins with three positive petitions. As there was an increase in the distress depicted by the verbs in the last strophe, so we see a development in the petitions here, as if

---

immediately following indicates that the question of a sensible punishment is not in the picture for the psalmist. Craigie, (*Psalms 1-50*, 92) thinks the psalmist merely asks Yahweh not to punish him for approaching him in prayer (cf. Gen. 18:30, 32). However, the context, especially the "how long" of v. 4b, tells us the wrath is experienced as a present reality, not only as a possibility. The prayer is for God to stop reproaching the psalmist.

[47]For the use of *kî* in prayers, see A. Aejmelaeus, *The Traditional Prayer in the Psalms* (Berlin: Walter de Gruyter, 1986), 68-79.

[48]Thus Airoldi, "Note Critiche al Salmo 6," 285, translates "le mie membra sono deperite," my limbs waste away.

the psalmist becomes braver in each petition he utters. First he uses an intransitive verb, שׁוּבָה, "turn around," not a definite prayer for help, but only for God to change. The object of the second petition "deliver" is "my life," thus making sort of a chiasm with v. 4: the petition "turn around" echoes the complaint "how long"; "O Yahweh" parallels "but you, O Yahweh"; and "deliver my life (נַפְשִׁי)" picks up "and my soul (נַפְשִׁי) is very terrified." The third petition, "save me," is followed by a motivation, "for the sake of your steadfast love." The psalmist cannot point to a reason in himself why God should help. He has above silently admitted to sin, but he knows that Yahweh is characterized by steadfast love and so he appeals to Yahweh's character. As in strophe 1 the psalmist adds a reason for his prayer. Now he does not speak of his present state but of what makes him so terrified: He may have to die soon, under God's wrath, and never more experience the love-relationship with Yahweh in worship and praise. He longs for a life where he can go with God's people to God's temple and praise him, but death is about to deprive him of that hope. However, by pointing to this relationship the psalmist is also motivating God to do something about his situation. He is not talking about sacred rituals before the wall. He stands in an I-you relationship to Yahweh. Israel's worship was instituted by Yahweh. Yahweh wants to be praised by his people. Thus Yahweh would not let those who praise him end up in a situation where they no longer are able to do so.[49]

What the psalmist wants restored is a life of continual praise of Yahweh, not simply a continued existence. The experienced "realities" move from Yahweh's wrath, via sickness, to death. The prayer is for grace and steadfast love to a life in praise and hope in Yahweh's steadfast love and will to fellowship.

The second stanza picks up the description of the psalmist's distress in vv. 3-4. Vv. 7-8 contain five complaints, three with "I" as subject, two with "my eye." The first stands by itself. The second is parallel to the third. These two have imperfects, picturing the action as ongoing. The fourth and fifth have perfects, giving the result brought

---

[49]Cf. J. Ridderbos, *De Psalmen*, 1:59. Note the motivation lies in God's will to fellowship.

about to his eye. The stress is on tears.[50] He is weary of sighing, he cries all night, and his eyes start failing.

The purpose of telling this to God is that the psalmist's tears should move God to pity. Notice the contrast between v. 6 and vv. 7-8: The psalmist wants to praise Yahweh, but now he weeps instead. In v. 8b the third group of actors in this psalm, the enemies, are brought in. Who they are, we are not told. Perhaps there were people who tried to take advantage of the psalmist's weakness—such people are always around[51]—or maybe they were mockers who would ridicule his claim of having a relationship with Yahweh.[52] "You who do injustice" in v. 9 would go well with that. Whoever and whatever they were, they were part of the situation that made the psalmist weep till his eyes were failing.

We saw that the "but you" at the end of the first strophe paved the way for the petitions and the appeal to Yahweh's steadfast love in the second. Similarly, the introduction of the enemies at the end of strophe 3 prepares for strophe 4. In the fourth strophe the enemies, rather than the sickness, are in focus. The imperative at the very beginning of this strophe is addressed to them rather than to Yahweh. The strophe is very different in tone from the preceding. How did that come about? I think the key is found in the phrase the psalmist uses for the enemies in v. 9a: "all you who do injustice." This designation stresses their anti-Yahweh character. "Injustice" (whatever the precise connotations of the word) displeases Yahweh, and the participle in construct chain depicts them in the habit of doing this, or as people whose personal character it is to do what God dislikes. As the psalmist focuses on these people and thinks of his own state, he suddenly knows Yahweh has heard him. Yahweh will not let the wicked vex him.[53]

---

[50]K. Seybold, *Das Gebet des Kranken im Alten Testament* (Stuttgart: Kohlhammer, 1973), 154, sees the weeping as ritual. Against this view weighs v. 8b: "it has grown old because of all my enemies."

[51]See Ps. 22:19.

[52]See Ps. 22:8-9.

[53]See M. Weiss, *The Bible from Within*, 312-313. This "rapid change of mood" has been differently interpreted. J. Begrich, "Das priestliche Heilsorakel", *Zeitschrift für die alttestamentliche Wissenschaft* 52 (1934): 81-92, thinks a priestly oracle of salvation comes between the complaint and the assurance. A. Weiser, *The Psalms, A Commentary*, The Old Testament Library. (London: SCM Press, 1962), 133, suggests that the whole psalm "was uttered after the cult community had partaken of the general

As in stanza I, the imperative is followed by a כִּי clause: Yahweh has heard and paid attention to his weeping (described in vv. 7-8). Yahweh, to whose steadfast love he appealed in stanza I, knows all about his situation and about what the doers of injustice do to him. As in v. 4, the psalmist elaborates on the כִּי clause, repeating the verb, but as Airoldi points out,[54] with a different nuance: "Yahweh has heard my supplication," not only paid attention to it but granted it. Also, note the reflection of v. 3a. There the psalmist prayed for grace; here he states that Yahweh has heard his petition for grace.

This expansion is then brought in chiastic parallelism to a second expansion: "Yahweh receives my prayer." We notice that the name Yahweh is repeated twice. Yahweh had brought about the miserable situation; Yahweh has made it cease. The enemies are made to be bystanders in this psalm. We have no verb to describe their actions against the psalmist. The only actions assigned to them are those followed by Yahweh's intervention: they will be put to shame and so forth. Then the psalmist's focus slides from giving the reason he could order the enemies to depart to speaking about them in third person on the basis of the fact that Yahweh has heard. The psalmist boldly states in four imperfects that the foes will be terrified and put to shame. The words "will be put to shame . . . will be put to shame suddenly" enclose the verse. Their scheme will fail. They will stand with shame as failures in what they tried to accomplish. The second verb, יִבָּהֲלוּ ("will be very terrified"), picks up vv. 3-4. I *was* very terrified, now the enemies *will be*. שׁוּב picks up v. 5a. Since Yahweh has *turned around* from his wrath toward me, now my enemies will *turn around* and leave. Notice also the connection between the very last word in this verse and v. 4. There the psalmist asked "how long." Here he has received the answer: the enemies will be put to shame "suddenly."

assurance of salvation." E. K. Kim, *The Rapid Change of Mood in the Lament Psalm*, Seoul: Korea Theological Study Institute, 1985, finds the background in the holy war tradition. Like Kim we see the psalm composed as a whole, not in a pre-oracle/post-oracle fashion. We think there is a close connection between the appeal of the psalm and the assurance, not as a sort of self-suggestion, but by giving attention to Yahweh and his *chesedh* (that the name Yahweh is mentioned eight times in this short psalm seems to support this).

[54]Airoldi, "Note Critiche al Salmo 6", 288-289 notes that the parallel of "receives" gives to "has heard" the meaning "esaudire" (Latin: exaudire).

The Problem

The physical distress in Psalm 6 seems to be bodily sickness (see vv. 3, 7-8), though the language is too general to say anything about what kind of sickness. Perhaps this is deliberate, to make the psalm available for many sorts of distress. Fear is very present. The psalmist is terrorized by the thought that he may have to end his life under Yahweh's wrath and go down to Sheol, forever excluded from the praise-relation to Yahweh (vv. 3-4 and v. 6). The enemies or doers of injustice play an obscure role in the psalm. They are clearly part of the distress, but no action on their part is described. The cause of the distress is Yahweh's wrath: "O Yahweh, do not reproach me in your anger, nor rebuke me in your wrath!" (v. 2). The wrath is depicted as active; God is actively punishing the psalmist.

The Prayer

The psalmist asks Yahweh not to punish him (for his sins) in wrath, but rather to be gracious to him and heal him from his sickness and save his life. He fears a death that separates him from Yahweh and wants to come back into the relationship with Yahweh where he can praise and worship him. It is worth noticing that there is no explicit prayer for rescue from the enemies, which seems to underscore that they are deliberately marginalized. God is the problem, and God is the solution.

The Appeal

The psalmist describes his distress to Yahweh, clearly with the thought that Yahweh should have compassion. The last strophe, where the psalmist declares that Yahweh has, indeed, paid attention to his weeping, confirms this. The reason for speaking of one's distress to God is "for the sake of your steadfast love," an appeal to Yahweh's "personal character." The psalmist grounds his appeal in the relation between himself and Yahweh. He is among those who will praise Yahweh, and this praise pleases Yahweh.

Conversely, the psalmist's tears move God to pity. Thus the threatening possibility of death, separated from the praise of God, is also an argument for Yahweh to act before the curtain falls. Finally, the way the enemies are handled is designed to motivate God to judge them. They are described as persons whose trait it is to do what God dislikes. The emphasis is not on what they have been doing to the psalmist. These are people that Yahweh is expected to punish, independently of their conflict with the psalmist.

Chapter Three

Psalm 44

1.   For the musical director. For the sons of Korah. A Maskil.

2a.   O God, with our ears we have heard;
 b.   our fathers have told us:
 c.   A deed you did in their days,
 d.   in days of old.
3a.   You with your hand dispossessed nations but them you planted;
 b.   you broke the peoples but made them send forth shoots.
4a.   For not by their sword did they take possession of the land,
 b.   and their arm did not gain victory for them.
 c.   No, for it was your right hand and your arm and the light of
       your face,
 d.   because you were well-disposed toward them.
5a.   You are my king, O God,
 b.   the one who appoints the victories of Jacob.
6a.   Through you we push down our enemies;
 b.   in your name we trample under foot those who rise up against
       us.
7a.   For not in my bow do I trust,
 b.   and my sword does not save me.
8a.   No, for you saved us from our enemies,
 b.   and those who hate us you have put to shame.
9a.   In God we boast all the time,
 b.   and your name we will praise for ever. Selah.

10a. But you have rejected us and brought disgrace on us,
 b.   and you did not go out with our armies!
11a. You made us retreat from the enemy,
 b.   and those who hate us plundered for themselves.
12a. You delivered us up like sheep for food,
 b.   and among the nations you scattered us.

13a.   You sold your people for nothing,
  b.   and you did not set the price for them high.
14a.   You made us a reproach to our neighbors,
  b.   a scorn and derision to those who surround us.
15a.   You made us a proverb among the nations,
  b.   a shaking of the head among the peoples.
16a.   All the time my disgrace is before me,
  b.   and the shame of my face covers me,
17a.   because of the voice of the reproacher and reviler,
  b.   because of the presence of the foe and avenger.
18a.   All this has come upon us, even though we have not forgotten you,
  b.   nor have we been unfaithful to your covenant.
19a.   Our heart did not draw back,
  b.   nor did our steps stray from your path,
20a.   that you have crushed us in a place of jackals
  b.   and covered over us with deep darkness.
21a.   If we had forgotten the name of our God
  b.   and spread our hands to a strange god,
22a.   would not God discover this?
  b.   For he knows the secrets of the heart.
23a.   No, for on account of you we are killed all the time;
  b.   we are regarded as sheep for slaughtering.

24a.   Rouse yourself! Why do you sleep, O Lord?
  b.   Awake! Do not reject forever!
25a.   Why do you hide Your face?
  b.   Why do you forget our misery and our affliction?
26a.   For bowed down to the dust is our soul;
  b.   our belly sticks to the ground.
27a.   Arise for our help,
  b.   and redeem us for the sake of your steadfast love!

Translation Notes

v. 1.   לִבְנֵי־קֹרַח מַשְׂכִּיל – "For the sons of Korah. A Maskil"

According to 1 Chron. 9:17-24 and 26:1-19, the Korahites were gatekeepers in the temple and responsible for guarding the thresholds. In 2 Chron. 20:19 they stand up in the public worship and praise Yahweh with loud voice. Several psalms are assigned to them: Psalms 42-49 (if Ps. 42-43 is regarded as one psalm), 84-85, and 87-88.[1] The meaning of the term "Maskil" remains obscure.[2]

v. 3a.   אַתָּה יָדְךָ – "You with your hand"

BHS suggests reading בְיָדְ, "with your hand." In favor of this solution, it makes the cola more even, and "you" is absent in LXX. However, LXX most certainly did not read a preposition before "hand," and LXX further attests to the same verse division as MT. Even though the construction sounds strange to us, it is well attested in Hebrew poetry to use two subjects, one of the person and the other of the instrument.[3]

---

[1] Cf. M. J. Buss, "Psalms of Asaph and Korah," *Journal of Biblical Literature* 82 (1963): 382-392. M. D. Goulder, *The Psalms of the Sons of Korah*, JSOT Supplement Series 20 (Sheffield: JSOT Press, 1982) thinks these psalms were composed by Danite clergy before the fall of the Northern Kingdom and became "Jerusalemized" as the Korahites later rose to prominence at the Jerusalem temple. Psalm 44 has been variously dated. For different views see H. M. Parker Jr., "Artaxerxes III Ochus and Psalm 44," *The Jewish Quarterly Review* 68 (1978): 152-168 (344 BC), Delitzsch, *Psalms*, 2:66 (At the time of David [2 Sam. 8:5-14]), E. Vogt, "Psalmus 44 et Tragoedia Ezechiae regis," *Verbum Domini* 45 (1967): 193-200 (time of Hezekiah). See further Beaucamp, *Le Psautier*, 1:191-192. An exilic date appears to us to be less than likely, given the strong profession of innocence. In all probability the psalm is pre-exilic, but whether it refers to the campaign of Sennacherib in 701, to the battle at Megiddo in 609, or to another war, is not possible to ascertain.

[2] Cf. Weiser, *The Psalms*, 281; Mowinckel, *The Psalms in Israel's Worship*, 2:209; and Kraus, *Psalms 1-59*, 32.

[3] GKC, § 144,l,m. Examples are Pss. 3:5; 27:7; 60:7; Hab. 3:15. So M. Girard, *Les Psaumes: Analyse structurelle et interprétation: 1-50*, Recherches Novelle série-2. (Montréal: Bellarmin–Paris: Cerf, 1984), 353. Jacquet, *Les Psaumes et coeur de l'homme*, 2:22 emends. Calès, *Le livre des Psaumes*, 1:458 and 462, retains MT, but connects the phrase to v. 2, and translates: "Aux jour d'autrefois,–de ta propre main."

v. 3b.　תָּרַע – "you broke"

MT points it as a hiphil of רעע I, "do evil, treat badly, harm." BHS and KB want to repoint it to read a qal from רעע II, a root that is common in Aramaic and corresponds to Hebrew רצץ. That the Aramaic influence was felt long before the time of the exile is now well established. More important, the qal of this verb is attested in Biblical Hebrew 10 times,[4] for example Ps. 2:9; Isa. 8:9 and Prov. 11:15. That later Jewish tradition would tend to read the more common Hebrew homonym is plausible. The Aramaic meaning fits the context somewhat better.

v. 3b.　וַתְּשַׁלְּחֵם – "but made them send forth shoots"

The suffix is ambiguous, but parallelism seems to demand that "our fathers" is the object. The rendering given above follows Dahood. He parses it as a piel of a denominative verb from שלח "sprout, shoot."[5] Whether that is correct or not, the verb is sometimes used with plants sending forth their shoots (Ps. 80:12; Jer. 17:8 and Ezek. 17:6).[6]

v. 4a+c.　כִּי . . . כִּי – "For . . . for"

The first כִּי is used as indirect explanation, and as such does not state the cause for what is actually said in the previous verse but rather the reason for saying it. The second כִּי introduces a positive alternative after a negative statement.[7]

---

[4]Even-Shoshan, 1088.

[5]Dahood, *Psalms*, 1:263,265.

[6]So also Leupold, *Exposition of the Psalms*, 346. For different translations, see Girard, *Les Psaumes*, 353; Sabourin, *The Psalms*, 2:145, and Weiser, *The Psalms*, 353.

[7]See A. Aejmelaeus, "Function and Interpretation of כִּי in Biblical Hebrew," *Journal of Biblical Literature* 105/2 (1986): 193-209. For the first כִּי in v. 4, see page 203; for the second, see page 200.

v. 4d.   וְאוֹר פָּנֶיךָ – "and the light of your face"

The phrase is applied to Yahweh also in Pss. 4:7 and 89:16. The
corresponding verbal phrase, הָאִיר פָּנָיו, is used nine times in the Old
Testament—eight with God as subject. It stands parallel to the verb חָנַן
in Num. 6:25 and Ps. 67:2. In Psalm 80 the phrase: וְהָאֵר פָּנֶיךָ וְנִוָּשֵׁעָה,
"let your face shine, that we may be saved," is used three times (vv. 4,
8, and 20). Similarly, in Ps. 31:17 the phrase is parallel to הוֹשִׁיעֵנִי,
"save me." Thus our phrase indicates that Yahweh is favorably
disposed so that he graciously saves. This is corroborated by the
secular use in Prov. 16:15: "In the light of the king's face is life, and
his favor (רְצוֹנוֹ) is like a cloud of the late rain."

v. 5a.   אַתָּה־הוּא מַלְכִּי – "You are my king"

This is what Waltke and O'Connor call an "identifying clause."
The particular use of הוּא serves to single out the subject and to
contrast it with other possible alternatives. The contrast in our verse is
not with other gods, but rather is a strong affirmation that the
psalmist's God is none other than the one who performed the mighty
deeds for the fathers.[8]

v. 5b.   [מְצַוֶּה] – "the one who appoints"

MT has an imperative. But we are now in the part of the psalm
where the psalmist says that the God of the fathers is the God of the
present generation and that he is even now the same as before. Later
the psalmist will emphasize how this perspective contrasts with what
the people currently experience from God. LXX reads a participle. We
think the MT text here is a result of haplography, and with the BHS
apparatus we read a participle.[9]

---

[8]Waltke-O'Connor, § 16.3.3b and c. See also Joüon-Muraoka, § 154j.

[9]So Calès, *Le livre des Psaumes*, 1:458 and 462 and E. Beaucamp, *Le Psautier*, 2
vols. Sources Bibliques (Paris: Gabalda, 1976), 1:190. Weiser, *The Psalms*, 353,
retains MT. Another possible solution is proposed by Dahood, *Psalms*, 1:263,265. He
simply moves the *mem* from אלהים over to make אלהי מצוה and lets the suffix do
double duty: "my God, my Commander" (and then he takes ישועות to mean "Savior").

v. 9a. בֵּאלֹהִים הִלַּלְנוּ – "In God we boast"

הלל in the usual sense "praise" does not take the preposition with the object. BHS and KB want us to read a hithpael, "make one's boast of" (an established meaning of the hithpael of this verb). BDB takes it in a similar sense but refrains from suggesting an emendation. That will also be our course, that is, assigning a hithpael meaning without deciding whether a piel could be used with this nuance.

v. 10a. אַף־זָנַחְתָּ וַתַּכְלִימֵנוּ – "But you have rejected us and brought disgrace on us"

For אף with an adversative function, see also Ps. 58:3. The suffix of the second verb does double duty.

v. 11b. שָׁסוּ לָמוֹ – "plundered for themselves"

Neither שׁסה nor the related שׁסס are elsewhere used with a reflexive pronoun (unlike הלך, see Gen. 12:1). We thus think the pronoun here is used to stress the inability of Israel to interfere with what they were doing. The enemies could do exactly what they wanted.[10]

v. 13a. בְּלֹא־הוֹן – "for nothing"

Literally: "for not-wealth." For ב with מכר to denote the price, see Amos 2:6 and Joel 4:3.

v. 13b. וְלֹא־רִבִּיתָ בִּמְחִירֵיהֶם – "and you did not set the price for them high."

Or: "and you did not increase (your wealth) by their price." רבה is used in the piel in Judg. 9:29; Ezek. 19:2 and Lam. 2:22, all with direct

[10]So, e.g., Delitzsch, *Psalms*, 2:63, 69-70; F. Nötscher, *Die Psalmen*, Echter-Bibel (Würzburg: Echter-Verlag, 1953), 87, and Craigie, *Psalm 1-50*, 330. For the preterital use of the *yiqtol* form in vv. 10-15, cf. Joüon-Muraoka, § 113h.

objects. Thus our verse will stand out against the other three instances no matter how we translate. We have taken the prepositional phrase as the object.

v. 15b. מְנוֹד־רֹאשׁ בַּל־אֻמִּים – "a shaking of the head among the peoples"

We understand the phrase as an expression of mockery (cf. הֵנִיעַ רֹאשׁ in 2 Kings 19:21 and Ps. 22:8).[11] The Leningrad codex has בַּל־אֻמִים, which does not make sense. The majority of Hebrew manuscripts have the text as we have rendered it.

v. 16b וּבֹשֶׁת פָּנַי – "and the shame of my face"

For this phrase, see Jer. 7:19; Dan. 9:7-8; Ezra 9:7; and 2 Chron. 32:21.

v. 17a+b. מִקּוֹל . . . מִפְּנֵי – "because of the voice of . . . because of the presence of"

It is possible to translate מִפְּנֵי, "because of."[12] However, the parallelism with מִקּוֹל seems to require a corresponding translation of the two phrases.[13]

v. 19a. לֹא־נָסוֹג אָחוֹר – "did not draw back"

The phrase has the connotation "become disloyal." For this meaning in a secular context, see Jer. 38:22 (where it is used with אָחוֹר); for disloyalty to Yahweh, see Ps. 78:57 and Isa. 59:13.[14]

---

[11]Craigie, *Psalms 1-50*, 331 takes it as a gesture of sorrow. In favor of this is the frequent use of the verb נוד in the meaning "shake one's head in mourning" (Job 2:11; Jer. 16:5 and 22:10). The context seems, however, to require a reference to mocking rather than to mourning rites. The substantive מנוד is a hapax.

[12]So Craigie, *Psalms 1-50*, 331.

[13]So Delitzsch, *Psalms*, 2:63, and Nötscher, *Die Psalmen*, 87.

[14]See further F. Reiterer, "סוג," *TWAT*, 5:769-774, and BK, 703.

v. 19b. וַתֵּט אֲשֻׁרֵינוּ – "nor did our steps stray"

The form of the verb seems to be either third person feminine singular or second person masculine singular of נטה in the qal conjugation. The subject is feminine plural, but it is not unusual that plural names of animals or things and abstracts are construed with a feminine singular (Ps. 37:31 and Jer. 4:14).[15]

vv. 20a and 23a. כִּי ... כִּי – "that . . . No, for"

With RSV we understand the first כִּי as consecutive (Gen. 40:15 and Ps. 8:5). "On account of you" in v. 23 is probably intended as the antithesis to what is argued in vv. 21-22: The reason does not lie with us. Thus the כִּי in v. 23 introduces a positive alternative after a negative statement (cf. vv. 4 and 8).[16]

v. 20a. בִּמְקוֹם תַּנִּים – "in a place of jackals"

Jackals as desert animals often belong to the picture of places having become ruins and wastelands after a divine judgment (Isa. 34:12-15; Jer. 10:22 and 49:33). Either the battle was held at a desolate place, or the battlefield was felt to be a desolate place as the armies had left and only the corpses remained. Some have taken תַנִּים here as a variant of תַנִּין, "the dragon" (compare Ezek. 29:3 and 32:2). A few manuscripts actually have תנין. M. Girard translates: "le lieu du monstre (marin)." He understands this place to be the nether world and thus parallel to v. 20b. E. Beaucamp takes במקום to mean "à la place de," an understanding that he shares with Gunkel. Dahood suggests a new word division: במק מתנים, "with festering of the loins."[17]

---

[15]Cf. GKC, § 145k. Many manuscripts read אשרנו, "our step", feminine singular. LXX seems to read a hiphil 2nd. person masculine singular and takes God as the subject.

[16]For the a consecutive use of כִּי, see Joüon-Muraoka, § 169e. For the use in v. 23, see Aejmelaeus, "Function and Interpretation of כִּי," 200.

[17]Girard, *Psaumes*, 354; Beaucamp, *Le Psautier*, 1:190-191; Gunkel, *Die Psalmen*, 184,188; Dahood, *Psalms*, 1:267.

v. 20b. בְּצַלְמָוֶת – "with deep darkness"

Ever since LXX the traditional translation of this word has been "shadow of death," taking it as a compound of צֵל and מָוֶת. The main problem with this translation is that the meaning appears not to fit most of the occurrences in the Old Testament. The phrase וצלמות חשֶׁךְ is found four times. In addition, there are six places where חשֶׁךְ, "darkness," and צלמות are parallel, always with חשֶׁךְ placed first. Only once is the word parallel to מָוֶת, "death." Thus it would appear צלמות must be a word that narrows down or intensifies חשֶׁךְ. Luther simply translated the word "Finsternis," "darkness." Further, compound words are very rare in Hebrew (except in proper names). Now, in cognate languages there exist words meaning "black, dark" that apparently are derived from the root צלם. KB,[18] and probably a majority of Biblical scholars today, derive צלמות from this root, translating "deep darkness." Some scholars have criticized this derivation, though, preferring the traditional one.[19] The word is attested in Ugaritic, but there is no agreement as to which conclusions may be drawn from the Ugaritic.

Both the "jackals" and "deep darkness" evoke strong negative connotations (for the latter, see Isa. 9:1; Amos 5:8 and Job 38:17). Jer.

---

[18]KB, 964.

[19]See D. W. Thomas, "צַלְמָוֶת in the Old Testament," *Journal of Semitic Studies* 7 (1962):191-200. He comes close to the meaning generally assigned to the word by modern scholarship, however, since he understands "shadow of death" to mean "deadly darkness." He is apparently followed by Craigie, *Psalms 1-50*, 331, J. Barr, "Philology and Exegesis: some general remarks with illustrations from Job," *Biblotheca Ephemeridum Theologicarum Lovaniensum* 33 (1974):39-61, and W. L. Michel, "SLMWT, "Deep Darkness" or "Shadow of Death"? *Biblical Research* 29 (1984):5-20. Michel maintains that the meaning "shadow of death" or "shelter of Mot" as an epithet of the underworld is appropriate in most of the occurrences. He seems to confuse meaning and reference. He is right that it sometimes (but by no means always, e.g. Job 24:17; 28:3) *refers* to the nether world (e.g. Job 10:21-22). However, the parallels with חשֶׁךְ, "darkness," even in these contexts (Job 3:5; 10:21), show that the *meaning* lies in the general area of "darkness." He further argues the root ṢLM, "dark," is rare or unattested in Hebrew. That, however, carries little weight since it is quite normal in languages that only one word from a certain root survives. See further H. Niehr, "צלמות," *TWAT*, 6:1056-1059.

2:6 has the expression בְּאֶרֶץ צִיָּה וְצַלְמָוֶת, "in a land of drought and deep darkness," which is precisely where we would find jackals.

LXX and a few Hebrew manuscripts make צלמות the subject of the clause.

vv. 21a-22a. אִם־שָׁכַחְנוּ . . . הֲלֹא אֱלֹהִים יַחֲקָר־זֹאת – "If we had forgotten . . . would not God discover this?"

Another possibility would be with Jacquet to take אִם in the meaning "certainly not" as in Isa. 22:14; Pss. 89:36; and 132:3,4.[20] Jacquet translates vv. 21-22: "Nul n'a donc oublié le Nom de notre Dieu, ni tendu les mains vers un dieu étranger. Est-ce que Dieu sur ce point se serait mépris, Lui qui connaît les arcanes du cœur?"[21]

v. 21b. וַנִּפְרֹשׂ כַּפֵּינוּ לְאֵל זָר – "and spread our hands to a strange god"

But for one instance (Prov. 31:20) פרש כפים always denotes prayer, and except for our verse, always (10 times) to Yahweh.

v. 24b. אַל־תִּזְנַח – "Do not reject"

R. Yaron has argued that this verb should be connected to Accadian zenû, "to be angry," rather than be given the traditional translation "reject."[22] His main argument is that the verb often stands without an object and that it sometimes is parallel to "be angry." Apart from Hos. 8:3, 5 and Lam. 2:7 his suggested translation would seem to be possible, but so is the traditional one. The Accadian word was known already by BDB, where it is said that it is not connected to the Hebrew verb. Neither KB nor TWAT[23] has taken up Yaron's

---

[20]Cf. Joüon-Muraoka, § 165j.

[21]Jacquet, Les Psaumes, 2:23 and 27.

[22]R. Yaron, "The Meaning of ZANACH," Vetus Testamentum 13 (1963): 237-239.

[23]KB, 265; H. Ringgren, "זנח," TWAT, 2:619-621.

suggestion. Further study seems to be needed on this word. We, accordingly, follow the traditional translation, although we do not rule out the one suggested by Yaron.

v. 25a. לָמָה־פָנֶיךָ תַסְתִּיר – "Why do you hide your face?"

When Yahweh hides his face, he does not listen to prayer (Pss. 69:17-18; 88:14-15; 102:2-3; 143:6-7; and Micah 3:4). He does not pay attention to the situation in which his faithful find themselves (Ps. 10:11). In Ps. 13:2, as in our verse, the expression is parallel to שכח, "forget." Deut. 31:17 tells us that when Yahweh hides his face, the people will be לאכל, "for consumption," and will experience much misery (רעות רבות). When Yahweh hides his face, people are terrified (Pss. 30:8; 104:29). S. E. Balentine[24] has shown that the phrase is used mainly in two contexts—judgment in the prophetic writings and lament in the Psalms.

v. 26.   כִּי שָׁחָה לֶעָפָר נַפְשֵׁנוּ דָּבְקָה לָאָרֶץ בִּטְנֵנוּ – "For bowed down to the dust is our soul; our belly sticks to the ground

Falling to the ground is the posture taken after Israel lost against Ai (Joshua 7:6), while the six men in Ezekiel's vision were killing the people of Jerusalem (Ezek. 9:8), and when Pelatiah son of Benayah died (Ezek. 11:13). In all these cases the posture is accompanied by fervent prayer to Yahweh not to destroy his people. In Joshua 7:6 Joshua and the elders remained on the ground until the evening. This picture fits well with the self-description of the people in our verse. They lie there struck by the serious blow Yahweh had administered to them, and they lie there to beg God to save his people. It is a posture of mourning,[25] but mourning taken before the face of God to obtain delivery.

---

[24]S. E. Balentine, *The Hidden God: The Hiding of the Face of God in the Old Testament*, Oxford: Oxford University Press, 1983. See also L. Perlitt, "Die Verborgenheit Gottes," in *Probleme biblischer Theologie*. Festschrift G. von Rad, ed. H. W. Wolf (Munich: Chr. Kaiser, 1971), 367-382.

[25]M. I. Gruber, *Aspects of Nonverbal Communication in the Ancient Near East*, 2 vols. (Rome: Biblical Institute Press, 1980), 463-465, 474-479. Gruber argues it is a

v. 27a.   קוּמָה עֶזְרָתָה לָּנוּ – "Arise for our help"

For the particular form of עזרה, see Pss. 63:8 and 94:17. With Delitzsch we understand עזרתה לנו as giving the purpose for the action requested by the preceding imperative.[26] An alternative would be to repoint it as a second person singular perfect of עזר and to understand it as a precative perfect (Deut. 6:5).[27]

v. 27b.   וּפְדֵנוּ לְמַעַן חַסְדֶּךָ – "and redeem us for the sake of your steadfast love"

With a human subject the verb פדה is used for the redemption of the firstborn. When God killed the firstborn of the Egyptians, he passed over the firstborn of the Israelites. Therefore all firstborn males, both of humans and livestock, are to be consecrated to Yahweh (Exod. 13:12). All the firstborn boys should be redeemed by paying redemption money (Exod. 13:13 and Num. 3:46-48),[28] and a donkey could be redeemed by a lamb (Exod. 13:13).[29] Apart from this particular use the word is generally used with God as subject and either Israel or an individual in Israel as its object (2 Sam. 7:23; Pss. 25:22; 49:16 and 71:23). When the object for the redemption is the people, the reference is very often to the exodus event (Deut. 13:6; Micah 6:4 and 1 Chron. 17:21). Since the word with God as subject is not found in the context of the sacrifices, the point of analogy is probably not the redemption sum[30] but the hopeless state of being handed over and the sole action of God with no human cooperation.[31]

---

posture of mourning and not a posture of prayer. The references he gives, however, are all accompanied with prayer.

[26]Delitzsch, *Psalms*, 2:72.

[27]So Dahood, *Psalms*, 1:268.

[28]That is, only for the firstborn who exceeded the number of Levites, since God had accepted the Levites instead of the firstborn (Num. 3:45-46).

[29]A special case is 1 Sam. 14:45, where the people redeem Jonathan after he unknowingly transgressed his father's oath.

[30]Contrast the usage in Mark 10:45.

[31]For למען חסדך, see our discussion in chapter 3.

Structure

Strophes

The psalm seems to have five strophes, vv. 2-4, 5-9, 10-17, 18-23, and 24-27.

Vv. 2-4: The fathers have told what God has done in their days. The strophe starts with the vocative "O God."

Vv. 5-9: The first colon of the second strophe connects with the vocative in the beginning of the first strophe, but now it is a strong affirmation that the God who performed the mighty deeds for the fathers is "my king." Notice the first person singular here and in v. 7. V. 6 has בך and בשמך, and v. 9 has באלהים and ושמך, thus framing vv. 6-9. Vv. 7-8 pick up v. 4 both in content and form.

Vv. 10-17: The strophe has six bicola (vv. 10-15) and concludes with a tetracolon (vv. 16-17). Vv. 11 and 12 have chiastic parallelism. All the bicola except v. 10 begin with an imperfect second person singular. (In v. 10 the first colon has a perfect and the second an imperfect.) The subject matter concerns the defeat in battle, and then from v. 14 on, the shame brought about by the military defeat. In vv. 14-15 the verb of the first colon does double duty for the second. Vv. 16-17 form an AA'BB' pattern. These two verses are in first person singular, as are vv. 5 and 7.

Vv. 18-23: The strophe forms an ABA'B' pattern. The people insist on their innocence (vv. 18-19), which is picked up by vv. 21-22 where it is stated that God would surely have discovered it if they had sinned. V. 20, a bicolon with initial כי, says that God has smitten them in spite of their innocence. Finally, v. 23, again a bicolon with initial כי, blames their misery on God.

Vv. 24-27: Petitions (v. 24 and v. 27) frame the complaint (vv. 25-26). V. 25 may be picking up on v. 4 (אור פניך) and is certainly referring to vv. 18 and 21 (לא שכחנוך).

Stanzas

The psalm consists of three stanzas, and the structure can be laid out as follows:

I. God is for the people (vv. 2-9)–God's past actions.
    God gave the fathers the land and gave them victories against
        their enemies (vv. 2-4).
    The God of the fathers is our God too (vv. 5-9).
II. God is against the people (vv. 10-23)—God's present actions.
    God has let us suffer defeat in war and the shame which
        follows from the defeat (vv. 10-17).
    God has done this to us even though we have been faithful to
        him (vv. 18-23).
III. Petitions that God return to being for his people (vv. 24-27)—
    God's future actions.[32]

Stanza I has 20 cola, stanza II 28 cola, whereas stanza III has eight
cola. Thus the first and the last stanza together are exactly as long as
the middle stanza.

Several words in stanza II pick up on the first stanza: צר and
משנאינו (v. 11) reflect v. 8 (the former is also found in v. 6). גוים and
לאמים (v. 15) remind us of v. 3. Further, בשת פני (v. 16) picks up on
הבישות of v. 8. These similarities heighten the contrast between the
"ideal" and the "reality," or between the past and the present.

An interesting feature of the structure of this psalm is the
alternation between first person plural and first person singular in the
second and third strophes. In strophe 2, "I" and "we" alternate; in
strophe 3 the "I" section is placed at the end of the strophe. There is
thus a parallel contrast between the "I" sections and between the "we"
sections.

Progression in Content and Mood

The psalm is generally regarded as a communal lament that
includes most of the elements associated with that genre. Broyles[33]

---

[32]Similar, though not identical: Craigie, *Psalms 1-50*, 332. Several scholars divide
the psalm into four stanzas, taking vv. 18-23 as Stanza III, and vv. 24-27 as the fourth.
So e.g. Gunkel, *Die Psalmen*, 184, J. Ridderbos, *De Psalmen*, 2:20-21, Briggs, *the
Book of Psalms*, 1:374-375, and Girard, *Psaumes*, 353-362.

[33]Broyles, *The Conflict of Faith*, 139-144.

assigns it to the subgenre of the complaint of the community. However, every psalm is unique, and we must try to trace how the complaint is put forward in this particular psalm.

The whole psalm is addressed to God. The speaker seems to be an individual speaking on behalf of the people. The psalm has a hymnic introduction. V. 2 opens with a vocative, "O God." Then the people recall how the fathers have told them about God's mighty works in the past. The phrase "you with your hand" stresses that the deeds to be related were performed by God and God alone. The things God did with his hand are then presented in an ABA'B' pattern: A and A' tell what he did to the nations/the peoples—He dispossessed them and broke them; B and B' tell what he did to Israel—He planted and made them send forth shoots (i.e., made them thrive and expand in the land).

V. 4 goes on to rule out any merit on the part of the fathers: It was not by their sword that they inherited the land; their arm did not save them. The latter verb does double duty for the rest of the verse: "No, it was your right hand and your arm (note the contrast with "their arm" and also the way this line underscores "you, with your hand") and the light of your face (that is, God's favor and blessing), because you were well-disposed toward them."

In v. 5 the psalmist shows how God's actions in the past are relevant for himself and for the people now: "You are my king, O God, who appoints the victories of Jacob." His God and king is the same who did those mighty works of past. The phrase "victories of Jacob" skillfully connects past and present. God gave "Jacob" victories in the past, and the people are still "Jacob." They can still expect the same. Note the first person singular here and in v. 7. The psalmist lets his personal confession and that of the people interchange, thus exemplifying that what is true for the people is true for the individual.[34]

---

[34]Mowinckel has suggested that the singular sections were spoken by the king or "one of the leading men of the congregation, such as the High Priest, or the governor, or the chairman of the council" (*The Psalms in Israel's Worship*, 1:226, cf. Craigie, *Psalms 1-50*, 332). This may be so, but it is easier to envision an individual praying on behalf of all throughout the entire psalm. We note that both the confession and the complaint of the "I" accord fully with the praise and the description of the distress of the "we."

V. 6 draws the consequences of this important fact with the crucial word בך: "Through you we shall push down (like a bull) our enemies; in your name we shall trample on those who rise up against us." With the same God as the fathers had, there should be nothing to fear! V. 7 parallels v. 4: "Not in my bow do I trust, and my sword (syntactically equivalent to "their arm" in v. 4b) does not save me." In v. 4 the verb does double duty, and here it is repeated: "No, you saved us from our enemies, and those who hate us you have put to shame (v. 8)." The same past actions of God are seen in the light of the confession in v. 5. God is the same, and the people are the same; thus it can be said: "You saved *us*." The stanza is rounded off with: "In (ב) God we boast all day long, and your name we will praise forever," picking up on v. 6, "through you" and "in your name." The victory comes from God, and the boast is in God. The ground for the boasting is God's deeds for "Jacob" in the days of the fathers. Therefore the people now boast in God all the time. "In God" also connects to "O God" in the first line of the stanza. *God* is what this stanza is all about.

Stanza II puts the current distress in bold contrast to how it should be according to stanza I. Vv. 10-13 retell what happened on the battlefield: "You have rejected us and brought disgrace on us" (v. 10a). This is spelled out more concretely in the second colon: "You did not go out with our armies." The next verse reverses the confident statement of v. 8: "You made us retreat from the enemy (instead of saving us from them); those who hate us plundered for themselves (instead of being put to shame by you)."

Vv. 11-15 all begin with second person singular imperfects, thus hammering home that God is the source of this misery. Notice that the military defeat and its consequences are depicted as active actions of God: You did this to us, you did that to us. V. 12 plays on the common metaphor of God as Israel's shepherd: "You delivered us up like sheep for food." No one took notice that sheep raised for food were slaughtered, for that was the very purpose for which they were raised.[35] God, the shepherd of Israel, has now treated his people as if they were just meant for the slaughter house. Instead of saving them in the land which he has given them as their inheritance, he spread them among

---

[35]Bentzen, *De gammeltestamentlige salmer*, 242.

the nations (that is, they were taken as prisoners of war), reversing the situation described in v. 3. He sold his people into slavery, and he did so for a very low price. It is as if they were of so little value to him that the most important thing was to get rid of them. Whether he was paid anything for the trade mattered little.[36] It should not be this way. The phrase "your people" assumes a covenant relationship between God and his people (this thought is picked up in v. 18). It serves to remind God who "we" are.

Vv. 14-17 describe the results of the defeat: "You made us a reproach to our neighbors." This is strengthened with two synonyms in the second colon. V. 15 reflects v. 3. In the past you dispossessed the *nations* and planted our fathers, but now you have made us a proverb among the *nations*; then you broke the *peoples* and made the fathers send forth shoots, but now you have made us a shaking of the head among the *peoples*. Again the psalm switches over into first person singular so as to let every single member of the people say, "This is how I experience it right now." In v. 9 it was said that the people boasted in God כל-היום, "all the time." Here "my disgrace is before me" כל-היום. Probably the phrase כל-היום is meant to do double duty for the second colon: "and the shame of my face covers me," that is, "it has overwhelmed my entire inward and outward being."[37] This is a far cry from what was said in v. 8b: "those who hate us you have put to shame." The reason for this vivid consciousness of shame is given in v. 17: "because of the voice of the reproacher and reviler, because of the presence of the foe and avenger."

In the present situation God has acted contrary to the norm set by his deeds in the past. He has not paid attention to the relationship he had established with the people. Could it be that God changed his course of action as a reaction to human infidelity? The fourth strophe negates this possibility in a most emphatic way. The people have not been unfaithful to God: "All this has come upon us even though we have not forgotten you, nor have we been unfaithful to your covenant. Our heart did not draw back (become disloyal), nor did our steps stray from your path." Disloyalty cannot explain that "you have crushed us

---

[36]Ibid., 242.

[37]Delitzsch, *Psalms*, 2:70.

in a place of jackals and covered over us with deep darkness"(v. 20).[38] We are crushed. We are in the darkest desolation and the deepest misery.

V. 21 picks up on vv. 18-19: If we had done so, God would surely have found out, "for he is the one who knows the secrets of the heart" (v. 22b). The underlying assertion is: But he has not found anything that could give him reason for doing what he has done. The conclusion is drawn: We are not to blame.[39] No, it is on account of you we are killed all the time; it is on account of you we are regarded as sheep for slaughtering (v. 23; compare v.12). God must take the full responsibility for what has happened.[40] There is no offense that can explain his present dealing with his people. This argument is clearly made under the assumption that God can be expected to treat his people *fairly.*

Note the repetition of כל־היום, "all the time." In v. 9 the people boast in God *all the time* because of what he did to the people in the days of the fathers, "in *days of old.*" However, as the focus is moved

---

[38]See translation notes to v 20.

[39]W. O. E. Oesterley remarks: "The unseemly tone of the psalmist's complaint is increased by the assertion of injured innocence (17-19); unlike the far more fitting attitude of many other psalmists when in trouble, whose sense of unworthiness bows their head in humility, we have here a claim of righteousness, and the implication that God has not been dealing fairly with his people." Oesterley, *The Psalms* (London: S.P.C.K., 1962), 248. But we should not take the statements in this psalm as claiming sinlessness in the theological sense of the word. Yahweh's covenant with Israel included provisions for how the people or an individual should deal with sins and weaknesses. When the people had repented of their sins, when they in their weakness set their heart to serve Yahweh, when the sacrifices were brought forward in accordance with Yahweh's stipulations, then the people could say: "We have not been unfaithful to your covenant."

[40]Kraus thinks the phrase עליך הרגנו, "on account of you we are killed," implies the suffering comes to the *community because it belongs to Yahweh.* He says: "Here the 'signs of the cross' already rest on the OT people of God (cf. Rom 8:36). Israel is chosen for suffering" (Kraus, *Psalms 1-59,* 448-449). But there is nothing in the psalm that would indicate that the mystery of righteous suffering has found its solution. On the contrary, the following verses very vividly point out that both the mystery and the terror remain. Thus it is more natural to see the statement as an antithesis to the preceding with the implication being: We have not caused this, so the blame must be on you—a protest to God. So Jacquet, *Les Psaumes,* 2:23. He translates: "Non, c'est pour Toi qu'on nous égorge tous les jour, qu'on nous . . . ."

from God's past actions to his present actions, v. 16 states, "my disgrace is before me" *all the time*. In v. 23 we see that God is the reason why they are killed *all the time*. With the people and the psalmist there is no change of attitude from past to present. The "I" confesses that God is his king (v. 5); he trusts in God and not in his own strength (v. 7). "We" boast in God (v. 9); "we" have not been unfaithful (v. 18). Only God's actions have changed.

Thus the foundation is laid for the prayer and the complaint in the last stanza. God has not been himself lately. He seems to be sleeping and therefore indifferent to his people: "Rouse yourself! Why do you sleep, O Lord? Awake! Do not reject (us) forever!" They want God to cease behaving the way he has been lately. The three petitions are followed by two complaints in question form: "Why do you hide your face" instead of saving us by the light of your face? "Why do you forget our misery and our affliction" when we have not forgotten you? These are not questions seeking a reasonable answer. They express bewilderment and inability to understand God's actions in the present. Their function is to protest against God's indifference and to implore God to end this intolerable state.[41]

This passivity and withdrawing of God describe the same situation that was depicted as God's active mistreatment of the people in the second stanza and in v. 20. God is both indifferent and hostile at the same time. This explains the urgency of the cries. God, the only possible savior according to stanza I, has rejected his people, has handed them over to their enemies, indeed, has himself become their enemy, and has withdrawn from their prayers. But they must persuade him to change his mind and to be favorable once more.

The next verse depicts the people as deeply moved by the distress: "For bowed down to the dust is our soul; our belly sticks to the ground." Joshua and the elders lie on the ground for hours after the defeat against Ai (Joshua 7:6). Now the people are continuously bowed down to the dust. Just as Joshua took his deep sorrow before Yahweh (Joshua 7:7), so they present their distress before God.

V. 27 contains two petitions: "Arise for our help and redeem us!" The people have need of God delivering them just as he delivered his

---

[41]See our translation notes to Ps. 74:1a, and to Ps. 88:15a.

people from Egypt. He has to go it alone. They are helpless.[42] Whereas
v. 24 had inserted a question or a complaint in question form, v. 27
adds a reference to Yahweh's character as a motivation for why God
should answer the prayer, "for the sake of your steadfast love." It was
unfair of God to crush the people when they were loyal to him.
However, the reason given why God should save them is not their
innocence but his character.

The Problem

Israel has suffered defeat in war. The enemies are national
enemies. Powerless, the people have had to watch them plunder just as
they pleased (v. 11b). Now Israel is ridiculed by its neighbors (vv. 14-
17). The military defeat and its consequences are interpreted as caused
by God. On the one hand, God is seen as actively delivering up his
people and selling them (vv. 10-13). He has made them a source of
mockery. On the other hand, God is depicted as absent, indifferent, and
hidden (vv. 24-25). To make matters worse, the people cannot
understand why God is doing this to them. They have been faithful to
him (vv. 18-23). Still he has acted contrary to the way they know him
from history.

The Prayer

The people want God to cease being inactive and hidden to their
prayers, to cease delivering them up to their enemies. They do not
want the present situation to go on forever (לנצח, v. 24). They want
God to go back to his previous way of behavior (vv. 2-9), when he
acted according to his covenant; they want the mutual relation between
God and his people restored (cf. vv. 6-9). They want God to help them
and to redeem them from their enemies, to give them victory over their
enemies: "Arise for our help and redeem us" (v. 27).

---

[42]See our translation note above.

The Appeal

The description of God's great saving works in the past (vv. 2-4) and the confession of the people that he remains the same as he was for the fathers (vv. 5-9) provide a *norm* according to which God should act. The argument is that the present situation by no means fits the description (v. 10-17). The people at present are one with the people of past (vv. 5 and 8). God was well-disposed toward the fathers, and he should still be so—the one who appoints the victories of Jacob. This relational appeal is supported by reference to God as Israel's shepherd (v. 12) and by the phrase "your people" (v. 13). The implicit allusion to the covenant in v. 13 is made explicit in v. 18: "We have not been unfaithful to your covenant." It is argued that the people have not been unfaithful so as to deserve God's punishment (vv. 18-22). The argument is that this is not fair! Vv. 25-26 appeal to the misery of the people: "Why do you hide your face? Why do you forget our misery and our affliction? For bowed down to the dust is our soul; our belly sticks to the ground." Nevertheless, what should make God act on their behalf is his steadfast love (v. 27).

Chapter Four

Psalm 74

1.   A Maskil by Asaph.

1a.   Why, O God, have you rejected forever?
  b.   Why does your anger fume against the flock of your
        pasturage?
2a.   Remember your congregation, which you acquired in ancient
        time,
  b.   which you redeemed as the tribe of your inheritance,
  c.   Mount Zion in which you dwelt.
3a.   Lift your footsteps to the utter ruins,
  b.   to everything which the foe has destroyed in the sanctuary.

4a.   Your enemies roared within your meeting-place;
  b.   they set up their own signs as signs.
5a.   He was known as one who brought up
  b.   axes into the thicket of trees.
6a.   So now her engravings all at once
  b.   with ax and clubs they were beating to pieces.
7a.   They set your sanctuary on fire;
  b.   to the ground they profaned the dwelling-place of your name.
8a.   They said in their hearts: "Let us oppress them all!"
  b.   They burned all the meeting-places of God in the land.
9a.   Signs for us we do not see; there is no longer a prophet,
  b.   and there is with us no one who knows how long.

10a.   How long, O God, will the enemy revile?
  b.   Will the foe disdain your name forever?
11a.   Why do you withdraw your hand, even your right hand?
  b.   (Take it) out from your lap! End it!

12a. O God, my king from ancient time,
  b. achiever of victories in the midst of the earth.
13a. You roused up in your strength the Sea;
  b. you broke the heads of the Tannins on the water.
14a. You crushed the heads of Leviathan;
  b. you gave them for food to seafarers.
15a. You divided spring and stream;
  b. you dried up perennial rivers.
16a. Yours is the day; yours is also the night.
  b. You established moon and sun.
17a. You fixed all the boundaries of the earth.
  b. Summer and winter, you formed them.

18a. Remember this: the foe reviles, O Yahweh,
  b. and a worthless people disdains your name!
19a. Do not give the soul of your turtle dove to the wild beasts;
  b. the life of your afflicted ones do not forget forever.
20a. Look at the covenant,
  b. for the hiding-places of the land are filled with dens of violence.
21a. Let not the oppressed turn back ashamed;
  b. let the afflicted and the poor praise your name.
22a. Arise, O God, conduct your case!
  b. Remember the reproach of you from the worthless all day long!
23a. Do not forget the noise of your enemies,
  b. the uproar of those who rise against you, which goes up constantly.

Translation Notes

v. 1#.　לְאָסָף – "by Asaph"

Twelve Psalms in the Psalter are assigned to Asaph: Psalm 50 and Psalms 73-83. The Chronicler describes Asaph as one of the chief singers appointed by David. Asaph, together with Heman and Ethan, was to sound bronze cymbals (1 Chron. 15:19 and 16:5). When David had appointed them, he committed a psalm to Asaph and his associates (16:7). Because at the time of David the temple was not yet built, let alone destroyed, it is hard to imagine that the title is intended to imply that Psalm 74 was written at the time of David.[1] "Asaph" probably refers to the Asaph-division of temple singers. Whether we then translate "by Asaph" or "for Asaph," the meaning is not much affected. The psalm originated and was used among the Asaph singers.[2]

The psalm is generally dated in the exile, although there are a few dissenting voices.[3]

v. 1a.   לָמָה אֱלֹהִים זָנַחְתָּ לָנֶצַח – "Why, O God, have you rejected forever"

Phrases starting with למה very often connote reproof (Gen. 12:18; Gen. 31:30; Exod. 2:13; and Jer. 44:7) or complaint (Pss. 10:1; 22:2; 44:24 and 88:15).[4] The phrase has this nuance in our verse. The psalmist is not primarily asking for God's reasons for rejecting them. He protests against this rejection and anger and wants God to stop it. For the verb זנח, see note to Ps. 44:24. W. A. Young calls attention to a certain ambiguity of the word נצח. It seems often to move back and forth from "forever" to "totally." This is reflected in his translation of the four instances of the word in this psalm, "unrelentingly" in v. 1,

---

[1] J. F. Brug holds the psalm to be written by David's contemporary through prophetic inspiration. J. F. Brug, *Psalms*, 2 vols. (Milwaukee, WI: Northwestern Publishing House, 1989), 2:11.

[2] See further M. J. Buss, "Psalms of Asaph and Korah," *Journal of Biblical Literature* 82 (1963): 382-392, and Mowinckel, *Psalms in Israel's Worship*, 2:95-97.

[3] Buttenwieser dates the psalm to 344 BC. Buttenwieser, *Psalms*, 606-616. H. Donner is very careful, but maintains that a Maccabean date is at least possible, H. Donner, "Argumente zur Datierung des 74. Psalms," in *Wort, Lied und Gottesspruch: Beitrage zu Psalmen und Propheten. Festschrift für Joseph Ziegler*, ed. J. Schreiner (Wurtsburg: Echter Verlag, 1972), 41-50.

[4] A. Jepsen has tried to show that למה, as opposed to מדוע, always has this sense. However, Barr has proved that this is not the case. Both words may have different nuances. The context will thus have to define the meaning more closely. A. Jepsen, "Warum? Eine lexikalische und theologische Studie," in *Das ferne und nahe Wort*, ed. F. Maass (Berlin: Alfred Töpelmann, 1967), 106-113; J. Barr, "Why in Biblical Hebrew," *Journal of Theological Studies* n. s. 36 (1985): 1-33.

"utter ruins" for מַשֻּׁאוֹת נֶצַח in v. 3a, and "forever" in vv. 10 and 19 where the context favors a temporal interpretation.[5] For v. 1, our understanding of the verb זָנַח prevents us from following Young's translation, but in the three remaining instances we follow him.

v. 1b.   יֶעְשַׁן אַפְּךָ – "Why does your anger fume"

"Why" of the previous colon does double duty. The expression probably refers to the sharp breath usually accompanying anger.[6]

v. 2a.   עֲדָתְךָ קָנִיתָ – "your congregation, which you acquired"

This is an asyndetic relative clause.[7]

v. 2c.   זֶה . . . בּוֹ – "in which"

זֶה is sometimes used as relative pronoun (Isa. 25:9 and Ps. 104:8).[8]

v. 3b.   כָּל־הֵרַע אוֹיֵב בַּקֹּדֶשׁ – "to everything which the foe has destroyed in the sanctuary"

This is an asyndetic relative clause, connected to v. 3a. The use of *maqqef* between כל and הרע in the Masoretic tradition supports this, since כל would have to be stressed if this were an independent sentence.[9]

---

[5]W. A. Young, "Psalm 74: A Methodological and Exegetical Study" (Ph.D. dissertation, University of Iowa, 1974), 62. The Greek translation "εἰς τέλος" has much of the same ambiguity, see P. R. Ackroyd, "נצח—εἰς τέλος," *Expository Times* 80 (1968-69): 126.

[6]See Gruber, *Nonverbal Communication*, 2:480-481 and 510-513.

[7]Cf. Joüon-Muraoka, § 158a, and GKC, § 155h.

[8]See GKC, § 138g.

[9]Young, "Psalm 74," 71-72, takes כל as an adverbial accusative.

v. 4b.   אֹתוֹת אוֹתֹתָם שָׂמוּ – "they set up their own signs as signs"

Some commentators think of military standards (compare Num. 2:2). Others maintain that the psalmist speaks of religious abominations so as to make it parallel to v. 9, "our signs."[10] However, military standards would most probably be the emblem of the victorious god, who was, if an exilic date is accepted, probably Marduk. Thus, the religiously abominable would be present with military standards. The signs in v. 9 could then be *their* equivalent to the signs of the victorious presence of Marduk, which would be signs that Yahweh is present and will save. Such signs could be his prophetic word or whatever God gave them as a pledge that he would intervene.[11]

v. 5.   יִוָּדַע כְּמֵבִיא לְמָעְלָה בִּסֲבָךְ־עֵץ קַרְדֻּמּוֹת – "He was known as one who brought up axes into the thicket of trees"

This and the following verse have been considered very difficult and definitely corrupt. However, the problems sometimes have been overstated. For the translation of these verses we are indebted to R. Sollamo. She calls attention to Hab. 2:17, where Nebuchadnezzar is condemned for "the violence done to Lebanon," referring to the king's felling program in the forests. Nebuchadnezzar boasts of the same in an inscription. Further, the height of Lebanon would explain לְמָעְלָה. Finally the plural, "axes" (another supposed corruption), would go well with a king using workers.[12] It is also possible that felling a forest was a well known metaphor for crushing an enemy. Compare Jer. 46:22-23

---

[10]Among the former is Beaucamp, *Psautier*, 2:10: "il y a hissé son blason (= Coat of arms). The latter view is forwarded e.g. by Donner, "Argumente zur Datierung," 43. Somewhere in between comes Calès, *Psaumes*, 2:15: "Ils y ont introduit leurs étendards de guerre et peut-être leurs idoles et les autres emblèmes de leurs superstitions, les substituant aux signes de la présence de Iahvé et de la religion révélée à Israël."

[11]See further Kraus, *Psalms 60-150*,98-99, and Gunkel, *Psalmen*, 324. Contra Delitzsch, *Psalms*, 2:330-331.

[12]R. Sollamo, "The Simile in Ps 74:5: A Wood-cutter Entering a Forest Wielding Axes," *Svensk Exegetisk Årsbok* 54 (1989): 178-187.

where the prophet says that Nebuchadnezzar (v. 13) will come against Egypt with axes (קַרְדֻּמּוֹת as in Ps. 74:5), like men who cut down trees and chop down her forest. This can hardly be taken literally, since there was no forest in Egypt. Thus v. 5 could well mean: "The enemy is known as one who destroys kingdoms." However, the traditional translation is by no means impossible: "It was known as when someone brings up axes in the thicket of trees."[13]

v. 6a.   וְעַתָּ – "So now"

ועת is a defective spelling of וְעַתָּה (see Ezek. 23:43).

v. 6a.   פִּתּוּחֶיהָ – "her engravings"

LXX has τὰς θύρας αὐτῆς, "her doors,"[14] which is a reading of the consonantal text before the *mater* letter *waw* entered. MT has the rarer word and should be followed. The feminine suffix is odd, since מוֹעֵד is masculine. Is the antecedent Zion?

v. 7a.   שִׁלְּחוּ בָאֵשׁ – "have set on fire"

For this idiom, see Judg. 1:8; 20:48 and 2 Kings 8:12.[15]

v. 8a.   נִינָם יָחַד – "Let us oppress them all"

This verse is not easy. With BHS apparatus and Even-Shoshan we have taken the word נינם as imperfect first person plural of the verb ינה, with third person plural masculine suffix. Peshitta supports this understanding. Gesenius' Hebrew Grammar reads with LXX the

---

[13]For a similar meaning of ידע niphal, see Gen. 41:21. KB, 375, proposes to read יגדעו, "they cut." Though the likelihood of a ג becoming a ו may be somewhat greater in some stages of archaic Hebrew script than in the square letters, they were never the letters most vulnerable to confusion. Further, for all its difference and difficulties, the text of LXX clearly witnesses to some form of ידע in the underlying Hebrew.

[14]So e.g. Briggs, *Psalms*, 2:153.

[15]For the missing dagesh, see GKC, § 20m.

substantive נִין, "progeny," with suffix.[16] If the Masoretic division of
the verse is retained, we would then have to read נִשְׂרְף, "Let us burn,"
with LXX instead of MT, שָׂרְפוּ, "They burned." A third possibility is
suggested by Young. He takes שָׂרְפוּ with the preceding and translates:
"Let all their progeny be burned, all the assemblies of El in the land."[17]

v. 8b.   כָּל־מוֹעֲדֵי־אֵל – "all the meeting-places of God"

The word מוֹעֵד often refers to the religious festivals of Israel (Lev.
23:4-8 and Isa. 1:13-14). The phrase אֹהֶל מוֹעֵד, "Tent of Meeting," a
phrase that refers to the tabernacle, is used 146 times in the Old
Testament. It is difficult to think of either the festivals themselves or
the festival assemblies being burned. Thus our verse is often taken to
refer to the place (or shrine) where the festivals were celebrated.[18] The
plural, however, creates problems with this understanding.

A. Gelston evaluates four possible solutions to these difficulties.
He rejects the idea that it may refer to non-Yahwistic shrines. That it
says "all meeting places" seems further to rule out the understanding
that it refers to the many buildings at the temple area. He finds a
reference to Yahwistic high places outside Jerusalem difficult because
of Josiah's reform and the psalmist's supposed deuteronomistic
sympathies. He thus settles for "non-sacrificial Yahwistic cultic
centers in Judah," forerunners of the synagogues.

He mentions 1 Macc. 3:46, which refers to a "place of prayer" at
Mizpah. He thinks it should be identified (correctly, I believe) with the
site where Gedaliah set up his administration after the fall of
Jerusalem.[19] He fails to see, however, that 1 Maccabees, rather than
reflecting an independent tradition, merely refers to the "house of
Yahweh" in Mizpah, which the book of Jeremiah mentions (Jer. 41:5).
To this place eighty men came from Shechem, Shiloh, and Samaria
bringing grain offerings and incense. Thus it is not absolutely non-

---

[16]GKC, § 76f.

[17]Young, "Psalm 74," 81-85.

[18]See K. Koch, "מועד," *TWAT*, 4:746.

[19]A. Gelston, "A Note on Psalm LXXIV 8," *Vetus Testamenum* 34 (1984): 82-86.
The reference to Mizpah is on page 85.

sacrificial. The question is whether this clearly legitimate "house of Yahweh" was a spontaneous creation after the temple was destroyed or whether it reflects a tradition of legitimate local cult places, where lesser offerings like the grain and incense offerings were offered and where people could come to pray and put their questions before God. Still, we do not know whether these (possible) "lower case shrines" were ever called מוֹעֲדִים.

v. 9a.   אוֹתֹתֵינוּ לֹא רָאִינוּ – "Signs for us we do not see"

The suffix is an objective genitive.[20] See our note to v. 4b.

v. 11a.   לָמָּה תָשִׁיב יָדְךָ וִימִינֶךָ – "Why do you withdraw your hand, even your right hand?"

The Masoretes divide the verse after יְמִינֶךָ, "your right hand." BHS suggests that the division be moved to follow "your hand." That gives us the common parallelism of יָד, "hand," and יָמִין, "right hand" (Ps. 139:10 and Judg. 5:26). However, if we follow the MT, v. 11b is not parallel to 11a. Then "even your right hand" intensifies the description of God's inactivity, which prepares well for 11b.

v. 11b.   חֵיקְךָ – "your lap"

We follow the Qere reading. The Ketiv, חוֹקְךָ, is probably a misspelling, as happens so often with *waw* and *yod*.

v. 11b.   כַלֵּה – "end it!"

LXX renders: εἰς τέλος, "to the end," which does not make much sense here. Many commentators think some form of כלא, "keep/keep back," must be what originally stood in this verse (final *aleph* and final *he* sometimes interchange). KB[21] suggests a second person imperfect תכלא, whereas BHS suggests כלאה. A less radical change could be

---

[20]GKC, § 135m.

[21]KB, 453 and 455.

obtained by reading an absolute infinitive, which is a good all-purpose form. With this emendation (and another verse division, see above) the two cola of this verse form a nice parallel. However, ancient Israelite poetry is not always that neat, and the MT makes perfect sense as conveying the climax of a complaint: "Why do you withdraw your hand, even your right hand? (Take it) out from your lap! End it!"[22]

v. 12a.   וֵאלֹהִים מַלְכִּי מִקֶּדֶם – "O God, my king from ancient time"

BHS suggests adding אתה before אלהים, which would go very nicely with the following verses.[23] There is, however, no textual evidence for this. H. D. Hummel suggests taking the *mem* in מקדם as enclitic and reading מלכ-ם קדם, "Ancient King," comparable to Babylonian *šar qudmi*. He notes that nowhere else in the psalm is the first person singular used.[24] Peshitta has "our God (is) king . . .", Targum: . . . ואלהא מלכא – "God (is) king . . ." LXX: ὁ δὲ θεὸς βασιλεὺς ἡμῶν πρὸ αἰῶνος, "But God, our king from ancient time." For the *waw* before "God," compare Jer. 11:20.

v. 13a.   פּוֹרַרְתָּ – "You roused up"

This verb has been variously translated. LXX translates ἐκραταίωσας "you strengthened." The traditional translation is "you split/cut/divided." This translation has the support of the Targum but is poorly attested in the texts. BDB takes it as פרר II but gives as

---

[22]See Tate, *Psalms 51-100*, 240 and 243. Another possible translation for the imperative is "destroy (i.e., the enemies)!" So Delitzsch, *Psalms*, 2:324 and 332. He refers to Ps 59:14 for a parallel use of this imperative. Young, "Psalm 74," 90-92, divides v. 11 as BHS does but moves כלה to the front of v. 12. He translates: "Why do you hold back your left hand? And your right hand in your bosom? Destroy them, O Elohim, my ancient King."

[23]Apparently first suggested by Gunkel (cf. his *Psalmen*, 320 and 324). It is followed by Kraus, *Psalms 60-150*, 99, and by others.

[24]H. D. Hummel, "Enclitic *MEM* in Early Northwest Semitic, Especially Hebrew," *JBL* 76 (1957): 97.

rationale: "so Ps. 74 seems to require."[25] Several more recent commentaries translate as פרר I: "break, frustrate, annul."[26] This verb is not used elsewhere for breaking an enemy or a thing. It is used for breaking a covenant (Judg. 2:1 and Jer. 14:21) or an alliance (1 Kings 15:19), for breaking commandments (Num. 15:31 and Ezra 9:14), and for annulling a vow (Num. 30:9, 14). This sense seems less suitable here.[27] We have followed KB פרר II, "rouse up," from pilpel "move convulsingly, move to and fro" in Middle Hebrew and Jewish Aramaic, supported by Syrian and Arabic cognates.[28]

vv. 13-14. לִוְיָתָן ... תַּנִּינִים ... יָם – "the Sea ... the Tannins ... Leviathan"

The Ugaritic Baal myth narrates how Baal defeated Yam, the personified sea, in a contest for kingship. The victory is followed by the building of a palace for Baal.[29] We note that יָם in our verse lacks the article. This, together with the parallel תַנִּינִים, leads us to capitalize the word. The tannins are mentioned in two texts from Ugarit.[30] In the first of these the connection with the Sea is clear. The latter also mentions "Lotan" (= Leviathan). A somewhat similar myth is known from Babylon, where Marduk slays the primordial sea *Tiamat*, divides

---

[25]BDB, 830. Recent scholars preferring this translation: A. A. Anderson, *Psalms,* 2 vols. New Century Bible (London: Oliphants, 1972), 2:543; Beaucamp, *Psaltier,* 2 (translation pages in front unnumbered), Jacquet, *Les Psaumes,* 2:462.

[26]So Young, "Psalm 74," 97-98 ("shattered"), Tate, *Psalms 51-100,* 240, 243 ("put down"), Lelièvre, "YHWH et la Mer dans les Psaumes", *Revue D'Histoire et de Philosophie Religieuses* 56 (1976): 254 (écrasé), M. Weiss, *The Bible from Within,* 289 ("drove back"), and Dahood, *Psalms,* 2:199, 204 ("shattered").

[27]Both BDB and KB give "destroy, shatter" for the D-stem of the Akkadian cognate *parâru.*

[28]KB, 917. So Gunkel, *Psalmen,* 320, 325, and J. Ridderbos, *De Psalmen,* 2:251 (Gij brengt . . . de zee in beweging." What lies behind the translation of Weiser, *Psalms,* 517, and Kraus, *Psalms 60-150,* 13, is not easy to say. They both render the verb with: "frightened" without providing a note on this translation.

[29]KTU 1.2-1.4 and also, apparently, 1.1.

[30]KTU 1.3 III 38-47 and 1.5 I 1-6.

her body and makes heaven from her upper half and earth from her lower half. Afterwards all the gods acclaim Marduk king and build his palace, Esagila, the Marduk temple in Babylon. In the Old Testament we meet Yam several places, for example Isa. 51:10 and Job 7:12. *Tannin* means "snake" in Exod. 7:9, 10, and 12 and probably also in Deut. 32:33. In Gen. 1:21 the "tannins" are large sea creatures which God created.

However, Isa. 27:1; 51:9, and Job 7:12 seem to refer to sea monsters hostile to Yahweh. *Leviathan* is mentioned six times in the Old Testament (Isa. 27:1 [twice], Ps. 104:26, Job 3:8; 40:25, and here). Isa. 27:1 is very similar to KTU 1.5. I 1-2. In Job 41 we may trace the picture of a crocodile, but all the other instances clearly talk of a hostile sea-monster (though made harmless in Psalm 104). H. Donner rightly warns us not to overrate the similarities with the Ugaritic literature.[31] However, I think we can safely say from the Old Testament, the context, and the corroborating evidence from Ugarit and Babylonia that Yam, the Tannins and Leviathan in our text are cosmic powers that challenged Yahweh's kingship and world order but found themselves utterly crushed and subdued. Yahweh reigns unchallenged in the cosmic realm. We should not, however, construct a sustained "creation myth" or "chaos myth," which the Old Testament material does not bear out.

v. 14b. לְעָם לְצִיִּים – "to seafarers"

MT has לְעָם לְצִיִּים. First, the rendering of צִיִּים is at best uncertain. KB posits either desert animals or demons. Holladay gives "demons" (as dwellers in צִיָּה). BDB settles for an unknown kind of

---

[31]H. Donner, "Ugaritismen in der Psalmenforschung," *ZAW* 79 (1967): 338-344. He concludes: "Man wird, aufs Ganze gesehen, nicht mehr als das Folgende sagen können: Es hat auf der von Kanaanäern bewohnten palästinisch-syrischen Landbrücke ein Repertoire mythischer Vorstellungen gegeben, die sich zu verschiedenen Zeiten, unter verschiedenen umständen und an verschiedenen Orten unterschiedlich formieren konnten. Auf dem Wege über die kanaanäische Vorbevölkerung Palästinas hat Israel aus diesem Repertoire ebenso geschöpft, wie es die ugaritischen Mythopoeten des Nordens getan haben. Darin besteht die Gemeinsamkeit. Sie sachgemäß zu interpretieren, ist eine noch nicht erledigte Aufgabe der Alttestamentler und Ugaritologen (p. 344).

desert animal[32] and Targum for some strange kind of desert bird. LXX lets the Ethiopians have the food. Secondly, the phrase as it stands in MT looks awkward, though not impossible. Delitzsch translates: "to a people [in the same sense as the ants and the rock-badgers in Prov. 30:25-26] to the creatures of the desert." The translation "to the creatures of the desert," given by many commentators, is merely short hand for this.[33] We follow Young and read צִי, "ship, fleet." לְעַם לְצִים or לְעַם לְצִי יָם is then simply "seafarers." This would go better with the picture of Leviathan as a sea monster than the traditional reading.[34]

v. 15.   אַתָּה בָקַעְתָּ מַעְיָן וָנָחַל אַתָּה הוֹבַשְׁתָּ נַהֲרוֹת אֵיתָן – "You divided spring and stream; you dried up perennial rivers."

The traditional understanding relates v. 15a to the water out of the rock (Exod. 17:6 and Num. 20:8) and 15b to the crossing of the Jordan River (Joshua 3).[35] However, there is nothing in v. 15a that points directly toward the wilderness experience, and the plural form of נהרות does not favor the view that it refers primarily to crossing the Jordan.[36]

---

[32]KB, 956; W. L. Holladay, *A Concise Hebrew and Aramaic Lexicon of the Old Testament*, 12th. corrected impression (Grand Rapids: William B. Eerdmans; Leiden: E. J. Brill, 1991), 305; BDB, 850.

[33]Delitzsch, *Psalms*, 2:324, 333. Compare Anderson, *Psalms*, 2:544, Jacquet, *Les Psaumes*, 2:462, and Tate, *Psalms 51-100*, 240 (He has a very full note on pp. 243-244). Beaucamp, *Psautier*, vol. 2, translates: "aux rapaces".

[34]Young, "Psalm 74," 101. A widely adopted but less convincing emendation is suggested by J. Löw, according to KB, 800. He repoints and redivides the phrase to לְעַמְלְצִי יָם—where the first word is conjectured from Arabic *maliṣ*, "slippery." Löw thinks an original *aleph* has become *ayin* in Hebrew (and disappeared in Arabic). Was ist denn glatt und schlüpfrig, lebt im Meer, und frießt Fleich?—Thus the reading becomes: "to the sharks of the sea." So Kraus, *Psalms 60-150*, 95-96, Nötscher, *Psalmen*, 147, and many others.

[35]Briggs, *The Book of Psalms*, 2:155, Delitzsch, *Psalms*, 2:333-334. Delitzsch explains the plural in 15b as referring to "the several streams of the one Jordan."

[36]J. Ridderbos, *De Psalmen*, 2:261: "Voorts vindt de gedachte, dat in 15a de geschiedenissen van Exod. 14 en Num. 20 worden vermeld in de uitdrukking 'bron en beek opengebroken' weinig steun. Evenzo kan het 'doen vertdrogen van sterk vlietende stromen' (vs 15b) moeilijk op de doortocht door de Jordaan zien, vooral vanwege het meervoud: Delitzsch' verklaring [see above] is weinig overtuigend." See further Lelièvre, "Yahweh et la Meer": "Donc, rien dans les vts 12-17, ni dans le reste

Today the verse is more often taken to refer to creation. J. A. Emerton takes his starting-point in the fact that the previous verses speak of God's attack on the sea and the dragon, and that 15b also seems to concern hostile action against water. He thus tries to find a negative interpretation that can fit the context. His suggestion is: God cleaved springs, holes in the earth, so the water could flow down to the subterranean sea and let the dry land come forth, that is, the opposite of what is described in Gen. 7:11. The נחל are surface brooks through which another part of the water escaped the dry land. The איתן נהרות are the mighty currents of the cosmic ocean attacked by God.[37]

K. Eberlein accepts Emerton's interpretation of 15b but rightly points out concerning his interpretation of v. 15a, "daß eine solche Vorstellung in keinem Schöpfungstext des ATs begegnet." He further points out that, whereas Gen. 7:11 spoke about "the springs of the great deep," here we hear about "spring and stream." He concludes: "Es dürfte also nicht verfehlt sein, V. 15a in dem Sinne zu verstehen, daß Jahwe Quelle und Bach als lebenspendende Elemente hat hervorbrechen lassen."[38]

We are not so sure that v. 15 should be limited to the original creation at all. It refers, as do the following verses, to God's activity as the victorious, unrivaled, and universal king. Young calls attention to the ambiguity of the language:

> The language of v. 15 is rich and multifaceted. We cannot limit the meaning of the verse to a reference to God's acts for the people in the Wilderness, or to an act of original creation, or to God's acts against a hostile enemy. The verse implies all of these and more. Nor can we conclude that v. 15a refers to creation and 15b to the Exodus. Both carry the connotation of God's original creation, his continued granting of fertility or withdrawing of it, and specific acts in the Wilderness.[39]

---

du Ps 74, ne nous pousse à faire un rapprochement avec le passage de la Mer Rouge."(258)

[37]J. A. Emerton, "'Spring and Torrent' in Psalm LXXIV 15," *Volume du Congrès: Genève 1965*, Supplements to Vetus Testamentum 15 (Leiden: Brill, 1966), 122-133.

[38]K. Eberlein, *Gott der Schöpfer-Israels Gott* (Frankfurt am Main: Peter Lang, 1986), 196-197. So also Gunkel, *Psalmen*, 325.

[39]Young, "Psalm 74," 105.

v. 16b. מָאוֹר וָשָׁמֶשׁ – "moon and sun"

מָאוֹר, "luminary, lamp," probably refers to the moon, reflecting "day and night" (16a).[40] Other possibilities are the stars[41] or a collective for heavenly lights.[42] Gunkel adds a *lamedh* before מאור and reads "du hast bestimmt zur Leuchte die Sonne."[43]

v. 17a. כָּל־גְּבוּלוֹת אָרֶץ – "all the boundaries of the earth"

Some have thought of the temporal zones,[44] apparently to make it parallel to 17b. However, neither גבול nor גבולה is ever used in this sense. A further question is how conscious the psalmist would be of the different temporal zones throughout the earth. Neither is it a strict parallel to the seasons. It makes better sense to follow Brigg's suggestion to think of the division between the seasons of the year (Gen. 1:14).[45] But the most probable interpretation is to take the word in the usual sense as referring to borders between peoples. The Old Testament is very clear that these borders are defined by God (Deut. 32:8). Therefore, it was punishable when the Assyrians boasted that they had removed the borders of the peoples (Isa. 10:13). Perhaps we should also think of the border between land and sea (Jer. 5:22).

v. 18a. זְכָר־זֹאת – "Remember this"

The object for זכר is not necessarily something belonging to the past (Isa. 47:7). The meaning seems to be "think of, consider," rather than "recall the past" (compare Eccl. 12:1).[46] Here Yahweh is called on

---

[40]So Young, "Psalm 74," 106, Tate, *Psalms 51-100*, 241. Nötscher, *Psalmen*, 147 translates "Leuchte" but provides a footnote saying "moon" is the likely reference.

[41]Lelièvre, "YHWH et la Meer," 254; Delitzsch, *Psalms*, 2:324.

[42]So J. Ridderbos, *De Psalmen*; 2:262, Jacquet, *Les Psaumes*; 2:463, Kraus, *Psalms 60-150*, 95.

[43]Gunkel, *Psalmen*, 321, 325.

[44]So Gunkel, *Psalmen*, 321, 325; Kraus, *Psalms 60-150*, 95; Nötscher, *Psalmen*, 147; Dahood, *Psalms*, 2:199, 207; and Young, "Psalm 74," 106.

[45]Briggs, *Psalms*, 2:156.

[46]See further H. Eising, "זכר," in *TWAT*, 2:571-593.

to pay attention to, to consider, what the enemies are doing. The demonstrative pronoun זאת can be used for reference backward or forward.[47] Here it refers to the following.[48]

v. 18b. וְעַם נָבָל – "and a worthless people"

The connotation of נבל is not so much "intellectually inferior" as "morally inferior." The נבל denies God (Pss. 14:1=53:2). He does what displeases Yahweh (Isa. 32:6) and blasphemes (Job 2:10). One who disgraces a daughter of Israel is a נבל (2 Sam. 13:13) and does נבלה (Gen. 34:7; Judg. 20:6 and 2 Sam. 13:12). In the same way a girl who has been adulterous has done נבלה (Deut. 22:21). When Israel turns away from Yahweh and worships idols they scoff at their Rock of Salvation (Deut. 32:15) and are themselves עם נבל (Deut. 32:6). Sometimes נבל seems also to have the connotation of "outcast" (2 Sam. 3:33 and Jer. 17:11). Thus to call the enemies עם נבל stresses their wickedness and their lack of respect for Yahweh.[49]

v. 19a. לְחַיַּת – "to the wild beasts"

Both LXX[50] and Targum translate this way. However, the text is not without problems. First, the word looks as if it is in construct form. If so, we would have to read לחית נפש, whatever that may mean in this context. It is possible, though, that we have an archaic feminine ending.[51] Second, the two occurrences of the word חית in this verse have totally different meanings. However, that may be a deliberate play on two different meanings of a word.[52]

---

[47]See Waltke-O'Connor, § 17.3d and Joüon-Muraoka, § 143b.

[48]So most commentators. Contra Gunkel, *Psalms*, 325.

[49]See further J. Marböck, "נבל *nābāl*," in *TWAT*, 5:171-185, and T. Donald, "The Semantic Field of "Folly" in Proverbs, Psalms and Ecclesiastes," *Vetus Testamentum* 13 (1963): 285-292.

[50]LXX reads plural, but it may be a plural translation for a collective in Hebrew.

[51]GKC, § 80f. Cf. Dahood, *Psalms*, 2:207, and Young, "Psalm 74," 112.

[52]Young, "Psalm 74," 113; Tate, *Psalms 51-100*, 244. A backtranslation from Peshitta would provide the text להוות (KB, 232, הוה II, "Verderben" (232)). KB

v. 19a.   תּוֹרֶךָ – "your turtle dove"

One Hebrew manuscript plus LXX and Peshitta read תּוֹדֶךָ, "the (soul) who praises you." A confusion between *resh* and *daleth* is easy and frequent. If we read "wild beasts" with MT and LXX, the figure of the turtle dove fits the context best.

v. 20b.   כִּי מָלְאוּ מַחֲשַׁכֵּי־אֶרֶץ נְאוֹת חָמָס – "for the hiding-places of
the land are filled with dens of violence"

The verse as it stands is difficult. There may be some textual corruption, but it is always easier to point to this possibility than to restore the original text. BHS suggests אֲנָחָה for MT נְאוֹת but without textual evidence. If we take the text as it stands, we should probably think of the desolation and lawlessness that would follow the war. With the land plundered and the governing structure broken down, the land is open for robbers and looters. They have filled all dark places suitable for hiding, from where they do their wicked work.

v. 21a.   אַל־יָשֹׁב דַּךְ נִכְלָם – "Let not the oppressed turn back
ashamed"

It is possible that we should read יֵשֵׁב, "sit" (compare Lam. 2:10 and Ps. 137:1).[53]

Structure

Stanzas

The Psalm has three stanzas preceded by a prologue. The individual stanzas seem not to be subdivided into strophes. The prologue plus the first stanza is as long as stanzas II and III together. In

---

prefers this reading. BHS proposes לִמּוֹת; BDB, 313, mentions further לְשַׁחַת and לְחָרֵב. The last three options are without textual support and appear to be pure guesses.

[53]So Young, "Psalm 74," 118; Tate, *Psalms 51-100*, 241, 244.

other words, the poem has two halves. The middle is marked by a first person singular form, "my king." The structure of the poem can be laid out as follows:

Prologue (vv. 1-3)
  Lament (v. 1)
  Hymn (v. 2)
  Call for divine intervention (v. 3)
Lament (vv. 4-11)
Hymn (vv. 12-17)
Call for divine intervention (vv. 18-23)[54]

The prologue begins with two complaints in question form, the "why" in the first doing double duty for the second. Then in a tricolon God is asked to remember his past actions toward and relation with the people. Finally, God is invited to come and see the destruction done by the enemy. The word נצח is found near the beginning and near the end of the prologue and thus frames it.

The rest of the poem is framed by the description of the enemies roaring in the sanctuary (note the assonance שאגו [v.4a], שאון [v.23b]). Both the prologue and the main body of the poem have three sections with a temporal progression from present to past to future.

Stanza I highlights the enemies, the people, and God in succession. Vv. 4-8 describe the enemies as creating havoc in God's dwelling place and burning it to the ground. The destructive character is underlined by very irregular parallelism. V. 9 gives us the effect on the people, whereas vv. 10-11 focus on the taunt that God receives. V. 8b, כל מועדי אל, reflects v. 4a, מועדך, whereas v. 9a, אותתינו, by contrast looks back to v. 4b, אותתם. Vv. 5-6 and 10-11 stand out by

---

[54]Following M. Weiss, *The Bible from Within*, 286-288. Young, "Psalm 74," 143, takes v. 3b with stanza I, but is otherwise in agreement with Weiss. Castellino, *Libro dei Salmi*, 307, also sees the three stanzas each corresponding to a part of the prologue (vv. 1-3), but he takes the call to consider the ruining work of the enemy (v. 3) together with vv. 4-11, the description of the case, whereas the prayer (vv. 18-23) expands on the complaint against God's wrath in v. 1.

having imperfects; the rest of the stanza has perfects. Vv. 10-11 harken back to the למה of verse 1 and with the prologue create a frame[55] for the first half of the poem.

Stanza II (vv. 12-17) starts with a disjunctive *waw* followed by two nominal clauses. The rest of the stanza consists of verbal clauses addressed to God. אתה is used seven times as subject for verbs in the perfect. Of the six bicola, five begin with the letter *'aleph*. The structural orderliness underlines the motif that under God's rule there is order. מקדם, "from ancient time," in v. 12a picks up קדם, "in ancient time" in v. 2.

Stanza III (vv. 18-23) is dominated by imperatives and negated jussives addressed to Yahweh. In total, there are ten expressions of the psalmist's wishes. זכר reflects v. 2 and occurs both in v. 18 and v. 22. Likewise the root חרף together with synonyms for "enemy" and the word נבל occur both in v. 18 and 22. אל תשכח appears in both v. 19 and v. 23. The whole third stanza recalls vv. 10-11. V. 10 reads: "How long, O God, will the enemy revile? Will the foe disdain your name forever?" V. 18 has: "The foe reviles, O Yahweh, and a worthless people disdains your name," and "forever" shows up in v. 19b. V. 21b contrasts the negative treatment of Yahweh's name: "let the afflicted and the poor praise your name."[56]

The prologue has 7 cola, about half the stanza length in this poem. Stanza I has 16 cola, whereas stanzas II and III have 12 cola each. Thus the prologue plus Stanza I have 23 cola, one less than the remaining stanzas together (24). Except for one tricolon in v. 2, the psalm consists of bicola.

Progression in Content and Mood

The psalm is generally regarded as a lament of the community.[57] Broyles assigns it to the subgenre of the complaints of the

---

[55]I hesitate to use the word "inclusio" for reasons given by Martin Kessler, "Inclusio in the Hebrew Bible," *Semitics* 6 (1978): 44-49.

[56]For the section on structure I am heavily indebted to W. A. Young, *Psalm 74.* He builds on M. Weiss, *The Bible from Within*, 281-293.

[57]An exception is F. Willesen, who regards it as a "ritual lament with a fixed position in the cult of the New Year Festival," "The Cultic Situation of Psalm LXXIV," *Vetus Testamentum* 2 (1952): 289.

community.[58] The psalm reflects the destruction of the temple in 586 B. C. The whole psalm is addressed to God. Jerusalem/the people is spoken of in third person (except v. 9, which has a first person plural). In v. 12, which is the middle of the poem, a first person singular suffix appears.

The psalm begins with a complaint against God's wrath, "Why have you rejected (us) forever?" This rhetorical question demands not an answer but a change in divine action (see translation note). To the psalmist the rejection appears total, eternal. If a shepherd is supposed to guard and feed his flock, "Why does your anger fume against the sheep of your pasturage?" This further underlines the hopeless situation of the people. When a wolf attacks the flock, the shepherd is there to kill him or drive him away. When the shepherd has turned against the sheep, there is no one to defend them. Such is the situation now, but it used to be different.

In v. 2 God is asked to remember his congregation, which he acquired in ancient time and redeemed as the tribe of his inheritance—the second colon making it clear that the reference is the Exodus.[59] The third colon takes us to the subsequent center of this "tribe of your inheritance" and the chief locus for Yahweh's relation to his people: "Mount Zion, where you dwelt." The present thus contrasts to the past. God, who seemingly has left the city,[60] is called on to lift his footsteps to what is left of his former dwelling place and to see the utter ruins.

As in v. 1, both the totality and the temporal aspect are present in נצח. The repetition of this word in the prologue underlines these aspects of the miserable situation. So far, the psalmist has only mentioned two actors, God and his people. The last colon of the prologue introduces a third, the enemy. In this way v. 3b functions as a transition to the first stanza, where the enemy plays a major role.

The enemy is singular in v. 3b and v. 5, presumably referring to the attacking king. The plural in vv. 4, 6, and 7-8 would then refer to

---

[58]Broyles, *The Conflict of Faith*, 150-154.

[59]For גאל with exodus, see Exod. 6:6 and 15:13. For the expression שבט נחלה, see Isa. 63:17; Jer. 10:16 and 51:19. The colon recalls Ex. 19:4-6, where Yahweh reminds Israel how he carried them "on wings of eagles" and brought them to himself with the intention that Israel should be his treasured possession out of all the peoples.

[60]Compare Ezekiel's vision of the glory of Yahweh leaving the temple (Ezek. 10:18-19) and the city of Jerusalem (11:22-23).

his soldiers. V. 3b places the enemy in the sanctuary. Then, in v. 4, the psalmist points the finger toward God: I am speaking of *your* enemies. They roared (like lions, Judg. 14:5; Hos. 11:10 and Amos 3:8) in *your* meeting place. There, in your meeting place, they set up their military standards carrying the emblem of their god (Marduk?). These would then not only show the victory of the enemy's armies but also symbolize that their *god* had been victorious.

If our translation of vv. 5-6 is correct,[61] the idea might be this: As the psalmist saw the soldiers coming with axes and clubs to hack out the valuable metals and precious stones that were engraved in the temple structure, he was reminded of wood cutters in the thick forest and thus recalled how the attacking king had workers in the forests of Lebanon chopping down the lofty cedars of God. Or, if cutting down a forest with axes was already a well known simile or expression for a total defeat of an enemy, then it means this: The attacking king, who had already defeated many armies and sacked many cities, now has turned against the dwelling place of God, and even in God's temple he was able to loot at will.

Not content with plundering, the enemies set the sanctuary on fire; again the psalmist takes care to say *your* sanctuary. In v. 7b he calls it "the dwelling-place of your name." An attack on the dwelling-place of his name must surely be an attack on God himself. The enemies have "profaned it to the ground" so that there is no longer a holy dwelling-place there. God no longer has a dwelling-place in Zion (vv. 2c-3a). Still the enemies were not satisfied: "They said in their hearts, 'Let us oppress them (the Israelites) *all*.'" With this in mind they went through the whole country burning every structure that was used for worshipping Yahweh.[62]

In vv. 4-8 the people are absent (but for the suffix of בָּם in v. 8). The enemy has destroyed *God's* place. In v. 9 the focus is on the people. V. 4 mentions the signs—the field standards—of the enemy. In contrast, "Signs for us we do not see." What the people wanted to see were not war emblems of Yahweh, if such ever existed. They needed signs assuring them of God's presence and intervention just as the

---

[61]See translation notes to these verses above.

[62]See translation note to v. 8b above.

emblems assured the enemies of their god's victorious presence. For Israel the assurance could be conveyed, for example, through a prophetic vision. But "there is no longer a prophet," a phrase that is explained by the next: "There is with us no one who knows how long." The misery had dragged on and on, and no one knew its end, if there was to be any. Yet, there had to be! For, "How long, O God, will the enemy revile? Will the foe disdain your name forever?" This never ending situation is insulting to *your name*, O God! How long will *you* tolerate it. How can it be (again with reproach and complaint as in v. 1) that you withdraw your hand, even your mighty right hand with which you formerly used to do all the mighty works. "Take it out of your lap! End it!"

The god of the attacker (Marduk?) had deprived Yahweh of his temple. What would that imply in an ancient Near Eastern context? The Babylonian myth of origin, *Enuma Elish*, tells how the chaos powers threatened to destroy the gods. No one was up to fight Tiamat and her allies. Then Marduk stood up and slew her. From her body he formed the inhabitable universe. All the gods acclaimed him as supreme king and built his palace (temple) in Babylon.[63]

A similar myth is found among the Ugaritic texts. Baal defeats Yam and is then acclaimed king. But he has no palace as the other gods. After a bit more back and forth, the palace is finally constructed and Baal can exercise his kingship of the universe.[64] Now Yahweh is seemingly defeated and has no palace. In a polytheistic environment this seemed to mean that Yahweh is not king. Marduk (or whoever the god of the attacking king is) is supreme. The second stanza opposes this position.

"O God, my king from ancient time, achiever of victories in the midst of the earth." God is king and he is *my* king. "From ancient time" reflects "in ancient time" (v. 2). Because several older or contemporary texts apply chaos-myth language to the crossing of the

---

[63]J. B. Pritchard, *Ancient Near Eastern Texts Relating to the Old Testament*, 3rd edition with Supplement (Princeton, NJ: Princeton University Press, 1969), 60-72, 501-503.

[64]KTU 1.2-1.4 (The role of KTU 1.1 is not clear). For an English translation, see e.g. Gibson, *Canaanite Myths and Legends*, 37-67. For the monsters associated with Yam, see our translation note to vv. 13-14.

sea (Ps. 77:17-21 and Isa. 51:9-10) and because creation language can refer to the beginning of the people of Israel (for example, Ps. 100:3 and Isa. 43:1), one may plausibly see a secondary allusion to Yahweh's historical defeat of the Sea in the Exodus event. In the midst of seemingly contrary evidence, the psalmist confesses that God and not the god of the invaders is king. He is the achiever of victories, not Marduk or Baal.

This is not a confession made in happy triumph. Rather, the perplexed and afflicted people who asked "Why do you withdraw your hand" are forced to remind God of who God is. The first person singular underlines the confessional character of the statement.[65] Notice that it comes exactly in the middle of the poem. The seven-fold אתה, "you," heightens the contrast to the god of the attacker. Not he, but *you* and *you alone* are supreme.

Vv. 13-14 relates God's victory over Yam and his allies. The imperfect in v. 14 may either be a stylistic variant or it may describe God as *portioning out* the heads of Leviathan to the sea-farers. The verses have one אתה per bicolon. It is to be noted that vv. 15-17 have one אתה in each colon (except for v. 16a, which begins with לך). This seems to favor Eberlein's thesis that they are to be seen as independent statements rather than as a coherent creation myth, as Gunkel understood these verses.[66] The point of vv. 13-14 is not to describe how God created the earth, or how and when he defeated the chaos monsters. The indisputable victory is described to depict God as the unrivaled achiever of victory, the creator and king of the universe.

It is in his capacity as king of creation that God does the things which are mentioned in vv. 15-17. God is the one who creates the springs and the streams. He is the one who dries up perennial rivers. He made and controls the different aspects of nature, such as day and night, moon and sun (seen as gods by the peoples surrounding Israel), all the boundaries of the earth, and the seasons of the year. *God* is the

---

[65]It is unnecessary to think of vv. 12-17 as sung by a soloist separate from the people or choir singing the rest of the psalm (so E. Bryn, K. Myhre et al, *Psalmenes Bok*, Oslo: Luther and Lunde, 1985-1987, 2:23).

[66]Eberlein, *Gott der Schöpfer*, 199; Gunkel, *Psalmen*, 325. Eberlein further uses his exegesis of v. 15 (see translation note above) to support his view. It should be noted, however, that Gunkel shares his interpretation of this particular verse.

unrivaled supreme king of the universe. He has shattered all cosmic forces. He is the author and governor of all creation. He is my king. This glorious confession is set in bold contrast to the miserable situation described in the first stanza.

Stanza III is dominated by imperatives and negated jussives rousing God to action on behalf of his people and on behalf of himself. It begins by picking up v. 10. The unrivaled creator and king of the universe is brought back to the present reality. "Remember this: the foe reviles (חֵרֵף cf. 10a), O Yahweh." Note the word-play on the alliteration חֹרֶף and חֵרֵף. God controls the winter but seemingly can not stand up to an earthly enemy. This verse is the first and only place in the psalm that the name Yahweh is used, and it is used as an object for the taunting of the enemies!

V. 18b follows up by saying his *name* is treated irreverently, reflecting v. 10b. The "foe" in v. 10 has become "a worthless people."[67] The נבל carries the day. This is what God is called on to consider.

V. 19 calls Israel God's turtledove. This little creature is helpless against the wild beasts: "Don't give her life to them, O God." The word חַיַּת, which in v. 19a is used for the enemies, is in 19b applied to the people of God: "The life of your afflicted ones do not forget forever." This is not a bold prayer for quick relief. The psalmist prays for the *survival* of his people and that the misery may *end* some time. לנצח picks up v. 10b.

In v. 20a the psalmist asks God to look at the covenant and consider the relationship he established with this people and the promises he gave. The reason for stating this prayer follows in 20b: In a ravaged land where justice has broken down, lawless people have occupied every dark place suitable for hiding a robber's den. The oppressed have turned to Yahweh in prayer; let them not have to turn back ashamed because there was no help. Instead of allowing your name to be disdained by your impious and taunting enemies, change the situation so that the afflicted and poor can praise your name.

V. 22 spells out the appeal that has been implicit in the whole psalm, "Arise, O God, conduct your case!" The enemy has brought

---

[67]See translation note to v. 18b above for the precise connotations.

forth evidence indicating that you are a defeated weakling, that you either do not care about your people or are unable to do anything. You have to clear your name and disprove the vicious charges! Remember the taunt directed against you (cf. v. 18a) from the worthless one all the time! Then the voice of the psalmist grows weaker, "Do not forget the noise of your enemies," and it is finally drowned out by the surrounding noise, "the uproar of those who rise against you, which goes up constantly."

The psalm ends as the main body began, with the enemies roaring. The tension is not resolved. The psalmist professes faith in God as the supreme unrivaled king of the universe and as the one who has entered into a relationship with Israel. The present reality bluntly contradicts this belief. The enemies have carried and still carry the day. The very existence of God's helpless people is in the balance. There is no theophany, no answer, no intervention. Only the constant uproar of the enemies can be heard.

The Problem

Enemies have sacked Jerusalem, looted, and burnt the temple (vv. 4-8). The psalmist interprets this as evidence that God has rejected his people, that he is angry with them (v.1), and that he no longer dwells in Jerusalem (vv. 2c-3a). Another interpretation lies close at hand, however, and must have frustrated many of the people: God is defeated. The god of the enemy, whose emblem shines from the field standards that were set up in God's city (v. 4b), is the supreme god, king of the universe. The psalmist is further distressed by the fact that he does not know how long God's anger and the enemies' triumph will last (vv. 9-10). Will it last forever (v. 19)? Finally, in this chaotic situation, where general lawlessness (v. 20b) adds to the misery caused by the enemy, the very existence of God's people appears in danger (v. 19a).

The Prayer

The psalmist prays for the survival of the people (v. 19). He prays that God end the present misery and stop his wrath that permitted it (v. 11b). He asks God to think of the covenant he has established with the people (v. 20a), begging him not to let his oppressed people down (v. 21a). He wants to return to a situation in which the afflicted people can praise Yahweh's name (v. 21b) instead of seeing it mocked and taunted by victorious enemies. Finally, God is asked to arise and demonstrate that he is the one the people have professed him to be—the supreme and only God, the unrivaled king of the universe (vv. 12 and 22-23). There is no prayer for the restoration of the temple or the city. Apparently the situation was too dark to think so far ahead. If only God would stop being an enemy!

The Appeal

Israel is God's tribe of inheritance. Zion is the place where he dwelt so that the temple's destruction is an attack on God himself. The enemies are his enemies (v. 4a). The enemies' idol emblems are highly visible, and Israel's God is quiet, which to the enemies implies that he is powerless. They have deprived him of his dwelling place. Has their god defeated Yahweh? They treat his name irreverently (vv. 10b and 18b). This stands in sharp contrast to the fact that he and he alone is the powerful and mighty God. He is really the unrivaled king of the universe. The psalmist brings this argument very vividly to the fore by dragging God to court and charging him to defend his reputation and prove that he is the one he is. Further, God has entered into a relation with his people. They are the sheep he tends (v. 1b). He acquired them in ancient time (v. 2a). He redeemed them and made them his special people (v. 2b). Zion was the place he chose for the dwelling place of his name (vv. 2c, 7b). Because Israel is his defenseless "turtledove," should not God defend it (v. 19a)? Because they are "your afflicted ones," do not forget them (v. 19b)! Because you have established a covenant with this people, pay attention to it, O God (v. 20a)! These people want to live in a relationship with you where they can praise your name. Let them do so, O God (v. 21b). Is that not better than having your name disdained by the worthless, impious enemy (v. 18)? The several designations applied to God's people—afflicted, oppressed, poor (vv. 19, 21)—are designed to move God to pity.

Chapter Five

Psalm 88

1. A Song. A Psalm of the sons of Korah. For the musical
    director. To Mahalath-leannoth. A Maskil of Heman the
    Ezrahite.

2a. O Yahweh, God of my salvation,
 b. by day I cry,
 c. in the night before you.
3a. Let my prayer come before you;
 b. incline your ear to my cry of supplication!
4a. For my soul is sated with troubles,
 b. and my life has come near to Sheol.
5a. I am reckoned with those who go down to the Pit.
 b. I have become like a man without strength.
6a. Among the dead I am "free,"
 b. like the slain,
 c. those who lie in the grave,
 d. whom you no longer remember;
 e. they are cut off from your hand.
7a. You have placed me in the nethermost pit,
 b. in the darkness of the depths.
8a. Against me your wrath has pressed,
 b. and with all your breakers you have subdued me. Selah.
9a. You have caused my close friends to stay away from me;
 b. you have made me an abomination to them,
 c. imprisoned, so I cannot escape.

10a. My eye has grown weak from affliction.
  b. I have called to you, O Yahweh, every day,
  c. I have spread out my hands to you.
11a. Do you do wonders for the dead?
  b. Do the ghosts rise and praise you? Selah.

12a. Is your steadfast love declared in the grave,
 b. your faithfulness in Abaddon?
13a. Are your wonders made known in the darkness,
 b. and your righteousness in the Land of Forgetfulness?

14a. But I, to you, O Yahweh, I cry for help,
 b. and in the morning my prayer meets you.
15a. Why, O Yahweh, have you rejected me?
 b. Why do you hide your face from me?
16a. I am afflicted and about to expire from my youth.
 b. I bear your terrors; I despair.
17a. Over me sweep your bursts of wrath;
 b. your alarms annihilate me.
18a. They surround me like water all the time;
 b. they close up against me together.
19a. You have caused to stay away from me beloved and friend,
 b. my close friends – darkness!

Translation Notes

v. 1.   שִׁיר – "A Song"

This is the unmarked word for song (Amos 5:23; 6:5). The word occurs a little more than thirty times in the superscription of psalms. Mowinckel thinks that here it had a more specialized technical meaning, since "there would be no point in stating in a heading that the text for cultic singing was a 'song' in a general sense." He cannot, however, provide any further information as to what that specialized meaning might be.[1]

v. 1.   לִבְנֵי קֹרַח. – "of the sons of Korah"[2]

See translation note to Ps. 44:1. Delekat points out that this psalm is the only one in which "to the musical director" is preceded by

---

[1]Mowinckel, *The Psalms in Israel's Worship*, 2:207-208, cf. *Psalmenstudien*, 2:2-3.

[2]See translation note to Ps. 44:1.

something else. He, therefore, proposes that the preceding words may originally have been a subscription to Psalm 87.[3] There is no textual support for this view, but some sort of fusing of two originally independent titles is not implausible.

v. 1.   עַל־מָחֲלַת לְעַנּוֹת – "to Mahalath-leannoth"

The meaning is uncertain. Tate provides a good survey of different opinions.[4]

v. 1.   מַשְׂכִּיל לְהֵימָן הָאֶזְרָחִי – "A Maskil of Heman the Ezrahite"

According to the Chronicler, Heman ben Joel (1 Chron. 15:17) was one of the chief temple singers appointed by king David (1 Chron. 15:19 and 25:6) and father of a family of Levitical temple singers (1 Chron. 25:1 and 2 Chron. 29:14). He is called "the seer of the king" in 1 Chron. 25:5. 1 Kings 5:11 mentions Heman together with Ethan the Ezrahite as men known for wisdom but surpassed by Solomon. 1 Chron. 2:6 has Ethan and Heman as sons of Zerah, grandsons of Judah. Ethan the Ezrahite is given as the author of Psalm 89. To make the picture even more complicated, there exists a word אֶזְרָח, "native" as opposed to גֵר, "foreigner" (Lev. 16:29 and 17:15). Dahood has thus suggested that "Ezrahite" describes Heman (and Ethan) as a native of a pre-Israelite Canaanite family.[5] But elsewhere the "natives" are always the Israelites and the "foreigners" those who do not belong to Israel. The derivation is therefore to be doubted. The meaning of "Maskil" is not clear.

v. 2b+c. יוֹם־צָעַקְתִּי בַלַּיְלָה נֶגְדֶּךָ – "by day I cry, in the night before you"

With Dahood we take both "I cry" and "before you" as doing double duty for both cola. His translation, "day and night I cry to

---

[3]L. Delekat, "Probleme der Psalmenüberschriften," *ZAW* 76 (1964):281.

[4]Tate, *Psalms 51-100*, 394-395.

[5]Dahood, *Psalms*, 2:302.

you,"[6] however, deprives the verse of some of the intensity achieved by adding "in the night."[7]

v. 3b.   לְרִנָּתִי – "to my cry of supplication"

רנה seems to denote a ringing cry with different connotations depending on the context. It connotes joy and praise in Pss. 105:43 and 107:22. It is parallel to תפלה in Pss. 17:1 and 61:2. Here the meaning must be something like, "cry of supplication."

v. 5a.   עִם־יוֹרְדֵי בוֹר – "with those who go down to the Pit"

The usual meaning of בוּר is "well, cistern" (Deut. 6:11 and Exod. 21:34), but it may also mean a pit used as a trap (Ps. 7:16). A cistern (or hole in the ground) could be used for prison (Exod. 12:29 and Jer. 37:16). Perhaps this use is the background for the usage of בור for Sheol, the underworld (Isa. 14:15 and Ezek. 32:23).[8] To "go down to the pit" accordingly means "to die." יורדי בור probably denotes those who are in the process of dying and not those who are already dead (Pss. 28:1; 30:4 and Isa. 38:18).[9]

---

[6]Dahood, *Psalms*, 2:301-302. The text is often emended to:

אלהי שועתי יומם צעקתי בלילה נגדך, "My God, I cry for help during the day, my crying is in the night before you" (Gunkel, *Psalmen*, 381-382; Nötscher, *Psalmen*, 177, G. Castellino, *Libro dei Salmi*, 889; cf. Calès, *Les Psaumes*, 2:118, 120-122). For a survey of different ways this verse has been translated, see Tate, *Psalms 51-100*, 395-396.

[7]Compare J. L. Kugel, *The Idea of Biblical Poetry: Parallelism and Its History*, 40-41.

[8]So J. G. Heintz, "בור באר," in *TWAT*, 1:500-503. Different: A. Bentzen, "Daniel 6: Ein Versuch zur Vorgeschichte der Märtyrlegende," in *Festschrift für Alfred Bertholet*, eds. W. Baumgartner et. al. (Tübingen: J. C. B. Mohr, 1950), 60.

[9]See KB, 112.

v. 5b.   כְּגֶבֶר אֵין־אֱיָל – "like a man without strength"

אֱיָל is a hapax. BDB[10] translates "help." It is then taken to be a loan word from Aramaic, although the word is apparently not attested in Biblical, Jewish, or Old/Imperial Aramaic, but only in Syriac.[11] By comparing with the words אַיָל I, "ram" and אַיָל II, "mighty tree," we should perhaps rather translate "strength" with KB.[12] This translation is supported by the Targum.[13]

v. 6a.   חָפְשִׁי – "I am 'free'"

The usual sense of the word is "free (from slavery), freedman" (Exod. 21:2, 5 and Job 3:19). This meaning does not seem to fit the context.

In a Ugaritic text the death-god Mot says to Baal:

wrd bt ḫptt. 'arṣ	and go down into the house of "freedom" in the earth;
tspr by rdm. 'arṣ	be counted among those who go down into the earth.[14]

It is noteworthy that the second line resembles v. 5a in our psalm, but the gain is limited since the translation of *bt ḫptt* in the Ugaritic text is at best uncertain.[15] Probably the only thing we can say from the

---

[10]BDB, 33.

[11]KB, 39 provides an Arabic cognate meaning "refuge".

[12]KB, 39. So most recent commentaries, e.g. Tate, *Psalms 51-100*, 394; Kraus, *Psalms 60-150*, 190; Nötscher, *Psalmen*, 177; Calès, *Les Psaumes*, 2:118.

[13]Targum to this verse translates חֵילָא, "strength"; targum to Ps. 22:20 (אֵילוּת) renders תּוּקְפִי, "strength, stronghold." Also Delitzsch argues for this translation (*Psalms*, 3:25, for Ps 22:20: *Psalms*, 1:321).

[14]KTU 1.5 V 14-16a. The English translation given here is from Gibson, *Canaanite Myths and Legends*, 72.

[15]G. Widengren, "Konungens vistelse i dödsriket," *Svensk Exegetisk Årsbok* 10 (1945): 71, translates *bt ḫptt 'rṣ* with: "jordens djupa boning," "the deep abode of the earth." Dahood, *Psalms*, 2:88, has: "the nether house of cots." P. Grelot sets forth as a hypothesis: "lieu de pourriture," "place of decay," from an Arabic cognate, Grelot,

Ugaritic evidence is that a cognate word of חפשׁי is used with reference to the nether world. If the word has its ordinary sense, the idea must be something like this: "Just as a slave is free from his master when he is dead (Job 3:19), so I am now free from being a servant of God. For a slave this is fortunate, since his slavery was hard; for me it is disastrous, since to serve God was my life." We thus have an ironical use of the word "free."[16] It has often been suggested to emend the text, but it still holds true what Gunkel concluded about the problem many years ago: "Konjekturen überzeugen nicht recht."[17]

v. 6c.   שֹׁכְבֵי קֶבֶר – "those who lie in the grave"

With BHS and most commentators we take this as an independent colon and not as part of 6b.[18] Since "the slain" is stronger than simply "the dead," and since a decent burial is not what generally characterizes those who die on the battlefield, Gunkel suggests emending this colon to "those deprived of a grave." Tate understands קבר here as a "common grave" of those "slain and buried without proper attention (compare Isa. 14:19 and Ezek. 32:20-32)."[19] As in v. 12, we should probably take קבר as referring to the underworld. Ezekiel 32 speaks of the slain "who went down uncircumcised to the nether world" (v. 24).

v. 6e.   וְהֵמָּה מִיָּדְךָ נִגְזָרוּ – "they are cut off from your hand"

והמה is used with a change of subject to heighten the contrast between the subjects: *You* no longer remember; *they* are cut off (Jer.

"Hofšī (Ps LXXXVIII 6)," *Vetus Testamentum* 14 (1964): 260-261. Grelot has a good survey of different translations and suggestions for emendation of חפשׁי in our verse.

[16]So Tate, *Psalms 51-100*, 396.

[17]Gunkel, *Psalmen*, 382. This holds true also for the suggestion made by J. L. Haddix, "Lamentation as Personal Experience in Selected Psalms" (Ph.D. dissertation, Boston University Graduate School, 1980), 115, to read śin instead of šin.

[18]Contra Widengreen, "Konungens vistelse," 70.

[19]Gunkel, *Psalmen*, 383. So also Jacquet, *Les Psaumes*, 2:669, and Tate, *Psalms 51-100*, 396.

31:1, 33 and Ps. 106:43). The niphal נגזר is used with a personal subject five times in the Hebrew Bible. Of these two are without an object (Ezek. 37:11 and Lam. 3:54), and both have the sense "as good as dead, beyond hope." King Uzziah was "cut off" from the house of Yahweh when he got leprosy (2 Chron. 26:21), and Yahweh's Servant was "cut off" from the land of living (Isa. 53:8). Thus in all these cases the subject is excluded from life before God and with others. God's hand very often suggests God's power and saving activity (Pss. 44:3; 74:11 and 139:10). Since both Isa. 53:8 and 2 Chron. 26:21 use the preposition מן in a privative sense, we should take it in the same sense here.

v. 7b.   במחשכי-ם ם-[מצלות] – "in the darkness of the depths"

MT has בְּמַחֲשַׁכִּים בִּמְצֹלוֹת, "in the darkness, in the depths." However, H. D. Hummel has pointed out that the second *bet* probably arose from a failure to realize that the preceding *mem* was not a plural ending but enclitic.[20] Except for Zech. 1:8 מצולה always refers to the depth of the sea (Zech. 10:11 of the Nile). In Psalm 69 the psalmist prays to God to save him from the waters "for the waters have reached to my neck, I sink in the miry depth (מצולה) and there is no foothold" (vv. 2b-3). In v. 16 שבלת מים, "floodwater", מחולה, and באר (= בור), "pit" are all parallel. We should probably think of the chaos waters that are often depicted as God's enemies (Ps. 74:13-14). To be in the grip of the depths of the sea and to be in the grip of death would then both imply being excluded from God's saving activity and thrown to the mercy of the life-threatening forces.[21]

In this way we must understand the statements implying that the psalmist already is in Sheol. Life and death are seen in relation to Yahweh. When Yahweh has rejected a person and the life threatening forces have come with sickness, in the form of enemies, or in other

---

[20]H. D. Hummel, "Enclitic *mem* in Early Northwest Semitic," 98. This reading is also adopted by Tate, *Psalms 51-100*, 394, 396-397.

[21]See further O. Keel, *The Symbolism of the Biblical World: Ancient Near Eastern Iconography and the Book of Psalms*, translated by T. J. Hallet (New York: Seabury Press, 1978), 73-75. Gunkel, however, thinks the background for putting "the depths of the sea" parallel to "the nethermost pit" is that "die Wohnung der Toten liegt unter den großen Wassern" (*Psalmen*, 383).

ways that threaten his life, then the sphere of death has entered his life. It is characteristic for the dead to be outside the actions of God. But this is exactly what the psalmist experiences. Thus he is really in Sheol.[22]

v. 8a.   עָלַי סָמְכָה חֲמָתֶךָ – "Against me your wrath has pressed"

סָמַךְ usually means "lay hand on" (for example, the head of a sacrificial victim) (Exod. 29:10; Lev. 1:4 and Num. 8:12), or "support, sustain" (Gen. 27:37 and Isa. 59:16). However, in Ezek. 24:2 it is said that the king of Babylon סָמַךְ אֶל, "has laid siege to," Jerusalem. In our verse a hostile action is clearly intended.

v. 8b.   וְכָל־מִשְׁבָּרֶיךָ עִנִּיתָ – "and with all your breakers you have subdued me"

The text is difficult, since the verb is second person and has no object suffix. We have taken "with all your breakers" as adverbial accusative,[23] though we have to admit an adverbial accusative of means is not well attested.[24] An alternative would be to read third person plural (emendation) and make "all your breakers" the subject of the colon. Gunkel and others read אִנִּית, "du hast treffen lassen." We further understand עלי in 8a as doing double duty for the B-colon.[25] מִשְׁבָּרִים is taken in the usual sense "breakers of the sea," as in several other descriptions of deep distress (Ps. 42:8; 2 Sam. 22:5 and Jon. 2:4).[26]

---

[22]H. J. Kraus, *Theology of the Psalms*, translated by K. Crim (Minneapolis: Augsburg Publishing House, 1986), 162-168. See further C. Barth, *Die Errettung vom Tode in den individuellen Klage- und Dankliedern des Alten Testamentes* (Zollikon: Evangelischer Verlag, 1947), 91-122.

[23]So Dahood, *Psalms*, 2:304; Tate, *Psalms 51-100*, 397. Haddix in his translation note takes "you" as subject for the עִנִּית; however, in his translation he translates with "all your breakers" as subject, "Lamentation as Personal Experience," 115 and 113.

[24]Joüon-Muraoka, § 127l.

[25]Dahood, *Psalms*, 2:305; Tate, *Psalms 51-100*, 397; Haddix, "Lamentation as Personal Experience," 115.

[26]*Pace* Dahood, *Psalms*, 2:304. He conjectures the sense "your outbursts," which he tries to undergird by the Ugaritic expression *ṯbr aphm*, "their nostrils" (Dahood's

v. 9a.　מְיֻדָּעַי　– "my close friends"

This is a pual participle of יד‎ע, "know." J. L. Haddix translates "my acquaintances," but, as can be seen from Ps. 55:14 and 2 Kings 10:11, the word implies more than mere acquaintance. For the word used with the motif of deprivation of friends, see Ps. 31:12 and Job 19:14.

v. 9b.　תוֹעֵבוֹת　– "an abomination"

With Gunkel we take this as a plural of amplification or intensity.[27]

v. 9c.　כָּלֻא　– "imprisoned, so I cannot escape"

We understand the word as a qal passive participle. For the meaning "lock up in a room, imprison," see 1 Sam. 6:10 and Jer. 32:2-3.[28] The participle is dependent on the suffix of שַׁתַּנִי in 9b.[29] BHS apparatus proposes to read either כלא אני or נכלאתי, both giving the meaning "I am imprisoned."[30] LXX and Peshitta translate in the same way, but whether they actually had a different *Vorlage* is difficult to decide. For the idea of God imprisoning a person, see Job 12:14 and Lam. 3:7.

---

translation). The text (KTU 1.2 I 13) is, however, badly broken, and *t.b.r.* may well have the usual meaning of שבר‎, "break". So Gibson, *Canaanite Myths and Legends*, 40.

[27]GKC, §124e, Joüon-Muraoka, §136f. Gunkel, *Psalmen*, 383. Many commentaries translate as a singular but do not indicate whether they emend (so BHS apparatus) or take the plural as intensive.

[28]Compare בית (ה)כלא = prison.

[29]So Dahood, *Psalms*, 2:305, and Haddix, "Lamentation as Personal Experience," 115. Gunkel, *Psalmen*, 383, and Kraus, *Psalms 60-150*, share this understanding of the MT.

[30]So Gunkel and Kraus, see previous note.

v. 10a.   עֵינִי דָאֲבָה מִנִּי עֹנִי – "my eye has grown weak from affliction"

Outside of this verse the verb דאב is used in Jer. 31:12, 25 and is traditionally translated "languish." For the whole phrase, compare Ps. 6:8 (note that "eye" is singular both there and here). We should probably understand the weakening of the eye as caused by the weeping that results from the distress.

v. 10c.   שִׁטַּחְתִּי אֵלֶיךָ כַפָּי – "I have spread out my hands to you"

To spread out the hands is a gesture of praying (Exod. 9:33 and 1 Kings 8:38). Our verse is the only place the verb שׁטח is used in this phrase. Gruber maintains a difference between שׁטח כפים, "stretch forth the palms, beg for help," and the more usual פרש כפים, "spread the palms, supplicate."[31] He does not, however, explain how he arrives at his translation of שׁטח. In the qal the verb clearly means "spread out" (Num. 11:32; 2 Sam. 17:19; Jer. 8:2 and Job 12:23). The piel is found only here. Thus it seems best to take the phrase as a variant of the more common פרש כפים without any significant difference in meaning.

v. 11a.   פֶּלֶא – "wonders"

The word is a collective (cf. Pss 77:12,15 and 89:6). The same is the case for פלאך in v. 13a.

v. 11b.   אִם־רְפָאִים יָקוּמוּ יוֹדוּךָ – "Do the ghosts rise and praise you?"

For רפאים, "ghosts, dead, dwellers of Sheol", compare Isa. 26:14, 19 and Job 26:5. יודוך is asyndetically attached to the previous verb.[32]

---

[31]Gruber, *Aspects of Nonverbal Communication*, 1:25 and 44.

[32]Cf. GKC § 120g.

v. 12a+b. חַסְדֶּךָ אֱמוּנָתְךָ – "your steadfast love, your faithfulness"

These words are a common pair often used in praise to denote God's characteristics (Pss. 36;6; 89:2, 25, 34 and 98:3). Here they are located in parallel cola.[33] We notice in our verse that these characteristics are not called into question.

v. 12b. בַּאֲבַדּוֹן – "in Abaddon"

The word is from the root אבד, "perish." It is used as a name for the underworld (Job 26:6; 28:22; 31:12 and Prov. 15:11).

v. 13b. בְּאֶרֶץ נְשִׁיָּה – "the Land of Forgetfulness"

Although נְשִׁיָּה is a hapax, its meaning is clear based on the verb נשׁה, "forget." Even the memory of God's gracious works is erased as people enter Sheol.

v. 14a. וַאֲנִי – "But I"

The pronoun stresses the contrast between the psalmist and the dead who do not pray to God. The *waw* is disjunctive.[34]

v. 14b. תְּפִלָּתִי תְקַדְּמֶךָּ׃ – "my prayer meets you"

The verb means "meet, reach, come before, confront" (Pss. 21:4 and 89:15). We translate "meet" to distinguish it from the expression translated "come before" in v. 3a.

v. 15a. לָמָה יְהוָה תִּזְנַח נַפְשִׁי – "Why, O Yahweh, have you rejected me"

Questions beginning with למה often express complaint or reproach (see our translation note to Ps. 74:1a). Balentine notes that the "why"

---

[33] See our treatment of these words in Part Three below.

[34] Cf. Waltke-O'Connor, § 39.2.3b.

questions in the psalms often go unanswered. It is the uncertainty, the inability to understand God's actions in the present situation, that gives rise to the questions (compare Pss. 10:1 and 44:24).[35] For the verb זנח, "reject," see translation note to Ps. 44:24.[36] נפשי is periphrastic for "I" (cf. Ps. 103:1-2).

v. 15b. תַּסְתִּיר פָּנֶיךָ מִמֶּנִּי – "Why do you hide your face from me"

"Why" of the A-colon applies also to the B-colon.[37]

v. 16a. עָנִי אֲנִי וְגוֵעַ מִנֹּעַר – "I am afflicted and about to expire from my youth"

גוע means "expire, die" (Gen. 25:8 and Job 3:11). Here it must mean something like "ready to die, about to expire."[38] The versions seem to have read יגע, "exhausted." Castellino emends accordingly.[39] The pronoun "my" before "youth" is needed in English but not in Hebrew. Dahood and Haddix take the *mem* of מנער as enclitic and read the root נער, "growl" (Jer. 51:38). A hapax in the Bible, the root is attested in post-biblical Hebrew and Jewish Aramaic. However, Dahood prefers to support it mainly by some quite shaky Ugaritic evidence.[40]

---

[35]Balentine, *The Hidden God*, 116-125.

[36]Ibid., 143-151.

[37]For the hiding of God's face, see translation note to Ps. 44:25.

[38]Briggs, *The Book of Psalms*, 2: 243-244; Delitzsch, *Psalms*, 3:22; Tate, *Psalms 51-100*, 394, 398. Gunkel, *Psalmen*, 383, takes MT to mean: "I die from my youth," i.e., while I am still young."

[39]Castellino, *Libro dei Salmi*, 214-215.

[40]Haddix, "Lamentation as Personal Experience," 114, 116; Dahood, *Psalms*, 2:306. Dahood quotes KTU 1.2 IV 6-7: *wttn gh yg̱r tht ks'i zbl ym*, which he translates: "And his voice was given forth, he groaned [*yg̱r*, from the root *ng̱r*] under the throne of prince Yam." Gibson, *Canaanite Myths and Legends*, 43, translates: . . . he sank (*yg̱r*) under the throne of prince Yam." A. Caquot, M. Sznycer, and A. Herdner, *Textes Ougaritiques. Tome I: Mythes et Légendes* (Paris: Cerf, 1974), 135-136: "Sa voix (ne) se fait entendre (qu') en *grognant* [*yg̱r*, root *g̱r*, from Arabic *wag̱r*] sous le thrône du Prince Yam." The other Ugaritic text quoted by Dahood is KTU 1.93: 1-2: *arh.td.rgm.bg̱r*, translated: "The wild cow throws her voice by mooing." C. Virolleau,

v. 16b. נָשָׂאתִי אֵמֶיךָ אָפוּנָה – "I bear your terrors; I despair"

The pronoun of "your terrors" is to be understood as a subjective genitive: the terrors that are caused by you. אפונה is a hapax, apparently from the root פון. The meaning is uncertain. LXX translates: καὶ ἐξηπορήθην from ἐξαπορέω, "be in great difficulty, doubt, embarrassment." With Tate we assume that LXX understood it.[41]

v. 17a. חֲרוֹנֶיךָ – "your bursts of wrath"

Tate considers it an intensive plural, but in view of the plurals both in v. 16b and v. 17b we should understand it as a real plural. Compare חסדות, "expressions of steadfast love," and צדקות, "deeds of righteousness." They sweep over the psalmist as waves (compare Pss. 42:8 and 124:4-5).

v. 17b. צִמְּתוּתֻנִי – "annihilate me"

For the form of the verb, see BDB.[42]

v. 19b. מְיֻדָּעַי מַחְשָׁךְ – "my close friends—darkness!"

The meaning seems to be: My close friends? My only close companion is darkness![43]

Le Palais Royal D'Ugarit V, Mission de Ras Shamra XI (Paris: Imprimerie Nationale and Librairie C. Klincksieck, 1965), 173, translates: "La génisse jette (cet) appel (du haut) de la montagne" (*ģr*). A. Caquot, J. M. de Tarragon, and J. L. Cunchillos, *Textes Ougaritiuies. Tome II: Textes religieux, rituels, correspondence* (Paris: Cerf, 1989), 37-38, translates: "La Génisse émet (cette) parole: un cri . . . " (*bģr* parallel to Arabic *faģara* and Hebrew פער).

[41]Tate, *Psalms 51-100*, 398. The word is often emended to אפוגה, "grow numb," e.g. Castellino, *Libro dei Salmi*, 214, 889. Nötscher, *Psalmen*, 178, takes it as a loan word from Akkadian, translating: "in högsten Maße." Haddix, "Lamentation as Personal Experience," 116, connects it with פנא, which he says means "to turn, to pass away," but the verb *never* means "pass away" in the sense required here. For the cohortative form, see GKC, § 108g.

[42]BDB, 856.

Structure

Stanzas

The psalm has three stanzas: vv. 2-9, 10-13, and 14-19. None of them are subdivided into strophes. Every stanza begins with an introduction depicting the psalmist as persistently praying to Yahweh. Stanza I contains 21 cola, stanza II has 9, and stanza III has 12. Thus the last two stanzas together are of equal length with stanza I. Stanza I is therefore a full stanza, whereas stanzas II and III are half-stanzas.

In the introduction to the first stanza (vv. 2-3) the first colon invokes Yahweh. Then follow two closely knit cola stressing the incessant nature of his prayer. Finally, a jussive and an imperative ask God to receive the prayer. Vv. 4-9 present an exposition of the situation. Except for a tricolon in v. 6, the description of the distress consists of bicola.[44]

In stanza II (vv. 10-13) v. 10 picks up v. 2 by stressing the psalmist's continuous prayer to Yahweh. The three bicola of vv. 11-13 are all rhetorical questions beginning with the interrogative ה. The questions give motives to persuade the psalmist that it may be worthwhile to go on praying and to persuade Yahweh that he should hear.

The third stanza (vv. 14-19) consists of six bicola. It begins with disjunctive *waw*. V. 14 picks up vv. 2-3. The vocative "O Yahweh" and the word "prayer" are found both places, but instead of "day" and "night" there, the psalmist here says "morning." As stanza II after the introduction continued with questions, so v. 15 has two rhetorical questions spearheaded by למה. V. 16 pretty well sums up the situation described in vv. 4-7. Vv. 17-18 pick up v. 8, and v. 19a repeats "you have caused to stay away from me" from v. 9a.

---

[43]Delitzsch, *Psalms*, 3:29. Dahood, *Psalms*, 2:307, thinks of "darkness" as designating Sheol, but we should probably take it as referring to the whole distressful situation.

[44]So Gunkel, *Psalmen*, 381-382, J. Ridderbos, *De Psalmen*, 2:365, and others (some take v. 10a with the preceding). Castellino, *Libro de Salmi*, 210, divides after v. 10 and regards vv. 11-19 as one stanza. So also Tate, *Psalms 51-100*, 398.

Progression in Content and Mood

The psalm is usually regarded as an *individual* lament psalm[45] or, more precisely, a psalm of sickness.[46] Broyles assigns it to the subgenre of the complaint of the individual.[47] Significantly, the psalm lacks several features generally associated with the genre of lament. Gunkel calls attention to the absence of any real petition (except for the call to attention in v. 3). Castellino further notes the lack of expressions of trust.[48] There is also no final doxology.

The psalm begins with an invocation of Yahweh. The phrase "God of my salvation" seems, in view of the rest of the psalm, to focus on the present rather than on the past. Yahweh is the one to whom the psalmist looks for help. There is no one else. The psalmist has cried to Yahweh by day; even in the night he has cried before him. So far there has been no response. Therefore the psalmist goes on to pray: "Let my prayer come before you; incline your ear to my cry of supplication." This is both an indirect complaint over God's indifference and a plea to end it and begin paying attention.

The reason for this prayer, the description of the distress, is introduced by יכּ (compare Pss. 6:3 and 22:12). The psalmist's soul (used as close synonym for "life" as in v. 15) is sated, filled with troubles. V. 4b intensifies this: "My life has come near to Sheol" so that I am about to die. The next colon takes this a step further: "I am

---

[45]Briggs, *The Book of Psalms*, 2:242, sees it as a national lament. Widengren, "Konungens vistelse," 79-80, finds the background in a text read by the king during a night of ritual suffering. Goulder, *The Psalms of the Sons of Korah*, 195-210 similarly sees it in the context of ritual suffering, originally during an autumn festival at the sanctuary of Dan.

[46]See e.g. Mowinckel, *The Psalms in Israel's Worship*, 2:1-2, and Seybold, *Das Gebet des Kranken*, 113-117. Seybold places it in the group: "Psalmen mit sicherem Bezug zu Krankheit oder Heilung des Beters." It has sometimes been suggested that the sickness in this psalm is leprosy (e.g., Delitzsch, *Psalms*, 3:26), but the psalmist does not give us enough concrete "symptoms" for making a diagnosis.

[47]Broyles, *The Conflict of Faith*, 206-209.

[48]Gunkel, *Psalmen*, 382; Castellino, *Libro dei Salmi*, 209.

reckoned with those who go down to the Pit," those who not only have come close to Sheol but are actually *entering* there. He has become "like a man without strength."[49]

According to v. 6, he is not only reckoned with the dying, he is among the dead. A slave is free from his master after six years of work (Exod. 21:2). The psalmist is "free" from his relation to Yahweh, "free" from his saving activity. He is not even like one who dies in honor and receives a decent burial. He is "like the slain, those who lie in the grave," who have gone down to Sheol from the battlefield (similar to the description in Ezek. 32:19-27). Of these dead, and thus of him, it is characteristic that Yahweh does not remember them any more. They are cut off from his care and his saving activity. The psalmist finds himself totally excluded and erased from the mind of the God of his salvation. Even worse, God is actively against him: "You have placed me in the nethermost pit," as far down in the realm of death and the underworld as one can possibly go, and it is Yahweh, "the God of my salvation," who did it. The parallel colon speaks of "the darkness of the depths." "The depths" refer to the chaos-forces of the Sea.[50] The powers of death and the chaos forces of the Sea are seen together as life threatening forces that try to challenge God's order. The psalmist is as deep into the grip of these powers as is possible. Still, Yahweh has not only placed him as far away from him as possible, he himself wages war against him. His wrath presses against him just as an enemy lays siege against a city (Ezek. 24:2). Then according to v. 8b, God himself has become, as it were, a chaos force. He is sending his breakers continually to roll over him and press him down.[51]

With each new statement we saw the psalmist sinking deeper and deeper into the realm of death. Death is first and foremost seen as separation from Yahweh, his care, and his saving activity (especially v. 6). In this way a person still alive can actually be in Sheol, outside of God's sphere of gracious activity and at the mercy of the life-

---

[49]גבר often connotes strength, BDB, 150.

[50]See translation note above. Compare Ps. 69:2-3.

[51]Cf. Ps. 42:8, see P. R. Raabe, *Psalm Structures: A Study of Psalms with Refrains*, 48.

threatening forces of chaos. As the psalmist sinks deeper into death, the distance from Yahweh increases. Then in v. 7 God is brought in but not as "the God of my salvation." He is the one who has thrown the psalmist so deep into death and as far away from himself as possible. Implicitly this affirms God's control even in Sheol. And what is implicit here becomes explicit in v. 8, for now the life-threatening force he has to face which presses him down again and again like breakers of the sea is none other than Yahweh himself.

In v. 9 a new accent is introduced. The separation and alienation from God has social consequences: "You have caused my close friends to stay away from me." The next colon intensifies this: "You have made me an abomination to them." Notice that it is *Yahweh* who has caused the break in social relations. The psalmist sees himself as "imprisoned," possibly a reference back to v. 7 but more likely a description of the isolation experienced by a sick, dying, friendless person against whom God acts as an enemy.

There is no escape; he cannot do anything to change his situation. What he can do and must do is go on weeping and praying. The second stanza begins by saying that weeping has weakened his eye (cf. Ps. 6:8). He has been calling to Yahweh every day, and his hands are spread out in the posture of supplication toward Yahweh. Yahweh is the God of his salvation. After the introduction the second stanza has six rhetorical questions, all requiring a negative answer. The motives in them can be seen as an elaboration of the phrase "God of my salvation" in v. 2.

The first bicolon consists of two parallel questions, both referring to the dead. God does not do wonders for them nor do they praise him. God's activity is for the benefit of the living. Only the living can enter into a relationship with him and praise him for his works. The next two bicola are each chiastically structured with the verb doing double duty. In the middle are two words describing God's character (v. 12) or his works (v. 13). They are enclosed by a name for the underworld in each colon. "Is your steadfast love declared in the grave, your faithfulness in Abaddon? Are your wonders made known in the darkness, and your righteousness in the Land of Forgetfulness." The parallelism with "wonders" shows that "righteousness" here denotes God's deeds of righteousness (see Ps. 103:6). They are not declared or even known, and if by chance they would be, then certainly they would be forgotten.

These rhetorical questions, on the one hand, function to remind God that if he wants his steadfast love, his faithfulness, his wonders, and his deeds of righteousness to be declared, known, believed, and praised, then he should save the psalmist before the psalmist finds himself irreversibly in the grip of Abaddon. On the other hand, they underline the urgency for the psalmist himself. He soon will be excluded forever from Yahweh's saving love and wondrous works. He soon will lack even the memory of Yahweh.

However, the questions also make it clear for the psalmist that he is not yet lost among the dead. He is different from them: "But I, to you, O Yahweh, I cry for help." Descartes once said: "Cogito, ergo sum." The psalmist could have said: "Supplico, ergo sum." This gives him courage to approach God once more. He had asked in v. 3 that his prayer might come before Yahweh. Now he states that his prayer meets Yahweh in the morning. The morning seems to have been the time especially associated with God's saving acts (Pss. 46:6; 90:14 and Lam. 3:22-23).[52] Yet, when his prayer meets Yahweh, the only thing that will come out is complaint: "Why, O Yahweh, have you rejected me? Why do you hide your face from me?" The questions do not look for an academic answer. They express bewilderment and protest (see translation note). God is not supposed to be like this, for he is the God of my salvation. He is characterized by steadfast love and faithfulness. He works wonders and acts of righteousness. Why does God not act toward me in conformity with the way he is? And as the psalmist moves on to describe his situation, he ends up rephrasing what he had said in his first complaint: "I am afflicted and about to expire from my youth." The possibility of a premature death has been hanging over him. But this time, since he just noted the difference between himself and the dead, he moves straight to the wrath of God: "I bear your terrors; I despair!"

V. 17a closely reflects v. 8a: "Over me sweep your bursts of wrath." Even more intense is the second colon which chiastically balances it: "Your alarms annihilate me." Then the water image from v. 8b is brought in: "They [the terrors, the bursts of wrath, the alarms] surround me like water all the time." Finally, the totality and the

---

[52]See J. Ziegler, "Die Hilfe Gottes `am Morgen'," *Bonner Biblische Beiträge* I (1950): 281-288.

inevitability of doom come to a climax in v. 18b: "They [again the terrors, bursts of wrath, and alarms of God] close up against me together." They join forces to attack him from every possible angle. He is drowning in God's wrath, engulfed in his alarms. As in the first description of the situation, the social aspect is mentioned and with almost the same words. Yahweh has caused those who formerly loved him and were his friends to stay away from him. What is left for him? Does he have any close friends remaining? The only companion that remains is darkness! With this darkness the psalm ends.

What is the function in the psalm of the second and third stanzas? Is the psalmist any different after v. 19 than he was after v. 9? He is more aware that the problem is not so much the miserable situation itself as it is God. He is not lost in Sheol, as he lamented in the first stanza; he is lost under Yahweh's wrath. He is more conscious that it is not too late for Yahweh to save him from death, that he can do it, that he should do it, but he does not do it. Darkness.

The Problem

The psalmist is apparently sick, although there is little or no description of symptoms. He is dying and has been in a critical state from his youth (v. 16a). All his close friends have left him (vv. 9 and 19). He has been praying day and night to Yahweh, but Yahweh has not paid attention (vv. 2-3, 10, 14). The psalmist sees himself in the grip of the powers of the underworld and chaos (vv. 4-6). He is radically separated from God, his care, and his saving activity (v. 6). What makes it even worse is that it is God who has separated himself (v. 7) and who continuously attacks as an enemy (vv. 8, 16-18). The psalmist does not understand God (v. 15). God is the God of steadfast love and faithfulness (v. 12) but not to him. God is the only one who is able to save him (v. 2), but he is precisely the one who fights against him to annihilate him (v. 17). What the psalmist fears more than anything else is death as utter separation from Yahweh (vv. 11-13).

The Prayer

The only explicit petition in this psalm is the prayer for attention in v. 3. There is no prayer for healing, not even for rescue from death.

And in one sense attention is what this psalm is all about. What the psalmist wants and needs is that God bring him into his presence, into the divine sphere of care and gracious activity (cf. v. 6). The psalmist wants God to end his strange wrath and to stop attacking him. He wants God to show him his steadfast love and faithfulness (v. 12). He wants God to do wonders and works of righteousness (v. 13). He wants God to act as the God of his salvation (v. 2). But he does not put these wishes into words. He goes no farther than to lament his misery and protest God's wrath (vv. 8, 16-18).

The Appeal

The psalmist begins his psalm by calling Yahweh "God of my salvation." The psalmist has been persistently praying for a long time (v. 2). It is time the God of my salvation hears my supplication (v. 3). Therefore, the description of his distress should move God to action. The second stanza spells out the implications of invoking "the God of my salvation" by mentioning Yahweh's steadfast love, his faithfulness, his wonders, and his deeds of righteousness (vv. 11-13). For this God gets no recognition in Sheol, which the psalmist is about to enter. But he is not there yet, since he continues to pray to Yahweh (v. 14). Thus, if Yahweh still wants to be known as the God he is, he should come quickly to rescue the psalmist. This all remains implicit, however, as the psalmist never gets courageous enough to verbalize a petition.

Chapter Six

Psalm 90

1.   A prayer of Moses, the man of God.

1a.   O Lord, an abode you have been for us,
 b.   from generation to generation.
2a.   Before mountains were born,
 b.   and before you brought forth the earth and the world,
 c.   even from eternity to eternity, you are God.

3a.   You turn man back to dust,
 b.   and you say, "Return, children of man."
4a.   For a thousand years in your eyes
 b.   are like yesterday, for it passes by,
 c.   and like a watch in the night.
5a.   You pour on them sleep;
 b.   they become in the morning like grass that passes away.
6a.   In the morning it blossoms, but it passes away;
 b.   toward the evening it withers and is dry.
7a.   For we vanish because of your anger,
 b.   and because of your wrath we are terrified.
8a.   You have fixed our offenses in front of you,
 b.   our secrets before the light of your face.
9a.   For all our days decline because of your fury;
 b.   we complete our years like a groan.
10a.   The days of our years, in them there may be seventy years,
 b.   or if with supreme strength, eighty years;
 c.   yet their pride is trouble and distress,
 d.   for it passes hastily by, and we fly away.
11a.   Who knows the strength of your anger,
 b.   and, according to the fear due to you, your fury?

12a.   To count our days, such teach us!
 b.   Then we will obtain a heart of wisdom.

13a.   Turn around, O Yahweh! How long?
 b.   And repent concerning your servants!
14a.   Satisfy us in the morning with your steadfast love,
 b.   so that we may shout for joy and be glad in all our days.
15a.   Make us glad as many days as you have humbled us,
 b.   as many years as we have seen misery.
16a.   Let your work be revealed to your servants,
 b.   and your grandeur for their children.
17a.   And let the kindness of the Lord our God be upon us,
 b.   and the work of our hands establish for us,
 c.   and the work of our hands, establish it!

Translation Notes

v. 1.   תְּפִלָּה לְמֹשֶׁה אִישׁ־הָאֱלֹהִים – "A prayer of Moses, the man of
        God"

This is the only psalm in the Psalter ascribed to Moses. Delitzsch
has pointed out affinities to Deuteronomy, especially the song of
Moses (chapter 32) and the blessing of Moses (chapter 33).[1] The title
"the man of God" is ascribed to Moses, for example, in Deut. 33:1 and
Josh. 14:6. It is applied to David (2 Chron. 8:14 and Neh. 12:24, 36)
but is mostly used as a title for prophets exclusively or primarily in
pre-exilic times (1 Sam. 9:10 and 1 Kings 13:4-11).

v. 1a.   מָעוֹן – "abode"

H. P. Müller argues for the meaning "help." He cites Pss. 31:3;
71:3 and 91:9 as examples.[2] Ps. 31:3 has "rock of refuge [מָעוֹן, variant:

---

[1]Delitzsch, *Psalms*, 3:49. In his exegesis of the psalm (pages 49-60) he pays close
attention to these affinities. Regarding Deuteronomy as of direct Mosaic origin, he sees
in this a strong argument that Moses really is the author of this psalm.

[2]H. P. Müller, "Der 90. Psalm: Ein Paradigma exegetischer Aufgaben," *ZTK* 81
(1984): 269, text and notes. Also Tate, *Psalms 51-100*, 431-432.

מָעוֹן, "abode"]," parallel to "a house of strongholds." Ps. 71:3 reads: "Become for me a rock of abode [variant: refuge] where I can always come; you have commanded to save me, for you are my rock and my stronghold." In Ps. 91:9 מָעוֹן is parallel to מַחְסִי, "my refuge." The traditional rendering is supported by all these examples. Furthermore, they all show that מָעוֹן when applied to God carries connotations of a place of refuge. Therefore, emendations to מְעוֹנָ[3] are unnecessary; LXX may very well have read מָעוֹן both here and in Ps. 91:9.[4]

v. 1b.   בְּדֹר וָדֹר – "from generation to generation"

Many manuscripts substitute the more familiar phrase לְדֹר וָדֹר, which one may also translate "from generation to generation" but as future (Pss. 10:6 and 79:13), whereas this verse looks back.

v. 2b.   וַתְּחוֹלֵל אֶרֶץ וְתֵבֵל – "and before you brought forth the earth and the world"

LXX reads a polal, making the colon passive as in v. 2a. Several scholars follow this.[5] J. Ridderbos calls the sense conveyed by MT ("God was, before he created") a tautology.[6] However, God is to be assumed as the actor behind the passive also in v. 2a,[7] and it is not obvious that the psalmist would have felt that an active verb was less adequate in the context than a passive verb. וַתְּחוֹלֵל is a polel second person singular imperfect waw consecutive of the verb חוּל, "bring

---

[3]E.g. Castellino, *Libro dei Salmi*, 342.

[4]Contra BHS apparatus.

[5]E.g. Weiser, *Psalms*, 594; Castellino, *Libro dei Salmi*, 342-343; B. Vawter, "Postexilic Prayer and Hope," *CBQ* 37 (1975): 460.

[6]J. Ridderbos, *De Psalmen*, 2:396.

[7]*Pace* Kraus, *Psalms 60-150*, 215. He argues from Job 38:4-11 for seeing a cosmogonic myth that contradicts the faith in creation. In the Job account Yahweh's honor and wisdom "consisted of this, that he was there already as the only God and was witness to the mythic primeval event." Kraus says: "understood thus, v. 2 is a statement about the supreme sovereignty and eternity of the God of Israel." However, in Job 38:4 God asks Job: "Where were you when I laid the foundation of the earth?" That passage does not attest to a cosmogonic myth where God had no part. In fact, no such myth can be found in the Old Testament.

forth, be in travail."[8] For the metaphor, see Job 38:28 (cf. Prov 8:24). בטרם in v. 2a does double duty for v. 2b.

v. 3a.　תָּשֵׁב אֱנוֹשׁ עַד־דַּכָּא – "You turn man back to dust"

תשב is the short form used with the sense of the long form (Pss. 11:6 and 25:9).[9] דכא used as noun is a hapax, derived from the verb דכא, "crush, break to pieces." An adjective דכא is found with רוח, "spirit," with the meaning "contrite, humble." Although both LXX and Vulgate have "to humility," this does not fit the context.

v. 4a.　כִּי אֶלֶף שָׁנִים – "For a thousand years"

For the use of כי to introduce circumstantial information, see Gen. 35:18.[10] This verse is sometimes transposed before verse 3[11] and would admittedly fit well there. As none of the versions reverse the order, it is more likely that the author purposely located this verse as a parenthesis in the flow of thought to strengthen the contrast between God's eternity and human frailty.

v. 4b.　יַעֲבֹר – "it passes by"

Gunkel and Castellino take the *yod* as dittography caused by preceding כי and read a perfect.[12]

---

[8]In theory the form could be 3rd. person feminine (so Gunkel, *Psalmen*, 400), but this seems forced.

[9]Müller, "Der 90. Psalm," 271 argues that the short form here is the old preterit form. If so, the meaning is: You have decided in ancient time that humans shall return to dust, i.e. die. The waw consecutive (relative) of the B-colon might be taken to support this view, although the waw consecutive after an imperfect can be used for present time (see Waltke-O'Connor, § 33.3.3c).

[10]See Aejmelaeus, "Function and Interpretation of כי," 203.

[11]Gunkel, *Psalmen*, 396; Nötscher, *Psalmen*, 183; Castellino, *Libro dei Salmi*, 344.

[12]Gunkel, *Psalmen*, 396, 400 reads plural, taking "a thousand years" as subject. Castellino, *Libro dei Salmi*, 344 (and BHS apparatus) reads singular.

v. 4c.   וְאַשְׁמוּרָה בַלָּיְלָה – "and like a watch in the night"

The כְּ ("like") of v. 4b does double duty for the third colon. The night was divided into three night-watches (Judg. 7:19; 1 Sam. 11:11 and Lam. 2:19).

v. 5a.   זְרַמְתָּם שֵׁנָה – "You pour on them sleep"

זרם in the qal is unattested elsewhere. KB conjectures a separate root (with a doubtful derivation from Arabic), "stop, put an end to life."[13] BDB gives "sweep away" for qal and "pour forth" for the one instance (Ps. 77:18) of a poel.[14] The versions had problems too. LXX translates: τὰ ἐξουδενώματα αυτῶν ἔτη (ἔσονται), "What they hold in contempt (will become) years." Jerome has: *percutiente te eos somnium (erunt)*, "When you strike them, (they become) a sleep." Peshitta has: "their generations are a sleep" (from which is conjectured: "you seed them year after year"[15]).[16] The translation given above must be credited to Castellino.[17] It has the advantage of making no emendations (except for moving the half-verse division, see below), and the meaning given the verb זרם is consistent with the meaning of the noun זֶרֶם, "rain-storm, cloudburst." "Sleep" indicates "utter human helplessness and liability to death as willed by God"[18] (cf. Ps. 76:6; Jer. 51:39 and Nah. 3:18).

---

[13]KB, 270.

[14]BDB, 281.

[15]Kraus, *Psalms 60-150*, 212-213. So also suggested in BHS apparatus.

[16]For surveys of different suggestions, see KB, 1480, and C. Whitley, "The text of Psalm 90:5," *Biblica* 63 (1982): 555-557.

[17]Castellino, *Libro dei Salmi*, 344. R. J. Tournay picks this up in "Notes sur les Psaumes," *Revue Biblique* 79 (1972): 50-53, making the translation known to those who understand French but not Italian. M. Tsevat supports the same by an Akkadian expression, "Psalm XC 5-6," *Vetus Testamentum* 35 (1985): 115-116. This translation is further followed by Th. Booij, "Psalm 90:5-6: Junction of Two Traditional Motifs," *Biblica* 68 (1987): 394-396, and Tate, *Psalms 51-100*, 431, 433-434.

[18]Booij, "Psalm 90:5-6: Junction," 395.

v. 5b.   יִהְיוּ בַּבֹּקֶר כֶּחָצִיר יַחֲלֹף – "they become in the morning like grass that passes away"

MT, LXX, and Jerome connect the verb with v. 5a. This would also make the verse more evenly divided. However, יחלף is singular and seems to have חציר as subject. The morning would be the time when the fatal result of what God had done became apparent,[19] although it is possible that בבקר has crept in from v. 6.[20] The Versions read "in the morning" in both verses. The verb חלף is sometimes taken as "become renewed, grow again."[21] Although this understanding has been around for centuries, it apparently is a guess from the context. יחלף, "that passes away," is an asyndetic relative verbal clause.[22] The relation between v. 5a and v. 5b seems to be temporal: "When you . . . then they."

v. 7a.   כִּי־כָלִינוּ בְאַפֶּךָ – "For we vanish because of your anger"

For the use of כי, see note to v. 4a. For the sense of כלינו, compare Pss. 39:11 and 71:13. For בְ, "because of," see Ps. 6:7; Gen. 18:28 and Lam. 2:19. So also v. 7b and v. 9a.

v. 8b.   עֲלֻמֵנוּ – "our secrets"

The word is a qal passive participle masculine singular (taken as a collective) of עלם: "hidden things," that is, secret sins (compare Ps. 19:13 נסתרות). Elsewhere the verb always occurs in the niphal. Many manuscripts have the plural, עלמינו.[23] In all other occurrences, עלמים means "youth." Targum accordingly translates "the iniquities of our

---

[19]Cf. Ziegler, "Die Hilfe Gottes 'am Morgen'," 286-287, for God's destruction of Israel's enemies as being revealed by the morning.

[20]Nötscher, *Psalmen*, 184; Kraus, *Psalms 60-150*, 212-213; Booij, "Psalm 90:5-6: Junction," 395-396.

[21]BDB, 322; Kraus, *Psalms 60-150*, 212; Jacquet, *Les Psaumes*, 2:719; J. Ridderbos, *De Psalmen*, 2:393.

[22]Joüon-Muraoka, § 158a.

[23]So Aquila, Symmachus and Jerome; LXX reads sg. and translates αἰών.

youth."[24] Castellino and Tate take it as a plural.[25] Delitzsch argues that the plural of עָלוּם would be עֲלָמוֹת in analogy with נִסְתָּרוֹת (Ps. 19:13) and not עֲלָמִים, "youth."[26]

v. 9b. כִּלִּינוּ – "we complete"

LXX seems to read a qal (the same form as in v. 7a) and connects it with the preceding word. BHS wants us to read כָּלוּ, "[Our years] vanish," apparently supported by Peshitta.[27] To make "our years" the subject would make the clause more parallel to v. 9a where "our days" is the subject, but a change of subject is not uncommon in parallelism (Pss. 77:10 and 16:6-7).

v. 9b. כְמוֹ־הֶגֶה – "like a groan"

The word הֶגֶה is used in Ezek 2:10, where it appears together with קִנִים, "dirge," and in Job 37:2, where it seems to refer to the rolling of thunder. The word derives from the verb הגה, "growl, murmur, groan." Curiously, both LXX and Peshitta have found a reference to a spider's web.[28]

v. 10a. יְמֵי־שְׁנוֹתֵינוּ בָהֶם שִׁבְעִים שָׁנָה – "The days of our years, in them there may be seventy years"

We understand this colon in the following way: "The days of our years" is synonymous to the span of our life, our age (see Gen 25:7). In the span of our life (בָּהֶם) there may be seventy years, or even eighty years. The number of years given is often taken as a normal life span.

---

[24]Dahood, *Psalms*, 2:321, 325, follows the rendering of the Targum. Briggs, *The Book of Psalms*, 2:271, 274, translates "our youth."

[25]Castellino, *Libro dei Salmi*, 344-345; Tate, *Psalms 51-100*, 434.

[26]Delitzsch, *Psalms*, 3:55.

[27]So Gunkel, *Psalmen*, 397, 401; Kraus, *Psalms 60-150*, 213.

[28]See A. A. Macintosh, "The Spider in the Septuagint Version of Psalm XC. 9," *Journal of Theological Studies* n. s. 23 (1972): 113-117, for the view that the spider crept into the LXX text from Ps. 28:12 and not from the translators' understanding of the Hebrew nor from an underlying text different from MT.

With Castellino, we relate v. 10 to the previous verse: Life is completed like a groan even if it may extend to seventy (and with exceedingly good health to eighty) years.[29] BHS suggests deleting the first two words *metri causa*, which seems careless, especially with a text as problematic and "non-metric" as this psalm. בהם, "in them," is often emended or deleted,[30] although MT is clearly supported by LXX and the other Versions. Targum solves the difficulties gallantly הדין בעלמא, "in this world/age," but we can be sure that this is an expansion. גבהם is frequently suggested[31] but has no textual support.

v. 10c. רָהְבָּם – "their pride"

This word is a hapax. The verb רהב is used two times in the qal (Isa. 3:5 and Prov. 6:3), and two in the hiphil (Ps. 138:3 and Cant. 6:5). In Isa. 3:5 it describes the young as *rising up against* the old. Prov. 6:1-5 gives advice to one who has put up security for someone. He should humble himself, go back to the person and plead with him (רהב) to be released from the pledge. The psalmist in Psalm 138:3 says to God: תרהבני בנפשי עז, "you have strengthened my soul." Finally, in Cant. 6:5 the eyes of the loving girl הרהיבו, "overwhelm" her lover. Targumic Aramaic has a word רהבא, "pride, arrogance."[32] Thus BDB translates the noun "pride," that is, the object of pride.[33] The Versions all translate as if they read רבם, "the majority of them."[34] Another possibility would be to read רחבם, "their span," suggesting that ה and ח had been confused some time before the versions appeared. We read the MT and translate "pride" on the strength of the Aramaic word.

[29]Castellino, *Libro dei Salmi*, 345. We refer to his commentary section, not to the translation (which is on the following page). Compare Tate, *Psalms 51-100*, 431.

[30]Kraus, *Psalms 60-150*, 213-214, and Nötscher, *Psalmen*, 184, delete.

[31]Müller, "Der 90. Psalm," 274, n. 49; Gunkel, *Psalmen*, 401.

[32]Jastrow, 1453.

[33]BDB, 923. See KB, 1113 for other translations and emendations suggested.

[34]BDB, 923, thinks the versions read רחבם but that is hardly the case.

v. 10d. גָּז – "it passes by"

This is a perfect third person singular of גוז, "pass over, pass away." The only other occurrence in the Bible is Num. 11:31, where a transitive translation is required. Targum translates plural, which would fit the context well, but LXX clearly had singular in its *Vorlage*. The subject is perhaps רהבם, "their pride."

v. 11b. וּכְיִרְאָתְךָ עֶבְרָתֶךָ – "and, according to the fear due to you, your fury"

For כְ "according to," see Gen. 1:26 and 1 Sam. 13:14. "Who knows" in v. 11a must be regarded as the subject and verb also for the B-colon. With respect to LXX, καὶ ἀπὸ τοῦ φόβου σου τὸν θυρόν σου, the meaning seems to be the same as that of MT, but LXX apparently read וּמִירְאָתְךָ instead of MT וּכְיִרְאָתְךָ. This has led some commentators to read וּמִי + verb, "and who fears your furor."[35] This would make the parallelism tighter, but the meaning would not be largely affected. The more radical surgery וּמִי רָאָה חֵץ, "and who sees the harshness of,"[36] has less to commend itself.

יִרְאָה is the right attitude toward Yahweh (Pss. 2:11 and 5:8). As such it is the source of life (Prov. 14:27 and 19:23). The promised king of David (Isa. 11:2-3) and the restored people (Jer. 32:40) are characterized by "the fear of Yahweh." It has ethical consequences (Prov. 8:13 and 16:6), as does the lack of it (Gen. 20:11). Of importance for our verse is the connection between "the fear of Yahweh" and "wisdom"/ "knowledge," which we find very frequently in Wisdom literature (Ps. 111:10; Prov. 1:7; 9:10; 15:33 and Job 28:28).[37]

---

[35]Nötscher, *Psalmen*, 184; Castellino, *Libro dei Salmi*, 346.

[36]Gunkel, *Psalmen*, 401; Maillot and Lelièvre, *Les Psaumes*, 2:243; Vawter, "Postexilic Prayer," 461; Kraus, *Psalms 60-150*, 213-214.

[37]See further H. F. Fuhs, "יָרֵא, יִרְאָה, מוֹרָא," *TWAT*, 3:869-893, especially pages 885-892.

v. 12b. וְנָבִא לְבַב חָכְמָה – "Then we will obtain a heart of wisdom"

The *waw* introduces the result of what is said in v. 12a.[38] The
hiphil of בוא means "to bring in, gather" (of the crops, 2 Sam. 9:10 and
Hag. 1:6). Proverbs 2 teaches us that wisdom is from Yahweh (v. 6,
compare Ps. 51:8). It is contingent on the "fear" of Yahweh (v. 5, see
above). It is given through instruction (vv. 1-4, cf. Ps. 34:12) and
enters the heart (v. 10, Prov. 23:15). The heart as the seat for the God-
given wisdom is mentioned several times in connection with the
artisans who built the tabernacle (Exod. 28:3; 31:6; 35:26, 35 and
36:2). Wisdom guides you and protects you from evil ways (Prov.
2:11-12) and saves you from sharing the disastrous end of the wicked
(Prov. 2:13-22).

v. 13. שׁוּבָה יְהוָה עַד־מָתָי וְהִנָּחֵם עַל־עֲבָדֶיךָ – "Turn around, O
Yahweh! How long? And repent concerning your servants"

For the form of the imperative שׁובה, see Ps. 6:5. The meaning is,
"turn from your anger" (see Exod. 32:12; 2 Kings 23:26 and Jonah
3:9). For עד מתי, see Ps. 74:10. הנחם, niphal imperative of נחם, is
often translated "have compassion on."[39] However, the instances
understood in this way[40] can all be understood in the sense "change
one's mind, change one's course of action" (the same is true for the
hithpaels which are traditionally translated in this way). We thus
translate "repent," not in the sense "be sorry for something done which
cannot be changed," but "to change one's course of action."[41] With
נחם in the niphal על mostly introduces the matter that one repents of

---

[38]GKC, § 109f.

[39]E.g. Delitzsch, *Psalms*, 3:48; Kraus, *Psalms 60-150*, 213; Nötscher, *Psalmen*,
184.

[40]BDB, 637, lists, apart from our verse, Judg. 2:18; 21:6, 15 and Jer. 15:6; in
hithpael Deut. 32:36 and Ps. 135:14. In Judges 21 we read how the Israelites changed
their mind concerning the tribe of Benjamin, from trying to exterminate them to trying
to save them as an independent tribe. For the other instances, see F. I. Andersen and D.
N. Freedman, *Amos*, The Anchor Bible (New York: Doubleday, 1989), 659, 666-671.

[41]For the meaning of "repent" see Andersen and Freedman, *Amos*, 638-679; H.
Simian-Yofre, "נחם," *TWAT*, 5:366-384. הנחם is translated "repent, change mind" by
Maillot and Lelièvre, *Les Psaumes*, 2:243, and Tate, *Psalms 51-100*, 432, 436.

(Exod. 32:14; Jer. 8:6 and Joel 2:13; an exception is Isa. 57:6). However, Deut. 32:36 and Ps. 135:14 have ועל־עבדיו יתנחם, "and concerning his servants he will repent" (hithpael).

v. 14a.   בַּבֹּקֶר – "in the morning"

The morning is often mentioned in connection with Yahweh's grace and saving acts (Pss. 46:6 and 143:8).[42]

v. 15a.   שַׂמְּחֵנוּ כִּימוֹת עִנִּיתָנוּ – "Make us glad as many days as you have humbled us"

ימות instead of the regular ימים is perhaps to be understood as *nomen unitatis*, stressing the many single days of suffering,[43] but it may be dictated by the desire for assonance with שנות (this form is also rare).[44] At any rate, the only other occurrence of the form is in Deut. 32:7. For עניתנו, compare Deut. 8:2-3,16. The preposition כ of כימות applies also to שנות, "years" in v. 15b.

v. 16a.   יֵרָאֶה אֶל־עֲבָדֶיךָ פָעֳלֶךָ – "Let your work be revealed to your servants"

LXX has καὶ ἰδέ, "and see," which corresponds to וראה. פעלך is a collective. Many manuscripts read the plural, but the singular form of this word is often used with a collective meaning (Job 34:11 and Ps. 143:5). With God as the subject, the word is used regularly to refer to his good, gracious, and marvelous deeds (Deut. 32:4 and Ps. 64:10)[45] and often his great works in the past (Ps. 44:2 and Hab. 3:2).

v. 16b.   וַהֲדָרְךָ עַל־בְּנֵיהֶם – "and your grandeur for their children"

---

[42]See Ziegler, "Die Hilfe Gottes 'am Morgen'," 281-288.

[43]Müller, "Der 90. Psalm," 278.

[44]So Dahood, *Psalms*, 2:326.

[45]Kugel, *The Idea of Biblical Poetry*, 41, translates "your active-force."

For הדר together with פעל, see Ps. 111:3. The idea is not that the parents shall see God's works, whereas the children are permitted to watch his grandeur. He is to reveal both to his servants, even for coming generations. The B-colon in terms of both what is seen and those made to see goes beyond the A-colon.[46] LXX reads והדרך as a hiphil imperative of דרך, "and lead."

v. 17c.   וּמַעֲשֵׂה יָדֵינוּ כּוֹנְנֵהוּ – "and the work of our hands, establish it"

This colon is lacking in a few Hebrew manuscripts and LXX. The repetition, however, is a very effective rhetorical device that serves to intensify the petition. Kraus says it "obviously has the force of an especially enduring petition."[47]

Structure

Strophes

We divide the poem into six strophes: vv. 1-2, 3-4, 5-10, 11-12, 13-15, and 16-17.

Vv. 1-2: After the opening vocative, "O Lord," the whole strophe is chiastically structured:

מעון – an abode

   אתה היית לנו – you have been for us

      בדר ודר – from generation to generation

         בטרם הרים – Before the mountains

            ילדו – were born

            ותחולל – and before you brought forth

         ארץ ותבל – the earth and the world

      ומעולם עד-עולם – even from eternity to eternity

   אתה – you are

אל – God.[48]

---

[46]See Mowinckel, *The Psalms in Israel's Worship*, 2:102, and Kugel, *The Idea of Biblical Poetry*, 40-41.

[47]Kraus, *Psalms 60-150*, 214.

[48]P. Auffret, "Essai sur la structure littéraire du Psaume 90," *Biblica* 61 (1980): 263.

Vv. 3-4: This strophe, like the previous, consists of a bicolon followed by a tricolon. The bicolon contrasts with the previous strophe in two ways. First, the statement with an imperfect תשב אנוש, "you turn man back," forms a contrast with the blessed reality expressed by the perfect מעון היית לנו, "an abode you have been for us," of v. 1. Second, the destiny of human beings returning to dust contrasts with the eternity of God. The tricolon (v. 4) restates the theme of the first strophe, the eternity of God, thus intensifying the contrast.

vv. 5-10: The strophe consists of 7 bicola and is structured as a thematic chiasm:

vv. 5-6 (2 bicola): The distressing reality of human life
> v. 7 (1 bicolon): We vanish because of your anger
>> v. 8 (1 bicolon): You have fixed our offenses before you
> v. 9 (1 bicolon): Our days decline because of your fury

v. 10 (2 bicola): The distressing reality of human life.[49]

V. 9 further picks up "day" and "year" from v. 4, again evoking the contrast between human beings and God. V. 10 contrasts a person's optimal lifespan with the thousand years that for God are like a night-watch (v. 4).

Vv. 11-12: V. 11 has two words for divine wrath; one is picked up from v. 7 and the other from v. 9. Vv. 11-12 are connected by the root ידע, by the fact that both verses have rhyme, and by the well-known connection between "the fear of Yahweh" and "wisdom." V. 11 pinpoints what is lacking while v. 12 supplies the solution. V. 12 picks up "our days" from vv. 9-10.

Vv. 13-15: This strophe has three bicola, each beginning with an imperative addressed to God. (V. 13 has two imperatives.) In v. 14 the B-colon gives the intended result of the petition in the A-colon, and the two cola in v. 15 form one petition. שובה in v. 13a reflects v. 3: God "turns" man back; now the psalmist prays that God himself "turn" around. Note the use of repetition: "in the morning" (v. 14, cf. vv. 5-6); the root שמח, "be glad" (vv. 14-15); the phrase "all our days" (v. 14, cf. v. 9); and the word-pair "day/year" (v. 15, cf. vv. 4 and 9).

---

[49]Ibid., 265-268.

Vv. 16-17: Whereas the previous strophe ended רעה ראינו, the present strophe begins, פעלך . . . יראה, "Let your work be revealed." Also, the last two strophes have "your servants" in the first verse (vv. 13, 16). "Lord" in v. 17 connects with v. 1 as does נעם, which is מעון spelled backwards. Note the repetition of the last line. This last strophe consists of a bicolon plus a tricolon like the first two strophes.

Stanzas

The first strophe (vv. 1-2), 5 cola, is an introduction to the poem. The next three strophes form the first stanza (vv. 3-12) and the last two strophes the second stanza (vv. 13-17). Stanza I has 23 cola, and stanza II is half as long with 11 cola.

Whereas the introduction stresses God's eternity and sovereignty and his past goodness to Israel, stanza I depicts human life under God's wrath. This life is short and miserable. The essence of the distress is that God has fixed human sin before his eyes. The stanza ends with a petition for the right attitude faced with God's wrath: "fear" and "wisdom."

The second stanza builds on this petition, and prays that God may once again be gracious to Israel. The psalmist prays for a reversal of the situation described in the first stanza (see under "strophes" for particular devices of contrast) and for a return of the reality described in the introduction (thus the reversed מעון and the repetition of אדני). Stanza II is sometimes regarded as a later addition to the psalm,[50] but as we have seen, the whole poem has a unified structure.[51]

Progression in Content and Mood

The psalm is often regarded as a communal lament.[52] Castellino considers it a lament influenced by wisdom, in which an individual

[50]Gunkel, *Psalmen*, 397; Müller, "Der 90. Psalm," 267-268.

[51]See further S. Schreiner, "Erwägungen zur Struktur des 90. Psalms," *"Biblica* 59 (1978): 80-90; Auffret, "la structure littéraire du Psaume 90," 262-276.

[52]E.g. C. Westermann, "Der 90. Psalm," in *Forschung am Alten Testament: Gesammelte Studien* (Munich: Chr. Kaiser Verlag, 1964), 344; G. Von Rad, "Psalm 90," in *God at Work in Israel*, translated by J. H. Marks (Nashville: Abingdon, 1980), 213.

laments the painful condition of the whole people.[53] Harrelson, on the other hand, views this psalm as a psalm of meditation.[54] The psalm contains most of the elements generally associated with the genre of lament (invocation, praise, complaint, petition). Broyles assigns it to the subgenre of "complaint of the community."[55] If it holds true for the psalms in general that each one advances the thought in its own unique way, this can be said even more of Psalm 90.

The psalm contains two movements, one of complaint and one of petition. After the invocation, "O Lord," the psalmist begins by extolling God's greatness and everlastingness. The introduction (vv. 1-2) has a chiastic structure. First, God is described in relation to the people as he has been experienced in the past: "An abode, a safe haven, a place of refuge, *you* (used with finite verb the pronoun carries stress, "you and you alone") have been for us from generation to generation." Then his eternity is contrasted with all creation: "Before the mountains were born, and before you brought forth the earth and the world." The verbs "were born" and "you brought forth" stand at the pivot of the chiasm, making the contrast even more effective. Finally, the thought of God's eternity is brought up again, this time not in connection with the past experience of the people, but as a reality valid from before creation and for all future, "from eternity to eternity." Notice that the people have disappeared from the picture. Now it is said that "you are God"; there is no "for us" as there is in v. 1. This leads over into the description of the present situation in stanza I.

This eternal God has decided to cut short the lives of human beings: "You turn man back to dust." Notice the clear allusion to God's curse upon man after the fall: עפר אתה ואל-עפר תשוב, "dust you are, and to dust you shall return" (Gen. 3:19). However, the psalmist has chosen a stronger word for dust, דכא, which probably connotes something crushed into pieces or pulverized. As God once said to Adam, so he continues to say to his descendants: "Return O

---

[53]Castellino, *Libro dei Salmi*, 342-343.

[54]W. Harrelson, "A Meditation of the Wrath of God: Psalm 90," in *Scripture in History & Theology: Essays in Honor of J. Coert Rylaarsdam*, eds., A. L. Merrill and T. W. Overholt (Pittsburgh, PA: The Pickwick Press, 1977), 181-182.

[55]C. C. Broyles, *The Conflict of Faith*, 173-177.

children of Adam" (בני-אדם)! Lest we miss the point, the author again reminds us that the very God who does this to people is himself totally unrestricted by time: "For a thousand years in your eyes are like yesterday." A third colon intensifies it, "and like a watch in the night," not a long period compared with a thousand years.

After this reminder we are back in the flow of thought from v. 3: "You pour over them sleep." This motif, which was usually reserved for the enemies of Israel (see translation note), is now applied to "the children of man" (v. 3) including Israel. It denotes death and destruction. When God thus overpowers humankind, in the morning, the time when God's nightly judgment is made manifest,[56] they become like grass that passes away quickly. The grass sprouts in the morning but may have withered at dusk.

The reason why human life is so frail and futile is God's judgment on sin (his righteous anger). The chiastic structure of v. 7 makes this fact stand out even more. We vanish. We are terrified.[57] Note that the psalmist from v. 7 on ceases to talk of "man" or "children of man" and turns back to the first person plural with which he opened the psalm. His interest is not with describing some general human experience but with God's people who at present are in distress because of God's anger.

God's wrath is directed against human sin. V. 8 is the pivot of the third strophe, framed by the "wrath" of vv. 7 and 9 and the description of the distress in vv. 5-6 and 10. "You have fixed our offenses before you, our secret faults before the light of your face" (v. 8). The point is not primarily to give a confession of sin. What the psalmist describes is God's reaction to the people's sins, even their secret faults. God scrutinizes their every shortcoming to punish them for it. God's focus on their sins is the reason for his wrath and thus the root of the distress.

This is the background for v. 9: "For all our days decline because of your fury; we complete our years like a groan." But what about those who attain advanced age in good health? The psalmist will not back off. Granted they may reach seventy years, and if they have extremely good health and a strong body perhaps even eighty, still "the pride of them," the very best they can come up with, is "trouble and

---

[56]See translation note to v. 5b.

[57]See Pss. 6:3-4; 30:8 for נבהל as human response to divine wrath.

distress," for it (the pride of their days and their years) passes by quickly, and they fly away.[58] Life under God's wrath is short and miserable. V. 10 lets us see that this is not so much a common experience of all as it is life seen by faith. That is to say, death is common enough, but the interpretation of life and death given by the psalmist is not one shared by every human. The psalmist describes a life under God's wrath.

V. 11 picks up the motif of God's wrath, holding together vv. 7 and 9 by picking one word for divine wrath from each. Now the problem is that the people do not *know* the strength of God's wrath. This may seem strange after the long description precisely of the human condition under God's wrath. The key is כיראתך, "according to the fear due to you." As seen in the translation note, the "fear" of Yahweh entails reverence, worship, and a living relationship to Yahweh. This seems to be lacking in the people. Therefore the psalmist turns to God in prayer: "To count our days, such teach us, that we may obtain a heart of wisdom." The combination of "fear" (v. 11) and "wisdom" (v. 12) and the focus on the verb "to know" evokes the proverb, "The fear of Yahweh is the beginning of knowledge," with "wisdom" in parallel (Prov. 1:7), or as Job has it: "The fear of the Lord, that is wisdom" (Job 28:28). The right way of understanding the precariousness of human life and the wrath of God is to be sought precisely with God. Notice how in this stanza time units such as days and years all pertain to humans (in v. 4 the point is the irrelevance of time units to God), whereas God is from eternity to eternity (v. 2c).[59] To count our days entails facing the reality of an impending death and having one's mind directed toward him who has been our abode from generation to generation.

As one who fears Yahweh, counts his days, and has wisdom in his heart, the psalmist confronts God, asking him to change the distressing situation. V. 13 begins a unit dominated by imperatives: "Turn around [away from your wrath, back to the earlier time when we learned to know you as an abode from generation to generation], O Yahweh!

---

[58]For the relation between v. 9 and v. 10, cf. Castellino's imaginative description, *Libro dei Salmi*, 345-346.

[59]See Castellino, *Libro dei Salmi*, 342.

How long [will your wrath last]? Repent [change your mind and your course of action] concerning your servants." The term "your servants" underlines the relation which exists between Yahweh and his people. The appeal to this relation is frequent in the prayer of lament psalms (for example Pss. 27:9; 31:17; 69:18).[60] The next petition is: "Satisfy us in the morning with your steadfast love." The psalmist does not speak of God's steadfast love as something new but as something known, obviously as part of the reality confessed in v. 1. The petition is that God may let the people enjoy it. In v. 5 the morning was the time when God's destructive activity against humans was made manifest. Here the psalmist prays that God may let them experience his steadfast love instead, precisely in the morning. The result that would follow when God does so is stated in the second colon: "so that we may shout for joy and be glad all our days," the very opposite of the situation painted for "all our days" in v. 9. Thus we have the contrast: When under God's wrath, our life declines with groans, but when experiencing God's steadfast love, all our days are filled with joy.

The motive of joy is carried into the next verse: "Make us glad as many days as you have humbled us, as many years as we have seen misery." Notice how it comes through that the psalmist prays as one whom God has taught to count his days: "in all our days" (v. 14b), "as many days as"(v. 15a), "as many years as" (v. 15b). In past days and years the people have *seen misery* (v. 15b), but now the psalmist prays that they may *see God's work* (v. 16a). As we observed in our translation note, God's פֹעַל is generally his gracious and salvific work and not the result of his wrath. The problem is that God's "work" has been hidden while God's anger lasts. The relational term "your servants" (v. 13b) is repeated in v. 16a. V. 16 is a good illustration of how Kugel describes parallelism, "A is so, and what is more B." The psalmist wants to see Yahweh's works, and what is more, God's "grandeur"; he wants it to be shown to Yahweh's servants, and what is more, even for their children.[61]

---

[60]Compare H. Ringgren, *TWAT*, 2:1000: "Er will sich durch diese Selbstbezeichnung als einen auf die Güte JHWHs angewiesenen Menschen darstellen, vielleicht auch sein 'æbœd-Sein als Grund für Gottes Eingreifen anführen (vgl. das kî in Ps. 143,12."

[61]Kugel, *The Idea of Biblical Poetry*, pp. 1-58.

V. 17 looks back to v. 1; the verse repeats the word אדני, and נעם is מעון spelled backwards. What the psalmist prays is for God to be "an abode for us" even now, as he has been from generation to generation. Finally, God is called on to establish (כון) the work of their hands for them, that is, to let them prosper under his care. The repetition underlines the thought that even the works of our hands are at the mercy of God. He is the one who establishes them.

The Problem

In Psalm 90 no physical distress is described, but the people seem to be in a situation that is interpreted by those who fear Yahweh as a prolonged period under God's wrath.[62] The distress is to live under the wrath of God. God is said to have fixed their sins in front of his eyes. Because of God's wrath they vanish (v. 7a); under God's wrath this short life becomes "trouble and distress" (v. 10). Even though the reality of death and the brevity of life are common human experiences, the psalm does not intend to describe life merely as it is generally experienced. Rather, it seems to present from a faith perspective a portrayal and an interpretation of the experience of God's people. Those who see their years declining are the same ones who could confess, "O Lord, an abode you have been for us from generation to generation."

The Prayer

The psalmist asks God to teach his people to count their days so that they may obtain wise hearts (v. 12). Thereby they can face the brevity of life and understand that God, their abode from generation to generation, is the only one and the only thing that really matters; thus they will put their trust and hope in him. Then he prays that God turn from his wrath (v. 13a), change his course of action concerning them (v. 13b), and grant them to enjoy his steadfast love (v. 14a). Then they

---

[62]This is sometimes taken to imply a post-exilic date, but it would fit any situation of prolonged wrath, including the forty years in the wilderness–with which the psalm is connected by the superscription–and the exile.

will rejoice for the rest of their days and years (vv. 14b-15). The psalmist wants to see God's "proper" works (v. 16a) and wants God's grandeur to manifest itself even to coming generations (v. 16b). He prays that God's kindness may be upon them (v. 17a) and that God may establish the work of their hands (v. 17b-c). In short, he wants God once again to let them experience him as an abode from generation to generation.

The Appeal

The emphasis on "*your* servants" in v. 13 and v. 16 underlines their total dependence on God and their relation to God as a motivation for why God should act. Note the prayer, "Let your work be revealed," as if God's present work is not *God's* work. One should probably understand this as an appeal to God's "proper" work. The same may be said of God's "grandeur" and "kindness." This is further strengthened by the connection that v. 17 makes with v. 1, where the Lord is said to have been an abode from generation to generation. As the opening would lead us to expect, the psalmist appeals to God's character as experienced in the past and still confessed and to the relationship between God and the people.

PART THREE

THEOLOGICAL ASSUMPTIONS AND IMPLICATIONS

Chapter Seven

Theological Assumptions and Implications

Introduction

D rawing together our findings from our investigation of the five psalms in Part Two, we now ask: What are the underlying theological assumptions and what are the implications? This consideration will lead us to an answer for our main question: What did the Israelite faithful do when they experienced God as their enemy?

In this chapter we will also use evidence from other psalms belonging to the subgenres of the complaints of the individual (Psalms 13, 22, 35, 39, 42-43, and 102) and the complaints of the community (Psalms 9-10, 60, 77, 79, 80, 85, and 89.[1]

Structure and Progression in Content and Mood

Each of the five psalms studied in Part Two has a unique structure and its own way of advancing the appeal. The different elements in a particular psalm function within the total progression in content and mood. Thus the same element may not have the same function in different psalms.[2]

Psalm 6 begins with petitions for God in his wrath to cease reproaching the psalmist. The enemies are not introduced before the last word of v. 8, and then only, in the next colon, to be ordered to leave. This effectively focuses attention on God's wrath as the cause of the distress and makes of the enemies a secondary problem.

---

[1]We have excluded Ps. 108. For a treatment of the individual psalms, see Castellino, *Libro dei Salmi*. For the psalms found in the first third of the Psalter, compare Craigie, *Psalms 1-50*; for those in the second, see Tate, *Psalms 51-100*. For Psalm 13, see Weiss, *The Bible from Within*, 298-314. For Psalm 42-43, see Raabe, *Psalm Structures*, 32-67.

[2]See also Raabe, *Psalm Structures*, 186-189.

Psalm 88 is very different. Like Psalm 6, it can be classified as a "sickness psalm" or an "individual near-death psalm." Here God is called "God of my salvation"(v. 2). The psalmist, after asking God finally to listen to his prayer, describes his distress. He sinks deeper and deeper into the realm of death. He sees himself as cut off from the sphere of God's saving activity (v. 6). Then God becomes his enemy (vv. 8-9). Whereas the description of the problem in Ps. 6:3-4a is from the very beginning linked to God's wrath, in Psalm 88 God's wrath only gradually becomes the problem.

The motif of no praise or recognition of Yahweh in Sheol functions differently in Psalms 6 and 88. In both it serves to warn God that he should act quickly if he wants the worship and praise of the psalmist. However, whereas in Psalm 6 the motif colors vv. 7-8 so that the weeping parallels the psalmist with those in Sheol, in Psalm 88 it leads the psalmist to realize that he is not yet in Sheol. He has not yet entered "the land of forgetfulness"; he is still praying. This situation motivates the new start in v. 14. For all the similarity between the third stanza and the first stanza, in stanza III the psalmist's problem is God, not the powers of Sheol.

The reference to God's steadfast love is also different in the two psalms. In Psalm 6 Yahweh is asked to save for the sake of his steadfast love, whereas in Psalm 88 the psalmist merely reminds God that his steadfast love is not recognized in Sheol. This accords well with the much more hopeless mood in Psalm 88. In Psalm 6 the psalmist becomes certain in the end that Yahweh has heard his prayer, but Psalm 88 ends in darkness.

The two laments of the community, Psalms 44 and 74, also have different structures. Psalm 44 begins by recalling how God was well-disposed toward the people in the past, gave them victory over their enemies, and made them thrive in the land. The psalmist then confidently asserts that this God is his king. He temporarily forgets the present realities and states: "With God we push down our enemies"(v. 6). The situation where God saves and the people praise him is pictured as the normal situation (v. 8-9).

Then, finally the present distress catches up with the psalmist. Vv. 10-17 contrast what God does now with what he did in the past. As the unchanged fidelity of the people enters the picture (vv. 18-23), the case is made that God has acted unfaithfully to his people. Against this background the questions of "why" are uttered (vv. 24-25). God's steadfast love with its element of faithfulness[3] is appealed to in the very last colon of the psalm.

The psalmist begins Psalm 74 with the complaint of the temple's destruction by the enemies of the people of God. Since the people are helpless, the question is how long God will tolerate the taunting of the enemies. The reference to God as "my king" in v. 12 does not connote confidence and trust as in Psalm 44. Here the tone is more one of complaint. If God is "my king from ancient time, achiever of victories in the midst of the earth," how is it that the enemy who taunts him can remain unpunished?[4] Thus the main argument made in this psalm is that God has to defend his reputation as king of the universe. Moreover, because he has entered into a relation with Israel, his role as their defender and his reputation as the only true God are joined together. The many relational expressions in this psalm make this clear (vv. 1-2, 19-21). Therefore, vv. 18-23 link together petitions that God should pay attention to the way the enemies mock him and petitions concerning his people.

The key to Psalm 90 is the opening motif of confidence and praise. The psalm describes such common human experiences as the brevity of life and the impending death. Without the opening, stanza I could be taken as a general description of the misery of life and a petition that God may teach us how to cope with it.[5] But v. 1 reveals that there was a past reality that is not being experienced at present. Therefore, after the petition that God may change us (vv. 11-12), the psalmist prays that God himself may change. The "how long" (v. 13) serves to motivate God to action. In Psalm 6 the phrase expresses both the hope that God's wrath will not last forever and the fear that the psalmist will die before God turns away from his wrath. This phrase in Ps. 74:9

---

[3]See our discussion of חסד below.

[4]See further Weiss, *The Bible from Within*, 278-280.

[5]This is the reason why Gunkel, *Psalmen*, 397, and Müller, "Der 90. Psalm," 267-268, see vv. 13-17 as a later addition. If the first stanza is read as a description of the way life necessarily is, there is nothing more to pray for than wisdom to cope with it. If so, vv. 13-17 must be seen as expressing disagreement with the view of life found in the first part of the psalm. If, however, we read stanza I in the light of v. 1, it becomes clear that there is more to say than "Help us cope with your wrath."

refers to the silence of God; there is no one who knows when the distress will end because God does not speak. The question of Ps. 74:10 is how long God will tolerate the insult of his enemies. Here in Ps. 90 we have a prayer for God's steadfast love, reference to the people as his "servants," and prayer that God will make them glad and reveal his work to them. The object of the prayer in the last stanza is the experience described in v. 1.

The Problem

Disasters Interpreted as Caused by God's Wrath

The complaint psalms reflect different troubles and distresses. In Psalms 6 and 88 the psalmist appeared to be *sick*. At any rate, he saw his death as impending. Sickness or near-death situations are the case also in Psalms 13, 22, 42-43, and 102.[6] *Enemies* are part of the distress in Psalm 6. The same is true for Psalms 9-10,[7] 13, 22, 35,[8] 42-43, and

---

[6]Pss. 13:3-4; 22:15-16, 18; 102:4-12, 24-25. Of these psalms Seybold, *Das Gebet des Kranken*, regards only Psalm 88 as a sure psalm of sickness (113-117). Psalm 102 is placed in the group "Psalmen mit sehr wahrscheinlichem Bezug zu Krankheit oder Heilung des Beters." Among his "Psalmen mit unsicherem Bezug zu Krankheit oder Heilung des Beters" are found Psalms 6 and 13. Seybold thinks Psalm 22 is not a psalm of sickness. For a discussion of the special problems of structure and unity of Psalm 102, see Castellino, *Libro dei Salmi*, 216-218.

[7]Broyles assigns Psalm 9-10 to the subgenre "the complaints of the community" (135-139). If so, the enemies should probably be taken to imply a military defeat. However, E. S. Gerstenberger, *Psalms part 1 with an Introduction to Cultic Poetry*, The Forms of the Old Testament Literature Vol. 15 (Grand Rapids: Eerdmans, 1988), 72-76, sees the psalm as individual. With Castellino, *Libro dei Salmi*, 775, we understand the psalm to have three parts. 9:1-11 praises God for a salvation in a past crisis. In 9:12-21 the psalmist approaches a present crisis, confident that Yahweh will help him now even as he did in the past. But to this "psalm of plea," as it would have to be classified in Broyles' system, the psalmist appends a complaint that God time and again permits the wicked to have their way (10:1-18). Only this last part qualifies as a "complaint psalm." Even though the enemies in Psalm 9 may be hostile nations, those in Psalm 10 appear to be whatever enemy there may be that rises up to oppress the poor and the godly. We therefore group the psalm with those featuring enemies rather than with those reflecting a military defeat.

[8]In Psalm 35 the problem seems to be false accusation, although see Castellino, *Libro dei Salmi*, 106-108, and Craigie, *Psalms 1-50*, 285-286.

Ps. 102.[9] In Psalm 44 the background is a *military defeat*, as it is in Psalms 60, 80, and 89.[10] Psalm 44 further mentions the *mocking done by the neighboring peoples* as a result of the defeat. In Psalm 74 the defeat is even more bitter and final, since Jerusalem is sacked and the temple looted and burnt. Such is also the case in Psalm 79. In Psalm 90 *death and a short life* under God's wrath for sin are the problem, as is also the case in Psalm 39.

We saw in Part Two that near-death situations, troubling enemies, military defeat, the destruction of the temple, and even a generally miserable life are all attributed to God's wrath. Personal and national disasters are not things that just happen. They are not caused by evil spirits or by the activity of sorcerers but by God's displeasure. What made the psalmists view misery in this way?

Yahweh is the living God (Ps. 42:3, 9). He is the creator and the only source of life (Pss. 89:48 and 90:2). Our life is in his hand (Ps. 39:6). This God had made Israel his own people (Ps. 74:2), rescued them from slavery in Egypt (Pss. 77:16 and 80:9), and planted them in the land of Israel (Pss. 44:3 and 80:9-11).

Yahweh had entered into a covenant relationship with this people (Ps. 74:20). How this was thought to influence life is seen in Deut. 30:15-19. Here Moses lays before the people "life and good" on the one hand, and "death and bad" on the other hand. If you will "love Yahweh your God, walk in his ways, and keep his commandments," then you will "live and multiply, and Yahweh your God will bless you in the land into which you enter to possess it." Life, blessing, and land belong together. On the other hand, if they do not obey God, but worship other gods, they will perish and not prolong their days on the land given them by Yahweh. Their life and well-being in its totality depend on their relation to Yahweh.[11]

This covenant relationship is spelled out in more detail in Deuteronomy 28, where the first part exemplifies blessings that will

---

[9]Pss. 10:3-11, 13, 15; 13:3, 5; 22:13-14, 17, 19; 35:1, 4, 7, 11-12, 15-16, 19-21; 42:10; and 102:9.

[10]Pss. 60:4, 12; 80:13-14, 17; and 89:39-46.

[11]See also G. Von Rad's treatment of this passage, "Statements of Faith in the Old Testament about Life and about Death," in *God at Work in Israel*, translated by J. H. Marks (Nashville: Abingdon, 1980), 199-200.

characterize their life with Yahweh, while the rest of the chapter gives numerous examples of what will happen if they forsake their God. The premonarchical Israelite traditions as recorded in the book of Judges are rich with examples of how Israel's life depended solely on its relation to Yahweh. The recurring pattern here is the following: The people sinned; God permitted neighboring peoples to oppress them; they cried to Yahweh; he saved them by his chosen judge; the judge ruled Israel for forty years; there was rest as long as he lived.

Life thus has no autonomy. Yahweh is the fountain of life (Ps. 36:10, Jer. 2:13, and 17:13). Life and good belong together and are at home in the realm of Yahweh's favor and blessing. Death and all kinds of misery [רַע] characterize an existence outside the sphere of God's goodness and saving activity, an existence under his curse. In this frame of reference, near-death situations, whether they were caused by sickness (Psalm 88), hunger, or wicked oppressors (Psalm 13), would be interpreted as evidence that God was angry.[12] When God is the absolute sovereign, the creator and unrivaled ruler of the universe (Pss. 74:12-17 and 90:1-2), there could be no place for military defeat where the people's relationship with Yahweh remained intact. Defeat had to be interpreted as Yahweh no longer guarding the land he had given them (Pss. 60:4; 80:13-14; and 89:41-42). Yahweh, who as a mighty warrior brought them out of Egypt and cleared the ground for them in the land he gave them (Pss. 44:3-4 and 80:9-10), has now turned their sword back and strengthens the enemy (Pss. 44:10-12 and 89:43-44).[13]

God's Wrath as the Heart of the Problem

If true life is to live with God, then his wrath is not only what brings death and misery, it is the core of the distress. What is so terrifying about death and Sheol in Psalm 6 is that there no one praises

---

[12]See P. R. Raabe, "Human Suffering in Biblical Context," *CJ* 15 (1989): 139-155.

[13]See further H. J. Kraus, "Der lebendige Gott," *Evangelische Theologie* 27 (1967): 190-195, which deals with God as the fountain of life, and Barth, *Die Errettung vom Tode*, 36-51. On pp. 50-51 Barth deals with the connection between life and the land: "*Überall gehören 'am Leben bleiben' und 'das Land besitzen' zusammen*" (50).

Yahweh (v. 6, compare Ps. 88:11-13). To be cut off from God's hand is central in the picture of death in Psalm 88; it is to be placed outside the sphere of his saving activity (vv. 6-7). Death is terrible because it separates from Yahweh, and sickness and near-death situations are a foretaste of this separation. In connection with these two psalms we saw how the reality of death reaches into the realm of physical life. The sick experience themselves as already being in Sheol, unable to praise Yahweh (6:7-8). This thought of separation from the praise of Yahweh is prominent in Psalm 42. Here the psalmist, caught up under God's "breakers and rollers" (v. 8), recalls a better past when he would go up with the festival crowds to the temple to praise Yahweh (vv. 5 and 9). He pants for God as a stag pants for water (v. 2).[14]

Psalm 88 gives us a vivid picture of a desperate man persistently praying to a deaf deity (vv. 2, 10, 14, and the end of it all in v. 19b, "darkness"). This unapproachability of God not only precludes any solution to the problem, it is very distressful itself. The psalmist wants to live in a praise-relation with God, yet God does not even bother to hear him. In Psalm 22 the psalmist describes a similar problem. In spite of his former close relation with God (vv. 10-11), God is now absent in his time of need (vv. 8-9 and 12). The fathers were saved when they cried to God (v. 5-6). He cries, but his salvation is far away (vv. 2-3). In Psalm 74 God's people are in danger of losing their faith, because it appears that the god of the conquerors has prevailed against their God. They are also in danger of losing their very lives. In this situation God remains silent. This is the problem in Psalm 74.

The silence of God made it impossible to know when this macabre situation would end (Ps. 74:9-10). The "how long" is a very common element in the psalms within our corpus (for example, Pss. 13:2-3; 35:17; 79:5, and 80:5). The theological assumptions and appeal value of these questions will be dealt with below. We will only mention here what they tell us about the problem. The "how long" questions sometimes express fear. The questions entail the possibility that it may be too long. Will death come before Yahweh's wrath ends (Ps. 6:4-6)? They may express bewilderment. How can it be that God for so long tolerates the enemies' taunting his name and oppressing his people?

---

[14]See Raabe, *Psalm Structures*, 48-50.

(Ps. 74:11). In all cases they add a note of urgency and can be seen as the negative formulation of the prayer in Ps. 22:20, "hasten to help me."

It makes a difference whether one says, "O Lord, here is a mighty army approaching, but I know you will save us," or one says, "Here is a mighty enemy, and you, O Lord, who always saved us before, have sold us to this mighty enemy." The latter is the situation in Psalm 44 (vv. 11-13). Consider also Psalm 89. After a lengthy section extolling Yahweh's might, love, faithfulness, and unbreakable promises to David and his dynasty, the psalmist abruptly breaks off: "Still, you have rejected and refused; you have become angry with your anointed. You have scorned the covenant with your servant; you have profaned to the ground the oath to him. You have broken down all his walls; you have made his fortresses into ruins . . . . You have lifted up the right hand of his enemies; you have made all his foes happy" (vv. 39-43). Thus the chief problem in these psalms is not the enemies but God who has acted as an enemy. God has disappointed them and bewildered them. He has ceased to be predictable. Now anything can happen. They experience "death and misery."

Psalm 90 describes the distress entirely as a short life under God's wrath. Even a life span of seventy or eighty years passes as a groan and has nothing better to offer than trouble when God is angry (Ps. 90:7-10 and Ps. 39:5-7).

In these psalms we note that the wrath of God is not only a problem insofar as it deprives people of health, social security, or national independence. God's wrath is a problem because it deprives people of God himself and of life with him. The heart of the distress in the complaint psalms is, therefore, the wrath of God.

The Character of God's Wrath

General

We have seen above that the wrath of God is not only an emotion. The psalmists view it as that which caused the intolerable situation they experience. God's anger is effective.[15] Still, we cannot reduce

---

[15]Compare Baloian, *Anger*, 98-99.

God's wrath to something like "retributive justice"[16] in order to defend a philosophical immutability and impassability of God. In many places the Old Testament depicts God as *provoked* to anger. He was not originally angry, but he became angry because someone made him angry. The God of the Old Testament and of the complaint psalms is a God who has passions.[17] Note the way the psalmists relate God to time and space. God rejects, and the psalmist asks how long he will go on rejecting. God forgets; what he was aware of before is no longer on his mind. God is far away, although he used to be close by. He does not go out with Israel's armies as he did before. He is sleeping but can wake up. Nevertheless, the strong statements of God's independence of time in Psalm 90 warn us against too tight of an interpretation of these motifs. The psalmists are not offering philosophical statements about God; they are describing how God is to them.[18]

We have discussed divine wrath in this study as depicting God's displeasure with people. Although only 10 of the 18 psalms (when

---

[16]The expression is mentioned as untenable by W. Eichrodt, *Theology of the Old Testament*, translated by J. A. Baker (Philadelphia: The Westminster Press, 1961), 1:259.

[17]See Eichrodt, *Theology of the old Testament*, 258-282; Baloian, *Anger*, 156-163, and F. Weber, *Vom Zorne Gottes: Ein biblisch-theologischer Versuch* (Erlangen: Andreas Deichert, 1862), 40-64. In his chapter "Die Gegensätze und ihre Ueberwindung," Weber refutes, on the one hand, the Augustinian view that God is impassible and that anger thus has no affect in God, and on the other hand, the view that a loving and caring God cannot be thought to be angry with anyone for anything. G. A. F. Knight misunderstands the nature of divine wrath when he writes: "Unlike human anger, which fluctuates with the passing mood and whim, the Wrath of God is permanent, unswerving, and undeviating. . . . The great thinkers of the OT accept this fact without any hesitation whatsoever. 'We are consumed in thine anger, and in thy wrath are we troubled' (Ps. 90:7)." (*A Christian Theology of the Old Testament* (Richmond, Virginia: John Knox Press, 1959), 133. On the contrary, in Psalm 90 the psalmist does not regard God's wrath as an unchangeable reality. He prays for a change. As we shall see below, it is an assumption of the psalmists that God's wrath is temporary toward his people.

[18]T. E. Fretheim interprets Ps. 90:4 as saying "one thousand of God's years are *like* one human day." He thus stresses that the relation of God to time is different from that of human beings. Nevertheless, "at least since creation, the divine life is temporally ordered" (*The Suffering of God*, Philadelphia: Fortress Press, 1984, p. 43. However, as we saw in chapter 2, Ps. 90:4 is not speaking of God's years but of how ordinary human years are to God. Moreover, note the contrast created in that psalm between the finite time of human beings and God's eternity.

Psalms 9-10 and 42-43 are each regarded as one psalm) included in our study explicitly contain a word for divine "wrath," in all the complaint psalms people are faced with evidence that God is against them. We shall see below that God is described in these psalms as actively hostile or as absent and hidden. We will now briefly overview the words in the semantic field of wrath which appear in these psalms.[19] Then we will look at the description of God as absent and as actively hostile.

Terminology for God's Wrath[20]

The most common word for "wrath" is אף, "nose, face, anger." The rationale for getting "anger" out of "nose" may be the snorting which often accompanies this emotion. The word is used with God as subject seven times in the complaint psalms. The word is parallel to חמה in Pss. 6:2; 90:7, and to עברה in Ps. 90:11, with אף placed first in all cases. Once אף is second in a parallel construction with the verb זנח, "reject" (Ps. 74:1). The expression חרון אף, which M. I. Gruber explains as the reddening of the nose/face of angry persons,[21] is parallel to עברה in Ps. 85:4. In Ps. 74:1b we find the phrase אפך יעשן, "your anger fumes."[22] The cognate verb אנף, "be angry" is used three times, all in parallel constructions. It stands as the A-word to קנאה in Ps. 79:5 and to אף in Ps. 85:6. In Ps. 60:3 it is found in the second colon, where the first contains זנח, "reject," and פרץ, "break through a wall."

---

[19]The word field given here is identical with that of Baloian, *Anger*, 6-7, with two exceptions: a) Words that do not occur in the complaint psalms are not included; b) the word קנאה is included since it is parallel with אנף in Ps. 79:5.

[20]For more thorough treatments of the words for "wrath", see F. Weber, *Vom Zorne Gottes* (Erlangen: Andreas Deichert, 1862), 14-28; E. Johnsen, "אנף," in *TWAT*, 1:376-389; K. D. Schunck, "חמה," *TWAT*, 2:1032-1036, and "עברה,"*TWAT*, 5:1033-1039; D. N. Freedmann and J. Lundblom, "חרה," *TWAT*, 3:182-188; N. Lohfink, "כעס," *TWAT*, 4:298-302; B. Wiklander, "זעם," *TWAT*, 2:621-626. A short summary is found in B. E. Baloian, *Anger in the Old Testament* (New York: Peter Lang, 1992), 5-7.

[21]Gruber, *Nonverbal Communication*, 2:491.

[22]See Gruber, *Nonverbal Communication*, 2:510-513.

חמה, "wrath," is usually connected with the verb יחם, "be hot." The word sometimes has the meaning "poison."[23] Gruber contests this derivation and sees "poison, venom, foam, wrath" as its range of meaning.[24] Apart from the two times it is parallel to אף, the word is used three times in verbal phrases: with שפך in Ps. 79:6, "pour out wrath" (or with the metaphor "pour out poison"),[25] in Ps. 88:8 with סמך, "lean, support,"[26] and in Ps. 89:47 with the metaphor of wrath "burning" as fire (בער). This last phrase stands parallel to נסתר, "hide."

עברה, "fury," is sometimes connected with the root עבר, "cross, pass by." The idea is that the heat inside boils over. Others trace the noun and the hithpael of עבר to a root meaning "be arrogant" (both the verb and the noun sometimes have this meaning). The verb is used once (Ps. 89:39) with זנח, "reject," and מאס, "refuse," in the first colon.[27] The noun is used three times in the complaint psalms: once with אף (Ps. 90:11), once with חרון אף (Ps. 85:4), and once alone (Ps. 90:9).

חרון, "wrath," is derived from the verb חרה, "burn." Thus once more we have the metaphor of wrath as fire. The verb is often used with אף (e.g. 2 Sam. 24:1 and Isa. 5:25) but is rare in the Psalms and absent in the complaint psalms. חרון אף is associated with כעס, "provocation," in Ps. 85:4-5.[28] In Ps. 88:17 חרון is used in the plural with עבר, "Over me sweep your bursts of wrath," and it is parallel to בעותיך, "your alarms." As mentioned above, in Ps. 79:5 קנאה,

---

[23] See Pss. 58:5 and 140:4.

[24] Gruber, *Nonverbal Communication*, 2:513.

[25] Gruber, *Nonverbal Communication*, 2:535.

[26] The phrase describes God's wrath as pressing against the sufferer (see translation note in Part Two above).

[27] Yaron, "The Meaning of Zanach," 237-239, has argued that זנח means "be angry" rather than "reject." He supports this view partly by parallelism. The three instances in the complaint psalms where the verb is parallel to words for anger/wrath do not, as far as we can see, strengthen his theory. In Ps. 60:3, for example, it is immediately followed by פרץ, "break through a wall," and in Ps. 89:39 by מאס, "refuse."

[28] The word is also used in Ps. 6:8 but in its passive meaning, "distress."

"jealousy" (used with בער, "burn") is parallel to אנף. In Ps. 102:11 the nouns זעם, "wrath" or "curse," and קצף, "anger," are used together in this order.

The words for wrath that are most common in the complaint psalms seem to have considerable semantic overlap and can, for our purposes, be treated as synonyms. We have applied the more common English word, "anger," for the more common אף, and the less common English words, "wrath" and "fury" for the less common Hebrew synonyms, חמה, חרון, and עברה.

God as Absent and Indifferent

In the complaint psalms the psalmists protest that God has *rejected* them, has *hidden* himself, has *forgotten* them, is *far away*, is *inaccessible*, and even *sleeps*. These complaints tend to cluster in the beginning of a description of the distress or, as negated jussives, in complaint-like petitions. These motifs have basically the same function; they protest that God has abandoned them and does not pay attention to their prayers. Still, each motif gives its own nuance to this complaint.

The most common verb for rejection[29] in the complaint psalms is זנח, which is used seven times in these psalms. עזב, "abandon," and מאס, "refuse," are used one time each (Pss. 22:2 and 89:39). Six times the motif of rejection is found in the first colon of a complaint section (Pss. 22:2; 44:10; 60:3; 74:1; 88:15; and 89:39). In Ps. 44:24 the vetitive, "do not reject forever," occurs in the second colon of the complaining prayer. In Ps. 77:8 the question, "Will the Lord reject for ever and never more be favorably disposed," is the first of several rhetorical questions complaining that God has seemingly stopped being good and asking him if this is final. The rejection motif is cast in a "why" complaint in Pss. 22:2; 74:1, and 88:15. In Psalms 44 and 89 the rejection motif is directly preceded by a hymnic section describing God's salvific acts in the past (44) or God's unbreakable promises

---

[29]We have grouped together words that are generally translated "reject," "abandon," "forsake," "refuse," etc. The discussion will make clear how the psalmists used these words.

(89). Immediately before the prayer in Ps. 44:24-27 the people had professed their innocence and unmistakably put the blame for their misery on God. In Ps. 22:2 the complaints following the rejection motif bear out the contrast between how God should have acted and how he in fact treats the psalmist. Thus the context of the rejection clauses presents a radical break between God's past, his promises, and his relation with the people, on the one hand, and the present, where God's promises are not kept and the relationship is not recognized, on the other hand. Sin or human unfaithfulness is not admitted in any of the complaint psalms in which the rejection motif occurs. When humans reject God or his commandments, it denotes apostasy (Lev. 26:15-16; Judg. 2:12; and 2 Kings 17:15). But now Israel or the individual has remained faithful to God, but God has broken faith with them.[30]

The motif of the hidden God is expressed four times by פָּנִים הִסְתִּיר, "hide the face" (including once [Ps. 10:11] in the mouth of the wicked), once נִסְתַּר, "hide oneself" (Ps. 89:47), and once הֶעְלִים, "hide" (Ps. 10:1). When God hides his face, he does not listen to prayer and pay attention to his people's misery. They are in the hands of whoever wants to oppress them and take advantage of them. S. E. Balentine mentions that the question "why do you hide your face" in the lament psalms receives no answer.[31] Interestingly, all instances where God is said to be hidden occur in contexts that stress temporal continuation. In Ps. 13:2 the phrase is found in a colon introduced by "how long." Although in both Ps. 44:25 and Ps. 88:15 the "hiding" motif is introduced by "why," the last word in 44:24b is "forever," and in 88:16 the psalmist complains that he has been dying "from (his) youth." Finally, the wicked in Psalm 10:11 says: "He [God] has hidden his face; he never sees." The hiddenness of God is depicted in the whole of Psalm 88, where the psalmist prays and prays but never gets through to God and ends up seeing only darkness. Similarly, the sufferer in Psalm 22 cannot understand why God does not answer his prayer (vv. 3-6).

---

[30]See our translation note to Ps. 44:24 above. See further Balentine, *The Hidden God*, 143-151, and H. Ringer, "זנח," *TWAT*, 2:619-621.

[31]Balentine, *The Hidden God*, 49-65. See our translation note to Ps. 44:25.

The verb שָׁכַח, "forget," which occurs nine times in the Psalms with God as subject and all within the complaint psalms,[32] seems to be closely connected to God's hiding of his face. Three times in our psalms (Pss. 10:11 [in the mouth of the wicked]; 13:2 and 44:25) it is parallel to הִסְתִּיר פָּנִים. A fourth, Ps. 10:12, reflects the bragging of the wicked in the previous verse and prays, "do not forget the afflicted."[33] The verb is found in questions (Pss. 13:2; 42:10; 44:25 and 77:10) which receive no response or in negated jussives (Pss. 10:12 and 74:19, 23). In Ps. 106:21[34] it is said about the fathers that they "forgot the God who saved them, who had done great things in Egypt," and so they built the golden calf (vv. 19-20). In the complaint psalms God is the one who does the forgetting; human sin does not enter the picture. In fact, Ps. 44:18 says that the people have not forgotten God. זָכַר, "remember, be mindful of," is used five times in these psalms, all in the imperative. Notice Ps. 74:18-23 where both "remember" and "do not forget" occur. In v. 20 God is asked to "look at the covenant," to pay attention to his promise and the relationship he has with the people. God has promised to be with his people, yet now he must be reminded, even petitioned, to be faithful to his promise lest the downtrodden, for whom he has pledged responsibility, be put to shame (cf. v. 21).[35]

Another motif is God's distance and aloofness. In Ps. 22:2 the psalmist complains that the words of his cry are "far away (רָחוֹק) from my salvation." This is followed by a description of how God has left him alone in his distress. In v. 12 he cries out, "Do not be far from me, for trouble is close by." After more description of the suffering and the threatening enemies he again prays, "Do not be far away"(v. 20). The psalmist in Psalm 10 asks why God stands far away and hides in times

---

[32]In Psalm 9-10 the verb is used three times. In 9:13 it is said that God did not forget the cry of the afflicted. In 10:11 the wicked brags that God does not pay attention to his oppression of the poor. Finally, in v. 12 the psalmist petitions God not to forget the afflicted.

[33]Balentine, *The Hidden God*, 136: "Clearly God's hiding and his forgetting are two aspects of the same lament."

[34]See also Pss. 78:11 and 106:13.

[35]Balentine, *The Hidden God*, 138. Our discussion of God's forgetting is indebted to pages 136-143.

of trouble (v. 1). Then he goes on to describe how the wicked have their way. A similar idea is expressed in Psalm 74 where v. 2c-3a implies that God has left Zion. The result is that the enemies have plundered and burnt his sanctuary and set up their standards there. In God's absence they have had free course. God's people see no sign, no revelation from God (v. 9). In Ps. 35:17 the psalmist complains that God merely stands and watches his distress without intervening. Pss. 44:10b and 60:12b say that God "did not go out with our armies." Ps. 74:11 asks, "Why do you hold back your hand, even your right hand."[36]

Finally, we must mention the motif of God sleeping, which we meet in Ps. 44:24.[37] It occurs together with the motifs of rejection, hiding the face, and forgetting. This implies that these motifs are different ways of expressing God's absence, inactivity, inattentiveness, and indifference. (In Ps. 121:4, in contrast, it is said that God does not sleep.)

God, as he is known from his deeds in the past, from his promises, and from his relationship to the people to which he has committed himself, has become for the psalmists impossible to reach. Past promises appear annulled and past patterns of action reversed. All communication between the psalmist and God is broken. The psalmist applies to Yahweh motifs associated with human unfaithfulness.

God as Actively Hostile

God is not merely absent or indifferent. The psalmists also depict him as actively hostile. In some psalms God is seen as having brought the psalmist near to death. In Psalm 6 God's persistent and angry reproaching (v. 2) makes the psalmist "feeble" and "terrified" (v. 3) and causes him to fear death as separation from God (v. 6). In Psalm 88 the psalmist says that God has placed him in "the nethermost pit," as far into Sheol as one can possibly go, and in "the darkness of the

---

[36]Ibid., 155-157.

[37]The same motif is apparently present in Ps. 35:23, where God is asked to rouse himself and awake. The imperative "arise" (44:27 and 74:22) may also be connected to this motif.

depth," an expression that evokes the picture of the chaos-forces. He sees the wrath of God as pressing (סמך) against him (v. 8a). In v. 8b God is even given the role of the chaotic Sea, "and with all your breakers you subdue me." This last motif is also found in Ps. 42:8. Similarly 88:17-18 says: "Over me sweep your bursts of wrath; your alarms annihilate me; they surround me like water all the time." Psalms 22 and 102 depict God's attitude toward the psalmist primarily as passive, but both also include complaints that God is actively causing the near-death situation (22:16 and 102:11, 24). The isolation from former friends connected with near-death experiences is said to be caused by Yahweh in Ps. 88:9 and 19.

Military defeat is interpreted as actively brought about by Yahweh in Psalms 44, 60, 80, and 89. God is said to have broken down the physical structures for defense (Pss. 60:4; 80:13 and 89:41). He has strengthened the enemy (Ps. 89:43) and weakened Israel (60:5). Thus he made them lose the battle (Pss. 44:11 and 89:44). Worse, he has actually delivered them up "as sheep for food" (Ps. 44:12a). He has scattered them among the nations (Ps. 44:12b) and sold them as slaves—on sale (Ps. 44:13). On the battlefield he has crushed them "in a place of jackals"[38] and covered them with deep darkness (Ps. 44:20). Yahweh has made them into a mockery for the peoples that live around them (Pss. 44:14-15 and 80:7). Generally he has let them experience sorrow and distress (Pss. 60:5 and 80:6). Thus the defeat from first to last with all its consequences is attributed to Yahweh. *He* is the one who has brought it upon them. In addition, Ps. 89:45-47 complains that God has thrown the king down from his throne, shortened the days of his youth, and brought shame upon him.

Psalms 39 and 90 describe the short and miserable life for sinners under God's wrath. Ps. 90:3 alludes to Gen. 3:19, "You turn man back to dust and say: return children of man." Like a hand-breadth you have set my days" (v. 6) is Psalm 39's counterpart to this. Ps. 39:10: "You have done this" also looks back to the description of life as short and distressful. In 90:5 God is said to pour sleep on[39] them and cause them to become like withering grass. According to v. 7, "We vanish because

---

[38]See the translation note.

[39]For this expression, see the translation note.

of your wrath" (also Ps. 39:11). God's wrath causes the people to be terrified (see Ps. 6:3-4, 11). God has fixed the people's sins in front of himself (v. 8). Similarly Ps. 39:12: "With reproaches over iniquity you correct man" (see Ps. 6:2 above). This is done in a such way that his wealth is consumed as by fire (39:12b). In 90:9 the psalmist complains that all their days decline under God's wrath. V. 15 speaks of the "days you have humbled us."

Sickness, near-death situations, military defeat, and a generally miserable life are the result of God's actively hostile action. All of this assumes that sickness and death are in God's hand, not in the hand of sorcerers or evil spirits nor caused by the law of nature or by a virus. When mighty military powers are able to invade Israel, it is not due to their military strength or tactical skill but because God has become Israel's enemy and gives their foes the victory. Distress is not just a part of life. It is an experience of God's wrath.

The Absence and Hostility of God Viewed Together

The same situation that is described as a result of God's absence is also described as an experience of God's hostile activity. God hides, forgets, and sleeps (Ps. 44:24-25), yet he also hands his people over "like sheep for food" (v. 12), sells them as slaves (v. 13), makes them a reproach to their neighbors (v. 14), and crushes them (v. 20). We see the same duality in Psalm 89. Yahweh has rejected his anointed (v. 39) and hides (v. 47), but he is also depicted as tearing down his strongholds and strengthening his enemies (vv. 41 and 43). God has left but is present in wrath. This tension is resolved if we see that what is absent is God as a loving and caring savior. He is inaccessible to their prayers. He does not defend his people against enemies. He does not pay attention to their affliction. Thus the experiences of God as absent and as hostile belong together. The same duality appears also in Deuteronomy 28 and in the text we looked at above from Deuteronomy 30. God's wrath deprives the people of a life with God, the source of life, in the land he had given them under his continuous blessing. It excludes them from the realm of God's gracious and saving activity. But at the same time the wrath also causes the people to be placed under God's curse. He is actively against them. With a sole, supreme, and sovereign God it has to be this way. Nothing happens that he has not permitted. Nothing comes that he has not sent (cf. Amos 3:6). There is no neutral position. God is either for or against a person, much like a person is either for or against God. It is important to note what a problem it is for the psalmists that God has hidden himself from them at the same time as his wrath terrifies them. It shows that they do not desire a life where God does not interfere.

Why is God Angry?

B. E. Baloian has emphasized two features of the wrath of God in the Old Testament: justice and rationality. Fifty-one percent of the pericopes that speak specifically of divine anger depict it as motivated by the wickedness of human beings in their behavior towards one another. Seventy-five percent of them have divine anger motivated by human rebellion against God's person. (Thirty-three percent include both motivations.) Baloian thus finds that Yahweh's wrath is predictable.[40] It is natural to start with the question whether this observation holds true in the complaint psalms. Is God's wrath depicted as a rational and predictable reaction to human sin and wickedness?

The verbs יכח and יסר used in Psalm 6 imply that the psalmist knows he is a sinner deserving Yahweh's chastisement.[41] However, his problem is not his sin as such but that God deals with him in his wrath rather than being gracious according to his steadfast love. In Psalm 90 the root of the problem is that God has fixed the people's sins in front of his eyes and scrutinizes their secret shortcomings. The psalmist's reaction to this is not, however, a quick confession that obtains a gracious God once again. He acknowledges his and the people's sins (that is clear from v. 8); he has his mind turned toward God and knows that only with him is true wisdom (v. 12). However, God continues to focus his eyes on secret sins and continues to be angry. This is the problem. There are two more complaint psalms where sin plays a role. In Ps. 39:9 the psalmist asks God to free him from all his sins. He, like the psalmist in Psalm 6, speaks of God as reproaching and correcting

---

[40] Baloian, *Anger*, 71-73.

[41] See translation note.

human beings (v. 12). But again, the problem is not lack of confession or any other reason that should provoke God to maintain his anger. The psalmist has confessed his sins and wants to be right with God, but God goes on reproaching and correcting. So in v. 13 the psalmist begs God to hear his prayer, "hear my prayer, O Yahweh, and listen to my supplication; be not deaf to my tears!" The other psalm is Psalm 79. While looking back to the destruction of Jerusalem and the temple, the psalmist asks, "How long, O Yahweh? Will you be angry forever? Will your jealousy burn like fire?" (v. 5). There was reason for God's jealousy: the psalmist mentions "the former sins" (v. 8). But why does this situation go on and on? The psalmist asks God to turn his wrath to the enemies who have offended him much more gravely than Israel does now (v. 6). He prays for forgiveness of Israel's sins (v. 9). Again, even though the reason for God's wrath is acknowledged, the problem now is not the sin but that God still does not turn his wrath away from them.[42]

In most of the complaint psalms sin is not mentioned. In Psalm 44 the people profess not to have given Yahweh any reason for his wrath: "All this came over us even though we had not forgotten you nor been unfaithful to your covenant" (v. 18); "Though we were loyal to you, you still crushed us" (vv. 19-23). We should not take this to be a profession of total sinlessness.[43] But, according to the covenant Yahweh had made with his people, they could see no reason why God should reject them and deal with them in wrath.

The wrath of God as it is depicted in these psalms ranges from explainable but burdensome (Psalms 90 and 39) to totally inexplicable (Psalms 22, 44, and 88). One cannot say that God's wrath is always predictable, that it is always a reaction to human sin, at least as God's behavior is experienced by the psalmists. There exist situations when God's dealings with humans can be given no justification. These psalms give no explanation. They simply affirm that there are times when God is experienced as an enemy.[44]

---

[42]In Psalm 85 sin is mentioned as already forgiven by God (v. 3). A *possible* allusion to sin may be found in Ps. 35:15, but it has no role in relation to God's wrath. It is rather a part of the description of the wickedness of the enemies.

[43]See Part Two above.

[44]S. Terrien, *The Elusive Presence: The Heart of Biblical Theology* (San Francisco: Harper & Row, 1978), 323, maintains that Psalm 22 is the only psalm where

Baloian maintains that the issue in these psalms is not Yahweh's involvement in unjust actions but rather the delay of his action: "These Psalms speak of those who await His merciful as well as just intervention. There is not contradictory evidence to characterizing Yahweh's person as just but there is a delay in its manifestation."[45]

However, the "how long" question is not just a matter of awaiting Yahweh's merciful intervention.[46] Furthermore, the "how long" is only part of the problem. The psalmists in several of these psalms clearly were faced with evidence indicating that Yahweh was not just. According to Psalm 44, God hands them over to the enemy even though the people have not been unfaithful to him. In Psalm 89 there is a stark contrast between what God has promised by an unbreakable oath and what he actually does. In Psalms 22 and 88 the psalmist keeps praying but gets no response; in the former the psalmist eventually becomes certain God has heard him, but in Psalm 88 by the end of the psalm there is nothing but darkness. This is exactly the core of the distress in some of these psalms. God appears to be either powerless or unjust; thus the many questions with "why."[47] We shall see below what the psalmists do about it.

---

the hiddenness of God is unrelated to sin. As can be seen from the discussion above, this is simply not the case. Balentine is right: There is a significant lack of references to sin in the complaint psalms in connection with God's absence and hiddenness. He says: "it may be suggested that for the psalmist the hiding of God's face was perceived as an inexplicable experience, at least in some instances" (Balentine, *The Hidden God*, 56).

[45]Baloian, *Anger*, 118.

[46]See below.

[47]Fretheim, *Suffering of God*, 66, mentions Pss. 44:23; 74:1, 10; and 89:46 as instances that speak of "an anguish over the divine absence because of sin." None of these psalms mention sin. If, as is likely, Psalm 74 looks back to the destruction of the temple in 586/7 BC, we can infer that the wrath spoken of in this psalm at least was initiated against sin. Still, it has reached a point when this no longer accounts for its persistence. Thus, "Why do you reject for ever?" However, in Psalm 44 the people deny any responsibility for this outburst of divine wrath. What has happened is unintelligible to them. Likewise in Psalm 89 there is no confession of any sin giving God a legitimate reason for being angry. In these psalms there is a striking *incongruence* between God as known by past revelation and God as he is experienced in the present situation. The Old Testament speaks of the inscrutability of God, the incomparability of God, the hidden God, and God apart from his revelation. Speculations centering on God apart from revelation are strongly discouraged. God should be approached as he is according to his revelation. It appears to me that Fretheim does not do justice to this aspect. His book read as a whole seems to leave no

The Prayer

Presuppositions for the Prayer

That the psalmists find it worthwhile to approach Yahweh in prayer assumes that he is a personal God. The psalmists address God as "you." It makes no sense to pray to a principle or a cosmic force. It is worth noting that in these psalms, several of which describe deep distress, we find no magical formulas or incantations. There is no way to force or manipulate God into action. In Psalm 88 the distress is both serious and protracted, but the sufferer can do nothing about it. The same is true for Psalm 74 and Psalm 6. The psalmists are talking to God, asking for a change, and even providing arguments why God should grant them their requests.[48] God is not only assumed to be personal but in such a way analogous to humans that a verbal communication in human language is possible.[49] This analogy is further underlined by the anthropomorphic language in which the prayers are cast: Stop being angry! (Ps. 6:2); Why do you stand at a distance? (Ps. 10:1); How long will you forget me and hide your face? (Ps. 13:2); Why do you sleep? (Ps. 44:24); Take your hand, your right hand out of your lap! (Ps. 74:11).[50]

To pray for a change further assumes that God can change and that he may change in response to human prayer. The psalmists ask God to "turn around" (שׁוב, Pss. 6:5; 80:15; and 90:13). We have seen that this means to turn away from his wrath and once again be gracious to his

---

room for a "Deus absconditus." In the psalms which form the basis for the present dissertation, however, the psalmists struggle precisely with a God that does not fit the description. They experience a God who deals with them contrary to what he has revealed about himself, what he has promised, and what he has previously done. See further Child's critique of Fretheim in B. S. Childs, *Biblical Theology of the Old and New Testaments: Theological Reflection on the Christian Bible* (Minneapolis: Fortress Press, 1993), 356-358.

[48]"God may not be coerced, but God can be persuaded." P. D. Miller, "Prayer as Persuasion: The Rhetoric and Intention of Prayer," *Word & World* 13 (1993): 361.

[49]Compare Gen. 1:26-27, God created man in his image.

[50]God's relatedness to the world and to humans is discussed by S. E. Balentine, *Prayer in the Hebrew Bible: The Drama of Divine-Human Dialogue*, 33-47. See also Fretheim, *Suffering of God*, 34-44.

people.[51] In Ps. 90:13 God is further asked to "repent" (נחם). The verb נחם with God as subject does not denote "to be sorry for what you have done and cannot change," as the word "repent" is often understood in modern usage, but to "change his mind about something he has planned to do, to change his course of action."[52] This also fits the context for the only occurrence of the word within the complaint psalms. In Psalm 90 Yahweh is not asked to be sorry for something he has done but to change his course of action concerning his servants, the people of Israel. He has been angry. The psalmist wants him to show his steadfast love.

Andersen and Freedman mention three conditions on which God's repentance occurs:

1. It can be a reaction to certain events or developments in the human scene.
2. It can occur in response to human intervention or intercession.
3. It can be a response to genuine repentance in word and deed on the part of the people.[53]

In Psalm 90 the prayer for divine repentance is preceded by a petition for God to give the people wise hearts (v. 12). Also in Psalm 6, where שוב is used, the penitent heart is implicit. Important for us here is that God can change his mind, and he can do so in response to human intercession or human actions.

> The language of repentance . . . has to do with divine affectability by the creation. The God who repents is also a God who is provoked to anger, who rejoices over the creation, who responds to prayer. This is a God who has chosen to enter into a relationship with the world such that it is a genuine relationship.[54]

---

[51]See Exod. 32:12; 2 Kings 23:16; Jonah 3:9; and translation notes to Ps. 6:5.

[52]Andersen and Freedman, *Amos*, 638-679.

[53]Andersen and Freedman, *Amos*, 644-645.

[54]T. E. Fretheim, "The Repentance of God: A Key to Evaluating Old Testament God-Talk," *Horizons in Biblical Theology* 10 (1988): 59.

It is sometimes said that prayer is primarily to change us, to open us for God's activity.[55] This is not what we see in these psalms. The psalmists pray to change God. They want him to relent from his wrath, to change his course of action concerning them, and to let them experience his steadfast love. They think that he may change in response to their prayers.

God is further seen as having the power to answer their prayers. When the psalmist in Psalm 6 cries out, "Be gracious to me . . . heal me" (v. 3), he assumes that it is in God's power to heal him. The same is underlined by the totally passive role assigned to the enemies in that psalm. Similarly, in Psalm 44 only the fact that God is sleeping and has hidden his face accounts for the tragedy that the people are subdued by the enemies. If God arises, he is able to redeem them (v. 27). The question is how long God will let his anger fume (Ps. 80:5). As soon as God chooses to let his face shine, they are saved (v. 8). In the meantime they are at the mercy of everyone else (v. 14). Even in Psalm 88 the psalmist never expresses doubt that God is able to end his distress. He is just bewildered why God does not do it.

Yahweh is not part of a polytheistic power balance. He alone is God; he alone is in control. Psalm 74 sets up a contrast between the way God appeared to the enemies and to all who were influenced by a Near Eastern polytheistic frame of reference and the way he really is. God is the one who once and for all crushed all the mighty life-threatening forces of chaos. He is the unrivaled king of the universe. He does not share his power with a sun god and a moon god. He does not have to fight Mot periodically to revive fertility after the dry season as the Canaanite god Baal did; "summer and winter, you formed them," the psalmist says (v. 17). There is no doubt that God is capable of snatching his turtle dove out of the teeth of the wild beasts and stopping their bragging. It is just that he holds back his hand, even his right hand.

We further see that their beliefs about God are not based upon their experiences in the present situation but on revelation and history.

---

[55]O. Hallesby, *Prayer*, translated by C. J. Carlsen (Minneapolis: Augsburg Publishing House, 1937), 12: "To pray is nothing more involved than to let Jesus into our needs. To pray is to give Jesus permission to employ His powers in the alleviation of our distress. To pray is to let Jesus glorify His name in the midst of our needs."

Although they experience God as absent (Ps. 22:2-3,12) and hidden
(Pss. 13:2 and 44:25), they still direct their prayer toward him and
come before him (Ps. 88:2)[56] as if he is present. They hope that God
will hear their prayer. Faced with a hostile God (88:7-9), they assume
that he is characterized by steadfast love, faithfulness, and
righteousness (88:11-13), and that his deeds are wonderful, even
though experience tells them the contrary.

T. E. Fretheim maintains that divine absence is "best understood
within the context of varying intensifications of presence." Thus it
means "the loss of one intensification of presence or another. . . .
absence always entails presence at some level of intensification, albeit
diminished."[57] That God in the Old Testament is present in different
ways is clear. We have also seen above that God's absence in these
psalms often is found together with the presence of divine wrath and
hostile action. However, although Fretheim's position may be a
workable way of holding God's absence and presence together in a
philosophical framework, it would be a misunderstanding to use it to
describe the theological assumptions of the psalmists. They are not in a
situation where God is "absent, but not that absent." Rather, God is
present *in wrath*. They experience God as being uninterested in their
distress, unapproachable by their prayers, and actively hostile to them.
Still, they turn from the God of their experience to the God of their
belief and assume that God does care about their distress, that he will
hear their prayers, and that he is rich in steadfast love.

Balentine writes that whereas "A major voice in the Hebrew Bible,
perhaps the majority voice, clearly espouses a type of contractual
theology that equates suffering with sinfulness, prosperity with
righteousness, in an unambiguous, quid pro quo distribution," these
psalms represent a counter tradition, "a virtual reservoir of protest
literature."[58] Although "quid pro quo" may be a caricature, there
clearly is the thought that God blesses those who are loyal to his

---

[56]In Psalm 88 the statement is so surprising in view of the situation that Dahood
suggests assigning a special meaning to נגדך for this verse (Dahood, *Psalms*, 2:301-
302).

[57]Fretheim, *Suffering of God*, 65.

[58]Balentine, *Prayer in the Hebrew Bible*, 147-148.

covenant and keep his commandments but punishes those who turn away from him (e.g. Exod. 20:5-6 and Deut. 28). It is, however, important to ask: *What kind of* protest do we find in the complaint psalms? As we have seen, it is *not* a protest against the theology of Exod. 20:5-6 or 34:6-7. The psalmists rather presuppose this theology.[59] They protest that what they experience flatly contradicts this theology (Ps. 44:18-23), or, at least, that the situation of wrath drags on when it should have ended (Pss. 6 and 74). They want God to act precisely according to the "majority voice" theology.

Do the psalmists then think that God really is angry, or do they just want to say that he appears to them as being angry? We may summarize their dilemma in five points:

1. What has happened to them is done by God (Ps. 39:10).
2. According to his self-revelation, God has done what he would do when provoked to anger.
3. According to his self-revelation and covenant, he would be provoked to anger by sin and unfaithfulness.
4. This time this reason does not apply.
5. Yahweh is good, just, and rich in steadfast love and faithfulness.

These five points express what is perceived as reality, and the psalmists never back down on any of them. They do not come up with a revised theology. They take the bewildering situation to the God whom they still believe and confess to be almighty, good, just, and rich in steadfast love. Is God really angry? Yes, he has handed his people over to their enemies and has made them a mockery to their neighbors. He has placed his faithful in Sheol. He has permitted the enemies to roar in his dwelling-place. Is God really angry? No, he is rich in steadfast love and faithfulness toward his people. The psalmists do not solve the tension. They take it to God.

The Contents of the Prayer

Turning now to what the psalmists pray for, as expected we find prayers for release from the distress. There is prayer for healing (Ps.

---

[59]For the punishment of the wicked, see Pss. 6:9-11 and 44:21-22.

6:3). There is prayer for rescue from the national enemies (Ps. 44:27). There is prayer for justice, that the wicked oppressor may be broken (Ps. 10:15). There is prayer for help against the enemies of an individual (Ps. 22:20-21). Moreover, just as the distress was seen to be theocentric, so also the content of the prayers is related to God.

In the individual near-death psalms the psalmists do not desire only that health be restored, personal enemies be put to shame, and bodily life continue. In Psalm 6 the worst thinkable situation for the psalmist is to be in death where "there is no remembrance of you" (v. 6). What he wants is for Yahweh to stop punishing him in his wrath and instead to be gracious to him so that he can return to that relationship with Yahweh wherein he can praise and worship him.

In Psalm 22 Yahweh is called the one "who is enthroned over Israel's songs of praise" (v. 4). The psalmist remembers how the fathers cried to Yahweh and were not put to shame (v. 6). He himself has put his trust in Yahweh since he was a child (v. 10-11). Thus, when he asks God to stop being far away, it is not merely a prayer for rescue. It is also a prayer for revival of the seemingly lost relationship. This is clear from his vow of praise when he knows for certain that Yahweh has heard his prayer (vv. 23-29).

In Psalm 42 the psalmist "pants" and "thirsts" for God and longs to see God's face (vv. 2-3). Instead, his tears are his bread (v. 4). As people mockingly ask, "Where is your God?" he remembers how he formerly used to join the crowd going up to God's house (vv. 4-5). In a distant area he is drowning in Sheol under God's rollers and breakers (vv. 7-8). He again thinks of how he used to sing of God's steadfast love (v. 9). What he desires is fellowship with God and that leads him to complain, "Why have you forgotten me?"(v. 10).[60]

Finally, Psalm 88 has no explicit prayer for healing. Apart from describing the situation and asking "why," the only prayer is for Yahweh to let the psalmist's prayer come before him (v. 3). The psalmist describes himself as dwelling in death, since he experiences himself outside the realm of God's saving activity. Life for him can only be a life with Yahweh.[61]

---

[60]See Raabe, *Psalm Structures*, 48.

[61]C. Barth, *Die Errettung vom Tode*, 44-51, has shown that life for the Hebrew is always a life "vor Jahwe." Thus the realm of death reaches into what can be described as physical life. A person is in the grip of death and Sheol when different kinds of

We see in all these psalms that the prayer is not directed only, not even mainly, toward a life of bodily health and social security. Their chief desire is the restoration of their relationship with Yahweh, a relationship where the psalmists can praise God and rejoice with all his faithful. The Old Testament focuses its attention on this earthly life. It is here that the blessings in relationship with Yahweh are experienced. There are a few glimpses of a future with God after death, notably Ps. 73:24, but not enough to alter the general picture. The complaint psalms fit in well with this perspective. Life in worship and praise to Yahweh, life under his steadfast love in the here and now, is what the psalmists petition God to restore. Death means separation from God. It should be noted, however, that death in these psalms is described by people who experienced themselves as being under God's wrath. The implications regarding death experienced by those in a good relationship with Yahweh, which the psalmists have lost and for which they pray, are not directly addressed in these psalms.

In psalms occasioned by military defeat, the defeat is not seen in isolation. In Psalm 44 the "normative" situation, against which the present distress forms a contrast, involves both victory over enemies and continuous praise of God's name (vv. 5-9).

In Psalm 80 the refrain is, "O Yahweh, God of Hosts, restore us; let your face shine so that we may be saved" (vv. 4, 8, and 20). Vv. 18-19 read: "Let your hand be upon the man of your right hand, upon the son of man you have strengthened for yourself. Then we will not turn away from you. Revive us, and we will call on your name." Whatever the reference of "the man of your right hand" may be, it is clear that the verses seek a restoration not only of military strength and security but of a good relation between Yahweh and his people. The desire is that God look on them with favor so that they will worship him.

Psalm 89 sets forth at length the character and power of God and the promises he made to David and David's offspring. This picture is then contrasted with the present situation. It is clear that the psalmist wants more than defeat turned to victory. He wants the return of the situation stipulated by the Davidic covenant.

---

affliction make him see himself as "cut off from God's hand" (Ps. 88:6) and handed over to the forces of death and chaos.

Thus, even in these psalms of military defeat, the primary request is to experience once again the relationship with Yahweh that existed in the past and that was prescribed through his covenant. What the people want is life with God.

Turning now to the psalms where the distress is less specified, we see that the psalmists want life under God's wrath to end and life under his steadfast love to begin. After lamenting the terrible distress of life when God is angry, the psalmist in Psalm 90 begins his petitions by asking for wisdom (v. 12), the wisdom that is connected with the fear of Yahweh (v. 11). After this he asks God to turn away from his wrath and to change his course of action concerning his servants (v. 13). He wants to see God's steadfast love, which will give the people gladness of life. Vv. 16-17 go on to ask God to show them his proper works, even his grandeur, and to establish their work. The psalmist testified in v. 1 that God had been an abode from generation to generation. This is precisely what he prays for in the present situation.

What is it the psalmist in Psalm 77 misses? Vv. 8-10 tell us what he is looking for but cannot find: "Will God no longer *be favorably disposed*? Is his *steadfast love* gone forever, his *promise* ended from generation to generation? Has God forgotten to *be gracious*? Has he shut up *his compassion* in anger?" He goes on to remember God's wonderful works in times past (vv. 12-21). Again, what is prayed for is life with Yahweh.

In situations where God is experienced as angry, absent, and an enemy, the primary prayer of the psalmists is for communion with Yahweh to be restored and for his steadfast love and wonderful works to be shown so that they can praise his name. These are prayers of faith, not protests of unbelief.

The Appeal

Appeal to Yahweh's Abiding Character

When the psalmists appeal to God's character, the attribute of "steadfast love" is mentioned most often; it occurs in eight of the complaint psalms. Since the word חסד has been understood in different ways, we shall include a discussion of its meaning here.

LXX and Vulgate translate חֶסֶד with ἔλεος and *misericordia* ("mercy"). The Targum uses derivatives of טוב ("goodness"). N. Glueck, in a very influential study,[62] defines the word in its secular meaning as "conduct corresponding to a mutual relationship of rights and duties" and maintains that "only those participating in a mutual relationship of rights and duties can receive or show *hesed*."[63] Thus it is often connected with the covenant and "constitutes the essence of a covenant."[64] God's *hesed*, he argues, denotes "Yahweh's covenantal relationship toward his followers."[65] He regards suitable translations to be "loyalty," "mutual aid," or "reciprocal love."[66]

H. J. Stoebe[67] notes that *hesed* often stands together with רחמים and is always first except for the cases where the words are in the plural. He concludes that "*häsäd* der übergeordnete Begriff ist und demzufolge in erster Linie als Ausdruck für eine gütige Gesinnung oder Freundlichkeit verstanden werden kann, während dann *rahamim* die konkrete Auswirkung dieser Gesinnung meint."[68] In its secular use the word expresses a goodness and friendliness going beyond that which one normally had the right to expect and beyond what was

---

[62]N. Glueck, *Das Wort hesed im alttestamentlichen Sprachgebrauche als menschliche und göttliche gemeinschaftsgemässe Verhaltungsweise*, Giessen: Alfred Topelmann, 1927; *Hesed in the Bible*, translated by A. Gottschalk, Cincinnati: The Hebrew Union College, 1967.

[63]*Hesed in the Bible* (Eng. ed.), 54. Glueck had to stretch some of his cases to find any relational obligation. In Joshua 2:12 he finds the obligation in the relation between host and guest (*Hesed in the Bible*, 36). This is aptly refuted by K. Sakenfeld, *The Meaning of Hesed in the Hebrew Bible*, Harvard Semitic Monographs 17 (Missoula: Scholars Press, 1978), 68: a prostitute had no obligation to help visitors that turned out to be spies for a hostile nation.

[64]Glueck, *Hesed in the Bible*, 55.

[65]Ibid., 102.

[66]Ibid., 102. Basically in agreement is A. R. Johnson, although on the basis of the close association with the root רחם he finds an emotional aspect in *hesed* which is not present in English "loyalty." He, therefore, suggests the translation "devotion." A. R. Johnson, "Hesed and Hāsîd," in *Interpretationes ad Vetus Testamentum pertinentes Sigmundo Mowinckel septuagenario missae* (Oslo: Forlaget Land og Kirke, 1955), 101-112.

[67]H. J. Stoebe, "Die Bedeutung des Wortes *häsäd* im Alten Testament", *Vetus Testamentum* 2 (1952): 244-254.

[68]Ibid., 247-248.

deserved. Through such action community becomes possible.[69] The word applied to God tells us *"dass Gott sich in bedingungsloser Freundlichkeit und Grossherzigkeit dem Menschen zuwendet. Er begibt sich also seines göttlichen Rechtes, um mit den Menschen Gemeinschaft zu haben."*[70]

For K. Sakenfeld,[71] *hesed* in secular usage denotes "the provision for an essential need" by a "situationally superior" party who has a "recognized responsibility" to act; nevertheless, the act is freely willed.[72] In theological usage it often refers to God's *hesed* for his covenanted people in the Mosaic tradition, either his "delivering, protective power on behalf of those who are obedient," or his "surprising forgiveness offered to the disobedient when they are penitent."[73] In basic agreement with Stoebe, and in some ways building on Sakenfeld, is F. I. Andersen.[74] His point of departure is four passages in the Pentateuch ascribing חסד to Yahweh, Exod. 20:5-6; 34:6-7; Num. 14:18-19 and Deut. 7:9-10. Exod. 34:6-7 is especially revealing. We will quote it in full:

> Yahweh is a merciful [רחום] and gracious [חנון] God, slow to anger [ארך אפים] and rich in steadfast love [רב-חסד] and faithfulness [אמת], who keeps [נצר] steadfast love for thousand generations [לאלפים], who forgives [נשא] iniquity [עון] and transgression [פשע] and sin [חטאה], but he will by no means clear the guilty [נקה לא ינקה], who punishes the iniquity of the fathers on the children and grandchildren, on the third and on the fourth generation.[75]

---

[69]Ibid., 248-249.

[70]Ibid., 254.

[71]K. Sakenfeld, *The Meaning of Hesed in the Hebrew Bible*, Harvard Semitic Monographs 17; Missoula: Scholars Press, 1978.

[72]Ibid., 234.

[73]Ibid., 237.

[74]F. I. Andersen, "Yahweh, the Kind and Sensitive God," in *God Who is Rich in Mercy*, eds. P. T. O'Brien and D. G. Peterson (Australia: Lancer Books, 1986), 41-88.

[75]Also Fretheim has called attention to the importance for Israel's faith of propositional statements about God's character. He calls them "generalizations of the history," without which the history is not "intelligible and coherent." These statements can then be viewed as "theological constants." See Fretheim, *Suffering of God*, 24-29. Compare Baloian, *Anger*, 67-71.

The people had just sinned gravely by making and worshipping the golden calf. According to the covenant they deserved punishment, but the punishment is withheld. In this context God provides this self-disclosure. Andersen finds that חסד here, far from describing "covenant obligations," can rather be said to describe Yahweh as characterized by a richness of amazing grace. After a lengthy survey of passages where the word חסד occurs, Andersen concludes:

> This study has located *hesed* outside the domain of duty and obligation, even though a promise to do *hesed* can bring it within the domain of commitment. . . . The act of *hesed* may be spontaneous, or in response to an open appeal. The receiver is usually in a desperate, helpless situation. . . . To sum up. First, in the old stories, *hesed* mainly describes exceptional acts of one human to another, meeting an extreme need outside the normal run of perceived duty, and arising from personal affection or pure goodness. Secondly, the earliest revelations of God's character (or "name") highlight his *hesed* as primal, elemental, enduring, and associated with his love, grace, compassion, rather than with justice. . . . Fourthly, in the Psalms, *hesed* is the supreme attribute of God, associated with both justice and compassion.[76]

Recently G. R. Clark has made a very thorough study of חסד.[77] He studied the word in association with other elements in the same lexical field, unlike previous word studies. His findings generally support those of Stoebe and Andersen but are more nuanced. He finds that three out of every four occurrences of חסד have God as *agent*. The word is never used with God as *patient*.[78] Already this would show that

---

[76] Andersen, "Yahweh, the Kind and Sensitive God," 81-82. See also H. J. Zobel, "חסד," *TWAT*, 3:47-71. Zobel finds in חסד a "Tatscharakter" (as seen from the phrase עשׂה חסד (used 36 times)), a "Gemeinschaftscharakter" (as seen from the contexts in which the word is used), and "Beständigkeit" (as seen from the hendiadys חסד ואמת [23 times, according to Even-Shoshan]). He rejects Glueck's subordination of חסד under the concept of the covenant.

[77] G. R. Clark, *The Word Hesed in the Hebrew Bible*, JSOT Supplement Series 157 (Sheffield: JSOT Press, 1993).

[78] Ibid., 65. For Clark's use of "agent" and "patient," see his glossary on pages 13-14. Note that the terms are not always equivalent to grammatical subject and object. E.g., in the sentence: "He was eaten by his pet crocodile," the grammatical subject is "he," whereas the crocodile is the agent.

Glueck's "mutual obligation" misses the mark. We will summarize some of Clark's findings. אמת and אמונה are essential components of חסד.[79] A commitment between the parties is involved with חסד but not with טוב.[80] When God is agent the most common benefit from חסד is deliverance. Other common benefits are assistance, forgiveness, preservation, and the Davidic dynasty. Very often Yahweh's חסד leads to worship.[81] חסד is close to חן; it includes 'grace' and 'mercy' but is much more. חן does not imply commitment.[82] חסד is close to רחמים; it includes 'compassion' but is not merely compassion. רחמים does not imply commitment.[83] The connotations of חסד are much broader than those of love.[84]

Several of the words that Clark found to be closest to חסד occur in Exod. 34:6-7 and the other passages Andersen used as the points of departure for his discussion. The statements in these verses are repeated and reflected several times[85] in the Old Testament and thus clearly qualify as "theological constants."[86] Although we find no repetition or even clear allusion to this particular formula in the complaint psalms, the theology—the "theological constants" in this and similar propositional formulas—is shared by the psalmists. We should remember that the formula in Exod. 34:6-7 and other formulas of God's character are presented as God's self-revelation and would be considered more than "generalizations from history."[87] Thus an appeal to God's חסד is an appeal to God's gracious character and amazing commitment to his people according to his self-revelation. In a shortened form, "Yahweh is merciful and gracious, slow to anger and

---

[79]Ibid., 259-260.

[80]Ibid., 260.

[81]Ibid., 262.

[82]Ibid., 267.

[83]Ibid., 267.

[84]Ibid., 268.

[85]Num. 14:18; Joel 2:13; Nah. 1:3; Pss. 86:15; 103:8; 145:8; and Neh. 9:17. The first part of the formula concerning grace is quoted more often than the last part.

[86]Fretheim, *Suffering of God*, 28.

[87]Fretheim's expression, *Suffering of God*, 28.

rich in steadfast love," the formula seems to have functioned as a quasi-creedal statement (Pss. 86:15; 103:8 and 145:8).[88]

The most direct appeal to חֶסֶד as "the supreme attribute of God" is the phrase לְמַעַן חַסְדֶּךָ, "for the sake of your steadfast love," in Pss. 6:5 and 44:27.[89] Yahweh's supreme goodness should motivate him to act and change the situation for the psalmist. Psalm 77 takes a more indirect course. Here the psalmist asks if God's חֶסֶד is gone forever. But by the way the question is asked, the psalmist makes clear that he regards doing חֶסֶד as an action characteristic for Yahweh. The incongruence of the present situation with this norm appeals to God to end the distress and once again to act according to his character.

In Psalm 88 the statements that Yahweh's חֶסֶד (as well as other attributes and characteristic actions of God) is unknown and unrecognized in Sheol (vv. 11-13) serve to motivate the psalmist's prayer (it will soon be too late) and to motivate God to act. He has to show who he is now and not when the psalmist is dead.

In Psalm 89 Yahweh's חֶסֶד as promised to David is part of (and may sum up) the normative pattern for the way God should act toward the Davidic king and his people. This pattern stands in the sharpest possible contrast to the shocking reality of recent events. Thus the psalmist can appeal to this חֶסֶד in v. 50: "Where are your former acts of steadfast love, O Lord, which you by oath promised to David in your faithfulness."[90]

In Psalms 77, 88, and 89 several of God's attributes are placed in clusters. In Ps. 77:8-10 חַסְדּוֹ, "his steadfast love," and רַחֲמָיו, "his compassion," describe God's character, while the two infinitives רְצוֹת, "be favorably disposed," and חַנּוֹת, "be gracious," depict his characteristic actions. These are found together with the obscure אֹמֶר, which is traditionally translated "promise." In Ps. 88:11-13 God's

---

[88]Joel 2:13 and Jonah 4:2 add an element to this: "and repents of the evil" (וְנִחָם עַל־רָעָה). Jonah uses this description of God to explain why he tried to flee to Tarshish. He did not want Yahweh to be gracious to Nineveh and change his course of action from the pronounced destruction.

[89]A similar phrase, כְּחַסְדֶּךָ, is found, for example, in Pss. 25:7; 51:3; and 109:26.

[90]Pss. 85:8 and 90:14 contain prayers for God's חֶסֶד. In Ps. 85:11 חֶסֶד is part of the blessed situation after the prayer is heard. In Ps. 13:6 God's חֶסֶד is the object of trust.

character is described by חסדך, "your steadfast love," and אמונתך, "your faithfulness," whereas his characteristic actions are פלא, "wonders," and צדק, "(works of) righteousness." In Psalm 89 the word חסד is used both to describe a characteristic quality of God (vv. 29 and 34) and the actions that flow from this quality (vv. 3, 15, and 50). It is found together with אמונה in vv. 2, 3, 25, 34, and 50. In v. 15 God's rule of the world is characterized by צדק ומשפט, "righteousness and justice," and by חסד ואמת, "steadfast love and trustworthiness." Yahweh's פלא is mentioned in v. 6.

For the distinction between the two cognates of אמן in general, it suffices to quote A. Jepsen:

> *"Während אמה das Wesen einer Person umschreibt, auf deren Wort und Tat man sich verlassen kann, bezeichnet אמונה das Verhalten einer Person, das ihrem eigenen inneren Sein entspricht. אמה ist Gottes Wort und Tat, auf die der Mensch sich verlassen kann; אמונה ist Gottes Verhalten, in dem er dem Wesen seiner Gottheit entspricht."*[91]

However, in his treatment of חסד ואמת Clark argues that this expression is a hendiadys, and that "[its] semantic area is closer to that of חסד than to that of אמת."[92] The use of אמונה in Psalm 89 is one of Clark's main arguments for calling it an essential component of חסד. Several times in the psalm the two words are used together in such a way that it is difficult to distinguish between them. In v. 50, however, אמונה is both the guarantee that God will keep his promise and the motivator for the promised חסד.[93]

The "how long" questions[94] indicate that God's wrath was not expected to last forever. The same is brought out by the complaints and protests that the distress is dragging on, apparently לנצח, "forever."[95]

---

[91] A. Jepsen, "אָמַן, אֲמָנָה, אֹמֶן, אָמֵן, אֶמֶת," *TWAT*, 1:344-345.

[92] Clark, *The Word Hesed*, 255.

[93] Ibid., 149-151.

[94] כמה in Ps. 35:17; עד אנה in Ps. 13:2-3; עד-מה in Pss. 74:9; 79:5; 89:47; and עד מתי in Pss 6:4; 74:10; 80:5; and 90:13.

[95] Pss. 44:24; 74:1, 10, 19; 77:9, and 89:47, נצח without ל is used with the same meaning in Ps. 13:2. לעולם and לעולמים are used with a similar function in Pss. 85:6 and 77:8.

This assumption coheres with the many statements found elsewhere in the Old Testament that God's wrath does not last long,[96] unlike God's steadfast love which endures forever (Isa. 54:8 and especially Psalm 136).[97] The point is not that the "how long" questions in the complaint psalms are dependent on any of these passages, but that they attest to the same theological assumption: God's steadfast love is lasting but his wrath is not. Perhaps the roots of this assumption lie in the contrast between the thousand generations to whom God's steadfast love is shown and the three or four generations that suffer his wrath according to Yahweh's self-presentation in Exod. 20:5-6 and 34:7.

Appeal to Yahweh's Relation to His People

Yahweh's saving acts in ancient times are appealed to in Psalms 22, 44, 74, 77, and 80. In Psalm 22 the psalmist contrasts his own situation with that of the fathers: "In you our fathers trusted; they trusted and you delivered them. To you they cried our and were safe; in you they trusted and were not put to shame" (vv. 5-6). For him it is different. He trusts, too, but God does not intervene (vv. 7-12).

In Psalm 44 the people look back to how God dispossessed the nations that formerly inhabited Canaan and planted Israel there. God did so because he was well-disposed toward them (v. 4). The psalmist goes on to confess that this God is his king. Then he contrasts this past glory with the present grim situation (vv. 10-23). Thus the distress is shown to be abnormal. My king did not act this way in the past and should not do so now.

Psalm 80 compares Israel to a vine. Yahweh brought it out from Egypt. He drove out the nations and planted it (v. 9). He cared for it, and it thrived and filled the land (vv. 10-12). But now God has torn down the wall around it (v. 13) and has delivered it up to the boars

---

[96]Pss. 30:6; 103:9; Isa. 10:25; 54:7-8; 57:16; Jer. 3:12; Micah 7:18-20; and Lam. 3:31-33.

[97]See P. R. Raabe, "The Two 'Faces' of Yahweh," in *And Every Tongue Confess: Essays in Honor of Norman Nagel on the Occasion of His Sixty-fifth Birthday*, eds., G. S. Krispin and J. D. Vieker (Chelsea, Michigan: Book Crafters, 1990), 286-288.

from the forest (v. 14). By this simile Israel's entire history is seen as a unity and directly related to what God did to establish the people.[98]

Also in Psalm 77 it is the events related to the Exodus that are remembered (vv. 12-21). Here the crossing of the sea is depicted in the language of the Storm-god's victory over the chaos forces of the personified Sea (vv. 17-20). In Psalm 74, because the god of the enemies has so blatantly challenged God's position as the king of the universe, it is precisely the primeval struggle with the chaos monsters (vv. 13-14) and Yahweh's role as creator and preserver (vv. 15-17) that are remembered as God's victories of ancient time. Also, a secondary allusion to the exodus event is probably intended.[99]

Westermann notes that when the lament psalms look back to God's earlier saving deeds, the events remembered are those belonging to the "series of events by which Israel first became a people."[100] The way this retelling of history functions as an appeal to God is stated well by C. Westermann:

> From the shock of contemporary (national) experience, what once happened suddenly emerged as that which was now to be held up before God, in the assumption that by forcing God to remember, he might heal the ruptures in the present. Recalling history had the immediate purpose of influencing history.[101]

God had made Israel into a people, his people, and given them the land. He had further established a covenant with them. Thus we find this appeal in Ps. 74:20: "Look at the covenant!" If God paid attention to the things to which he had pledged himself in the covenant, he would change the situation for his people. In Ps. 44:18 there is the charge that "All this has come upon us, even though we have not forgotten you nor have been unfaithful to your covenant." Thus God will have to do something about it if he is not to be marked as a covenant breaker.

---

[98]C. Westermann, *Praise and Lament in the Psalms*, translated by K. R. Crim and R. N. Soulen (Atlanta: John Knox Press, 1981), 217-218.

[99]See Chapter Four above.

[100]Westermann, *Praise and Lament*, 219.

[101]Ibid., 220.

In Psalm 89, where the miserable situation of the Davidic king is the focus of the complaint, the appeal is to the promises of the covenant which Yahweh established with his servant David. These unbreakable promises confirmed by oath have now been disregarded by God. He has done just the opposite of what he had said. The force of this contrast is to say that Yahweh now should restore the king to the position to which he is entitled according to the Davidic covenant if God still wants to be regarded as characterized by "faithfulness."

As God has entered into these relations with the people, almost all the complaint psalms contain relational appeals in one form or another. This is true both for communal and individual psalms. God is "my God" (Pss. 13:4; 22:2, 3, 11; 35:23, 24; 42:7, 12; 43:4, 5; 89:27; and 102:25) or "our God" (Pss. 44:21 and 90:17). He is "God of my salvation" (Ps. 88:2). The people are God's people (Pss. 44:13; 60:5; 77:16, 21; 79:13; 80:5; and 85:3, 7). It is called "your congregation" and "the tribe of your inheritance" (Ps. 74:2). The land is Yahweh's (Ps. 85:2). The image of a shepherd and his flock is evoked (Pss. 44:12; 74:1; and 80:2). The psalmist in Psalm 90 confesses that God has been an abode for his people from generation to generation (v. 1). He addresses God as "Lord" and refers to the people as "your servants" (vv. 13 and 16; cf. Ps. 89:40 [singular], 51). In Psalm 22 the psalmist appeals to a close personal relation with God: "For you are the one who drew me out from the womb, who made me secure at the breasts of my mother. Upon you I was thrown from the womb; from my mother's womb you are my God" (vv. 10-11). Then follows the prayer in v. 12 asking that God not remain far away.

The relation between the people and Yahweh entails worship and praise (compare Exod. 3:12, 15 and Deut. 8:10). The references to this in the complaint psalms assume that God desires to be praised by his people. The warning that no one praises or acknowledges God in Sheol (Pss. 6:6 and 88:11-13), besides expressing the urgency of the psalmist's plight, also should motivate God to intervene.

Several psalms have so-called "vows of praise."[102] Note also those where the promise of praise follows the assurance of salvation (Psalms 13 and 22). In Psalm 35 the prayer that God may vindicate the psalmist against the enemies (vv. 1-8) is followed by a vow of praise. If God

---

[102]Ibid., 52-54.

will hear his prayer and let the enemy fall into his own trap, then the psalmist will "rejoice in Yahweh and delight in his salvation" (v. 9). A description of how the enemy threatens and harasses the psalmist follows in vv. 11-16. In v. 17 the psalmist asks God how long he will passively look at this, "Rescue my life from those who hate me, my precious one from lions!" Then once more a promise of praise follows, "I will praise you in a large congregation" (v. 18). Here we see the idea: If God saves, he will receive praise. The same can be seen in Pss. 43:3-4 and 79:13. Ps 74:21 has this petition: "Let the afflicted and the poor praise your name!"[103] The prayer is clearly formed in contrast to v. 18, where it is said that a worthless people (the enemy) ridicules God's name. Thus, in addition to giving voice to the people's longing for restoration to a normal relationship with Yahweh, the petition also serves as a motivation for Yahweh to save under the assumption that he desires praise.

Appeals to God's compassion for the poor and needy could have been placed under "appeal to God's abiding character." They assume that God *pities* the helpless and afflicted and that he is not cold-hearted. But since a relational aspect is often present in these appeals, we deal with them here.

In Ps. 6:7-8 the psalmist tells about his weeping. The point of this description must be that his tears should move God to pity. He is in some ways like the dead who cannot praise Yahweh (v. 6). Similarly, in Psalm 88, where God is addressed as "God of my salvation," the long description of the psalmist's suffering is intended to move God to compassion. In Ps. 22:7-11 the psalmist's misery is laid out in contrast to his close relationship with God that previously existed. In Ps. 44:25 the psalmist complains that God forgets his people's misery and affliction. Ps. 74:19 speaks of "your turtledove," which God must defend against the wild beasts, and of "your afflicted one," whom he has forgotten. V. 21 mentions the "afflicted and poor" in relationship with Yahweh, "Let them praise your name." The psalmist of Psalm 10 knows that Yahweh as the eternal king will have compassion on the afflicted and marginalized (vv. 16-18). Here it seems to allude to the responsibility of the king to care for the oppressed, as evidenced both

---

[103]I hesitate to call this a vow of praise (Westermann, *Praise and Lament*, 54), since it is obviously a petition for salvation. On page 59 Westermann calls it an "implied vow."

in the Old Testament (2 Kings 8:1-3) and extra-Biblical literature.[104] In the exodus narrative God heard the outcry of the oppressed descendants of Abraham in Egypt and came to rescue them (Exod. 2:23-25; 3:7-12, and 6:2-8). A direct promise that God would see to it that the rights of the helpless were not suppressed is given in Exod. 22:20-23.[105]

Appeal to Yahweh's Reputation

Yahweh is the creator of the earth and the only true God (Pss. 90:1-2 and 74:12-17). He has entered into a covenantal relationship with Israel (Pss. 44:18 and 74:20) and has revealed his abiding character (Exod. 34:6-7). The psalmists assume that God wants this to be acknowledged both by Israel and by the nations.

In our discussion of Psalm 74 we saw the important role played by the argument of reputation. God is called to court to conduct his case and to show that he, not Marduk or any other god of the nations, is the only powerful and unrivaled king of the universe. In Psalm 10 the arrogant oppressor boasts that God has forgotten, has hidden, will not see the evil deeds, and will not hold him accountable (vv. 11 and 13). So the psalmist asks, "Why does the wicked man revile God?" (v. 13a). The assumption must be that God cares about his reputation. Also Psalms 44 and 89 present challenges to God's reputation. In Psalm 44 God appears to be unfair (vv. 18-23). In Psalm 89 the present circumstances are contrasted with God's promises in such a way that Yahweh is stigmatized as a liar if he does not change the situation and restore the Davidic king.

God is a person also in this way, in that it matters for him what people say and think about him. He wants his integrity to be recognized. Yahweh is zealous for the first commandment, for he is God and wants to be acknowledged as such by all the nations (cf. the argument used by Moses in Exod. 32:12). The psalmists point out the consequences that God's present actions or inactivity have for what kind of God he appears to be. By doing this they intend to move God

---

[104]See the Ugaritic legend of king Keret, KTU 1.16 VI 45-50. For an English translation, see Gibson, *Canaanite Myths and Legends*, 102.

[105]See further R. N. Boyce, *The Cry to God in the Old Testament*, SBL Dissertation Series 103; Atlanta: Scholars Press, 1988.

to act so that he once again can be seen by his oppressed people and by the mocking nations to be the one he really is. Note further that in Psalm 74 it is the destruction of the place where God dwelled among his people for their benefit that presents the challenge. God has bound himself to his people in such a way that his reputation is at stake.

Other Appeals

First, there is the appeal to the people's innocence in Ps 44:18-23. It is important to note, however, that whereas the innocence provides a reason why God should not act as he does, the motivation given in the prayer for rescue (v. 27) is God's own steadfast love.

Second, the brevity of life is used to give added urgency to different appeals. In Ps. 89:48-49 it motivates God to act quickly, lest he be seen as a liar forever. In Pss. 6 and 88 its function is to add urgency both to the psalmist's situation and to God's chances of having his gracious character and wonderful works recognized and praised.

Third, the psalmists depict the enemies as wicked, impious, and doers of injustice so as to present them as people Yahweh ought to punish (Pss. 6:9; 74:18 and 79:6). This presupposes God's justice. His justice should move God to punish, but his steadfast love should motivate him to save.

We have seen in connection with the different psalms that the "why" questions express reproach, protest, and bewilderment. In Ps. 10:1, 13[106] the psalmist protests the bewildering situation that God does not care for the afflicted but rather permits the wicked to have their way unrestricted. Pss. 22:2; 42:10; 43:2; and 74:1 protest God's present dealings with his faithful in view of the relation that had existed between them. In Pss. 74:11 and 79:10 the psalmists complain and are bewildered that God permits his reputation to suffer. In Ps. 80:13 God's present actions toward his people compared with what he had done in the past give rise to the "why." In Ps. 44:24-25 we should probably think of the cumulative force of the broken relation, God's endangered reputation, and his indifference to the afflicted as the

---

[106]V. 13 has עַל־מָה, all the others instances have לָמָה.

backdrop for the bewildered reproach expressed by these questions. These questions thus underline the theological assumptions mentioned above.

Conclusion

In these psalms the psalmists experience God's wrath as the heart of their problem and the cause of their present distress. They interpret the distress in the light of Yahweh as the Lord of life who promises a life rich in blessings to all who would be faithful to him. They know that those who are unfaithful are entitled to a broken relationship with Yahweh that ends in death and misery. In some of the psalms it is assumed that God originally was provoked to anger by the people's sin. His wrath, however, has dragged on beyond what is reasonable. In other psalms no explanation is given for why God should be angry. God appears to act contrary to his character, contrary to his way of acting in the past, in violation of the relationship into which he has entered with his people, and in violation of his promises. The result is that his own reputation suffers.

In this situation the psalmists hold these discrepancies up to God's nose. They tell him exactly how they experience his current actions and inactivity toward them. They complain and protest and ask God to be the one he has told the people he is and the one he has revealed in the past. They firmly believe, in total disregard of present evidence, that God is still rich in steadfast love and compassion, that he is still the one who forgives sin, that his promises and covenant are still valid and unchangeable, and that his former actions when he made Israel into his people are still characteristic of the way he deals with his people. They protest God's work of wrath as not being his proper work, and they seek his steadfast love and help that is given for the sake of his steadfast love.

They further assume that they matter to God. Because he has chosen them to be his people, he is "stuck" with them. Thus their situation affects his reputation. God is zealous for the first commandment (Exod. 20:2-5) and does not want to have his reputation damaged among the nations.

The psalmists do not explain away their suffering either by pretending that it is not real or by seeing it as what one simply has to expect in this world. They do not grant that anything is beyond their God's control. Still, they do not accept the affliction as God's will in a fatalistic manner or in such a way that one has to submit to it as good, just, and inescapable. They also do not assume that God's wrath in their cases is provoked by some unknown sin of which they need to repent. They protest God's work of wrath and pray that he may work according to his character.

Bentzen states regarding Psalm 44: "The psalm is an expression of the religious attitude which the prophets attacked. Its climax, that the people have a *claim* on God, is also as diametrically opposite to prophetic religion as possible."[107] He has either misunderstood the psalm or the prophets or both. These psalms are not expressions of impenitence (see Ps. 44:18-22), but they take Yahweh's covenant seriously. Faith sticks to God's self-revelation in the midst of conflicting evidence. That is the contribution of these psalms.

---

[107]"Salmen giver derefter udtryk for den religiøse opfattelse, som profeterne angriber. Dens højdepunkt, at folket har *krav* paa Gud, er ogsaa profetisk religion saa diametralt modsat som vel muligt." Bentzen, *Fortolkning til de gammeltestamentlige salmer*, 246.

Selected Bibliography

Ackroyd, P. R. "Some Notes on the Psalms." *The Journal of Theological Studies* n.s. 17 (1966): 392-399.

_____. "נצח - εἰς τέλος." *Expository Times* 80 (1968-69): 126.

Aejmelaeus, A. "Function and Interpretation of כי in Biblical Hebrew." *Journal of Biblical Literature* 105/2 (1986): 193-209.

_____. *The Traditional Prayer in the Psalms*. Berlin: Walter de Gruyter, 1986.

Airoldi, N. "Note critiche al Salmo 6." *Rivista Biblica* 16 (1968): 285-289.

Alter, R. *The Art of Biblical Poetry*. New York: Basic Books, 1985.

Andersen, F. I. "Yahweh, the Kind and Sensitive God." *God Who is Rich in Mercy*, eds. P. T. O'Brien and D. G. Peterson, 41-88. Australia: Lancer Books, 1986.

Andersen, F. I. and D. N. Freedman. *Amos*. The Anchor Bible. New York: Doubleday, 1989.

Anderson, A. A. *The Book of Psalms*. 2 vols. New Century Bible. London: Oliphants, 1972.

Anderson, G. W. "Enemies and Evildoers in the Book of Psalms." *Bulletin of John Rylands Library* 48 (1965-1966): 18-29.

Ap-Thomas, D. R. "Appreciation of Sigmund Mowinckel's Contribution to Biblical Studies." *Journal of Biblical Literature* 85 (1966): 315-325.

Auffret, P. "Essai sur la structure littéraire du Psaume 90." *Biblica* 61 (1980): 262-276.

_____. "Essai sur la structure littéraire du Psaume LXXIV." *Vetus Testamentum* 33 (1983): 129-148.

_____. "Note complémentaire sur la structure littéraire du Psaume 6." *Biblische Notizen* 42 (1988): 7-11.

Balentine, S. E. *The Hidden God: The Hiding of the Face of God in the Old Testament*. Oxford Theological Monograph. Oxford: Oxford University Press, 1979.

_____. *Prayer in the Hebrew Bible: The Drama of Divine-Human Dialogue*. Overtures to Biblical Theology. Minneapolis: Fortress Press, 1993.

Baloian, B. E. *Anger in the Old Testament*. American University Studies, Series VII, vol. 99. New York: Peter Lang, 1992.

Barr, J. "Philology and Exegesis," *Bibliotheca Ephemeridum theologicarum Lovaniensium* 33 (1974): 39-61.

_____. "Reading the Bible as literature." *Bulletin of John Rylands Library* 56 (1973-1974): 10-33.

_____. *The Semantics of Biblical Language*. Oxford: Oxford University Press, 1961.

_____. "Why? in Biblical Hebrew." *Journal of Theological Studies* 36 (1985): 1-33.

Barth, C. *Die Errettung vom Tode in den individuellen Klage- und Dankliedern des Alten Testaments*. Basel: Zollikon, 1947.

Beaucamp, E. *Le Psautier*. 2 vols. Sources bibliques 7. Paris: Gabalda, 1976.

Becker, J. *Wege der Psalmenexegese*. Stuttgarter Bibelstudien 18. Stuttgart: Katholisches Bibelwerk, 1975.

Begrich, J. H. "Das priestliche Heilsorakel." *Zeitschrift für die alttestamentliche Wissenschaft* 52 (1934): 81-92 = J. Begrich, *Gesammelte Studien zum Alten Testament*. Herausgegeben von Walther Zimmerli. Munich: Chr. Kaiser Verlag, 1964: 217-231.

Bentzen, A. "Daniel 6: Ein Versuch zur Vorgeschichte der Märtyrlegende." In *Festschrift für Alfred Bertholet*, eds. W. Baumgartner, O. Eissfeldt, K. Elliger, and L. Rost, 58-64. Tübingen: J.C.B. Mohr, 1950.

_____. "Der Tod des Beters in den Psalmen". In *Festschrift Otto Eissfeldt*. J. Fück, ed. Halle an der Saale: Max Niemeyer, 1947: 57- 60.

_____. *Fortolkning til de gammeltestamentlige salmer*. Copenhagen: G. E. C. Gads forlag, 1939.

Berlin, A. *The Dynamics of Biblical Parallelism*. Bloomington: Indiana University Press, 1985.

_____. "Grammatical Aspects of Biblical Parallelism." *Hebrew Union College Annual* 50 (1979): 17-43.

Birkeland, H. *Die Feinde des Individuums in der Israelitischen Psalmenliteratur*. Oslo: Grøndahl & søns forlag, 1933.

Booij, Th. "Psalm 90:5-6: Junction of Two Traditional Motifs." *Biblica* 68 (1987): 393-396.

Boyce, R. N. *The Cry to God in the Old Testament*. SBL Dissertation Series 103, Atlanta, GA: Scholars Press, 1988.

Briggs, C. A. and E. G. Briggs. *A Critical and Exegetical Commentary on the Book of Psalms*. 2 vol. International Critical Commentary. Edinburgh: T & T. Clark, 1906-1907.

Brown, F., S. R. Driver, and C. A. Briggs. *A Hebrew and English Lexicon of the Old Testament.* Oxford: Clarendon, 1907.

Broyles, C. C. *The Conflict of Faith and Experience in the Psalms: A Form-Critical and Theological Study.* Journal for the Study of the Old Testament Supplement Series 52, Sheffield: JSOT Press, 1989.

Brueggemann, W. "From Hurt to Joy, From Death to Life." *Interpretation* 28 (1974): 3-19.

_____. *The Message of the Psalms.* Augsburg Old Testament Studies. Minneapolis: Augsburg, 1984.

_____. "Psalms and the Life of Faith: A Suggested Typology of Function." *Journal for the Study of the Old Testament* 17 (1980): 3-32.

Brug, J. F. *Psalms.* 2 vols. The People's Bible. Milwaukee, Wisconsin: Northwestern Publishing House, 1989.

Bryn, E., K. Myhre, J. O. Mæland, and K. Valen. *Salmenes bok.* 2 vols. Bibleverket. Oslo: Nye Luther Forlag and Lunde Forlag, 1985-1987.

Buss, M. J. "Psalms of Asaph and Korah." *Journal of Biblical Literature* 82 (1963): 382-392.

Buttenwieser, M. *The Psalms.* Chicago: The University of Chicago Press, 1938.

Calès, J. *Le livre des Psaumes.* 2 vols. Paris: Gabriel Beauchesne et ses fils, 1936.

Caquot, A., M. Sznycer, and A. Herdner. *Textes Ougaritiques. Tome I: Mythes et Légendes.* Paris: Cerf, 1974.

Caquot, A., J. M. de Terragon, and J. L. Cunchillos. *Textes Ougaritiques. Tome II: Textes religieux, Rituels, Correspondance.* Paris: Cerf, 1989.

Castellino, G. *Libro dei Salmi.* Rome: Marietti, 1955.

Childs, B. S. *Biblical Theology of the Old and New Testaments: Theological Reflection on the Christian Bible.* Minneapolis: Fortress, 1993.

Clark, G. R. *The Word Hesed in the Hebrew Bible.* Journal for the Study of the Old Testament Supplement Series 157. Sheffield: JSOT Press, 1993.

Coppens, J. "Les Psaumes 6 et 41 dépenant-ils du livre de Jeremie?" *Hebrew Union College Annual* 32 (1961): 217-226.

Craigie, P. C. *Psalms 1-50.* Word Biblical Commentary Vol. 19. Waco, TX: Word Books, 1983.

Crenshaw, J. L. "The Human Dilemma and Literature of Dissent." In Dahood, M. "Hebrew-Ugaritic Lexicography VII." *Biblica* 50 (1969): 337-356.

_____. *Psalms*. 3 vols. Anchor Bible 16, 17 and 17a. Garden City, NY: Doubleday, 1965-1970.

_____. "Ugaritic-Hebrew Syntax and Style." *Ugarit-Forschungen* 1 (1969): 15-36.

_____. "Vocative *Lamedh* in Psalm 74:14." *Biblica* 59 (1978): 262-263.

Delekat, L. "Zum hebräischen Wörterbuch." *Vetus Testamentum* 14 (1964): 7-66.

Delitzsch, F. *Psalms*. Translated by J. Martine. Grand Rapids: Eerdmans, 1871.

Donald, T. "The Semantic Field of "Folly" in Proverbs, Psalms and Ecclesiastes." *Vetus Testamentum* 13 (1963): 285-292.

Donner, H. "Argumente zur Datierung des 74. Psalms." In *Wort, Lied und Gottesspruch*. Festschrift für J. Ziegler, ed. J. Schreiner, 2:41-50. Wurzburg: Echter, 1972.

_____. "Ugaritismen in der Psalmenforschung." *Zeitschrift für die alttestamentliche Wissenschaft* 79 (1967): 322-350.

Eberlein, K. *Gott der Schöpfer - Israels Gott: Eine exegetisch-hermeneutische Studie zur theologischen Funktion alttestamentlicher Schöpfungsaussagen*. Frankfurt am Main: Peter Lang, 1986.

Eichrodt, W. *Theology of the Old Testament*. 2 vols. The Old Testament library. London: SCM, 1961-1967.

Emerton, J. A. "Notes on Three Passages in Psalms Book III." *Journal of Theological Studies* n.s. 14 (1963): 374-381.

_____. ""Spring and Torrent" in Psalm LXXIV 15." *Volume du congrès Genève 1965*. Supplement to Vetus Testamentum 15 (1966): 122-133.

Even-Shoshan, A. *A New Concordance of the Old Testament*. 2nd ed., Grand Rapids, MI: Baker Book House, 1993.

Fenton, T. L. "Ugaritica-Biblica." *Ugarit-Forschungen* 1 (1969): 65-70.

Freedman, D. N. "Another Look at Biblical Hebrew Poetry." In
Directions in Biblical Hebrew Poetry, ed. E. R. Follis, 11-22.
Sheffield: JSOT Press, 1987.

_____. "Divine Names and Titles in Early Hebrew Poetry." In
*Magnalia Dei: The Mighty Acts of God: Essays on th Bible and
Archaeology in Memory of G. Ernest Wright*, eds. F. M. Cross, et
al, 55-107. Garden City: Doubleday, 1967.

Fretheim, T. E. "The Repentance of God: A Key to Evaluating Old
Testament God-Talk." *Horizons in Biblical Theology* 10 (1988):
47-70.

_____. *The Suffering of God: An Old Testament Perspective.*
Overtures to Biblical Theology. Philadelphia: Fortress Press, 1984.

Gelston, A. "A Note on Psalm LXXIV 8." *Vetus Testamentum* 34
(1984): 82-86.

Gerstenberger, E. *Psalms, Part I, With an Introduction to Cultic
Poetry.* The Forms of the Old Testament Literature XIV. Grand
Rapids: Eerdmans, 1988.

Gibson, J. C. L. *Canaanite Myths and Legends*, Edinburgh: T. & T.
Clark, 1977.

Girard, M. *Les Psaumes: Analyse structurelle et interprétation 1-50.*
Montréal: Editions, Bellarmin, 1984.

Glueck, N. *Das Wort hesed im alttestamentlichen Sprachgebrauche als
menschliche und göttliche gemeinschaftsgemasse Verhaltungsweise.* Giessen: Alfred Topelmann, 1927. English edition: *Hesed in
the Bible.* Translation: A. Gottschalk with an introduction by G. A.
Larue. Cincinnati: The Hebrew Union College Press, 1967.

Goulder, M. D. *The Psalms of the Sons of Korah: A Study in the
Psalter.* Winona Lake, IN: Eisenbrauns, 1982.

Gruber, M. I. *Aspects of Nonverbal Communication in the Ancient
Near East.* 2 vols. Rome: Biblical Institute Press, 1980.

Gunkel, H. *Die Psalmen.* Göttinger Handkommentar zum Alten
Testament. Göttingen: Vandenhoeck & Ruprecht, 1926.

Gunkel, H. and J. Begrich. *Einleitung in die Psalmen: die Gattungen
der religiösen Lyrik Israels.* Göttinger Handkommentar zum Alten
Testament. Göttingen: Vandenhoeck & Ruprecht, 1933.

Haddix, J. L. "Lamentation as Personal Experience in Selected Psalms." Ph.D. diss., Boston University Graduate School, 1980.

Hallesby, O. *Prayer.* translated by C. J. Carlsen. Minneapolis: Augsburg Publishing House, 1937.

Harrelson, W. "A Meditation on the Wrath of God: Psalm 90." In *Scripture and Theology.* Festschrift J. C. Rylaarsdam. Pittsburg Theological Monograph Series 17, eds. A. L. Merill and T. W. Overholt, 181-191. Pittsburg: Pickwick, 1977.

Holladay, W. L. A. *A Concise Hebrew and Aramaic Lexicon of the Old Testament.* 12th. corrected impression. Grand Rapids: William B. Eerdmans; Leiden: E. J. Brill, 1991.

_____. *The Root šubh in the Old Testament.* Leiden: Brill, 1958.

Hummel, H. D. "Enclitic Mem in Early Northwest Semitic, especially Hebrew." *Journal of Biblical Literature* 76 (1957): 85-107.

Jacquet, L. *Les Psaumes et le coeur de l'homme. Étude textuelle, littéraire et doctrinale.* 3 vols. Gembloux: Duculot, 1975-77.

Jastrow, M. *A Dictionary of the Targumim, the Talmud Babli and Yerushalmi, and the Midrashic Literature.* 2 vols. New York, 1903; reprint New York: The Judaica Press, 1992.

Jepsen, A. "Warum? Eine lexikalische und theologische Studie." In *Das Ferne und nahe Wort.* Festschrift L. Rost. Beihefte zur Zeitschrift für die alttestamentliche Wissenschaft 105, ed. F. Maass, 106-113. Berlin: Töpelmann, 1967.

Johnson, A. R. "Hesed and Hasid." *Norsk Teologisk Tidsskrift* 56 (1955) = *Interpretationes ad Vetus Testamentum pertinentes Sigmundo Mowinckel septuagenario missae.* Oslo, Forlaget Land og Kirke, 1955, 100-112.

Joüon, P. and T. Muraoka. *A Grammar of Biblical Hebrew.* 2 vols. subsidia biblica 14/I-II. Rome: Editrice Pontificio Istituto Biblico, 1991, corrected reprint 1993.

Keel, O. *Feinde und Gottesleugner: Studium zum Image der Widersacher in den Individualpsalmen.* Stuttgarter Biblische Monographien 7. Stuttgart: Katholisches Bibelwerk, 1969.

_____. *The Symbolism of the Biblical World: Ancient Near Eastern Iconography and the Book of Psalms.* Translated by T. J. Hallet. New York: Seabury Press, 1978.

Kessler, M. "Inclusio in the Hebrew Bible." *Semitics* 6 (1978): 44-49.

Kim, E. K. *The Rapid Change of Mood in the lament Psalms.* Seoul: Theological Study Institute, 1985.

Koch, K. *The Growth of the Biblical Tradition. The Form Critical Method.* Translated by S. M. Cupitt. New York: Charles Scribner's Sons, 1969.

Koehler, L. and W. Baumgartner. *Lexicon in Veteris Testamenti Libros*. 3rd edition. Leiden: Brill, 1967-1990.

Kraus, H. J. "Der lebendige Gott." *Evangelische Theologie* 27 (1967): 169-200.

_____. *Psalms 1-59: A Commentary*. Translated by H. C. Oswald. Minneapolis: Augsburg, 1988.

_____. *Psalms 60-150: A Commentary*. Translated by H. C. Oswald. Minneapolis: Augsburg, 1989.

_____. *Theology of the Psalms*. translated by K. Crim. Minneapolis: Augsburg Publishing House, 1986.

Kugel, J. *The Idea of Biblical Poetry: Parallelism and its History*. New Haven: Yale University Press, 1981.

Lelièvre, A. "Yahweh et la mer dans les Psaumes." *Revue D'Histoire et de Philosophie Religieuses* 56 (1976): 253-275.

Ludwig, A. G. "Remembrance and Re-Presentation in Israel's Worship." STM Thesis, Concordia Seminary, St.Louis, 1991.

Lund, N. W. *Chiasmus in the New Testament: A Study in Formgeschichte*. Chapel Hill: The University of North Carolina Press, 1942.

_____. "Chiasmus in the Psalms." *American Journal of Semitic Languages and Literature* 49 (1933): 281-312.

Macintosh, A. A. "The Spider in the Septuagint Version of Psalm XC. 9." *Journal of Theological Studies* n.s. 23 (1972): 113-117.

Maillot, A. *Les Psaumes*. 3 vols. Vol. 1, 2nd. ed. Vol. 2-3, 1st. ed. Geneva: Labor et Fides, 1972, 1966, 1969.

Michel, W. L. "ṢLMWT, "Deep Darkness" or "Shadow of Death?" *Biblical Research* 29 (1984): 5-20.

Miller, P. D. "Current Issues in Psalms Studies." *Word and World* 5 (1985): 132-143.

_____. "Prayer as Persuasion: The Rhetoric and Intention of Prayer." *Word & World* 13 (1993): 356-362.

_____. "Trouble and Woe: Interpreting the Biblical Laments." *Interpretation* 37 (1983): 32-45.

Mirsky, A. "Stylistic Device for Conclusion in Hebrew." *Semitics* 5 (1977): 9-23.

Mowinckel, S. O. P. *Psalmenstudien*. 6 vols. Kristiania (= Oslo): Jacob Dybwad, 1921-1924.

_____. *The Psalms in Israel's Worship*. 2 vols. translated by D. R. Ap-Thomas, Oxford: Basil Blackwell, 1962, Reprint Sheffield: JSOT Press, 1992.

Muilenberg, J. "The Linguistic and Rhetorical Usage of the Particle *kî* in the Old Testament. *Hebrew Union College Annual* 32 (1961): 135-160.

_____. "A Study in Hebrew Rhetoric: Repetition and Style." *Supplement to Vetus Testamentum* 1 (1953): 97-116.

Müller, H. P. "Der 90. Psalm: Ein Paradigma exegetischer Aufgaben." *Zeitschrift für Theologie und Kirche* 81 (1984): 265-285.

Nötscher, F. *Die Psalmen*. Echter-Bibel. Würzberg: Echter-Verlag, 1953.

Oesterley, W. O. E. *The Psalms*. London: S.P.C.K., 1962.

Perlitt, L. "Anklage und Freispruch Gottes." *Zeitschrift für Theologie und Kirche* 69 (1972): 290-302.

_____. "Die Verborgenheit Gottes". In *Probleme biblischer Theologie*. Festschrift G. von Rad, ed. H. W. Wolff, 367-382. Munich: Chr. Kaiser, 1971.

Pritchard, J. B., ed. *Ancient Near Eastern Texts Relating to the Old Testament*. 3rd. ed. with Supplement. Princeton: Princeton University Press, 1969.

Raabe, P. R. "Deliberate Ambiguity in the Psalter." *Journal of Biblical Literature* 110 (1991): 213-227.

_____. "Human Suffering in Biblical Context." *Concordia Journal* 15 (1989): 139-155.

_____. *Psalm Structures: A Study of Psalms with Refrains*. Journal for the Study of the Old Testamant Supplement Series 104. Sheffield: JSOT Press, 1990.

_____. "The Two 'Faces' of Yahweh: Divine Wrath and Mercy in the Old Testament." *And Every Tongue Confess: Essays in Honor of Norman Nagel*, ed. G. S. Krispin and J. D. Vieker, 283-310. Chelsea, Michigan: Book Crafters, 1990.

Ridderbos, J. *De Psalmen*. Commentaar op het Oude Testament. Kampen: N. V. Uitgeversmaatschappij J. H. Kok, 1955.

Ridderbos, N. H. *Die Psalmen: Stylistische Verfahren und Aufbau mit besonderer Berucksichtigung von Ps 1-41*. Beihefte zur Zeitschrift für die alttestamentliche Wissenschaft 117. Berlin: Walter de Gruyter, 1972.

Ringgren, H. *The Faith of the Psalmists*. Philadelphia: Fortress, 1963.

_____. *Psaltaren 1-41*. Kommentar till Gamla Testamentet. Uppsala: EFS-förlaget, 1987.

Roberts, J. J. M. "Of Signs, Prophets, and Time Limits: A Note on

Sabourin, L. *The Psalms: Their Origin and Meaning*. 2 vols. Staten Island: Alba House, 1974.

Sakenfeld, K. D. *The Meaning of Hesed in the Hebrew Bible: A New Inquiry*. Harvard Semitic Monographs. Missoula: Scholars Press, 1978.

Schmidt, H. *Das Gebet der Angeklagten im Alten Testament*. Beiheft zur Zeitschrift für die alttestamentliche Wissenschaft 49. Giessen: Alfred Topelmann, 1928.

Schreiner, S. "Erwägungen zur Struktur des 90. Psalms." *Biblica* 59 (1978): 80-90.

Seybold, K. *Das Gebet des Kranken im Alten Testament*. Stuttgart: Verlag W. Kohlhammer, 1973.

Smit Sibinga, J. "Gedicht en getal. Over de compositie van Psalm 6." *Nederlands Theologisch Tijdschrift* 42 (1988): 185-207.

Sollamo, R. "The Simile in Ps 74:5: A Wood-cutter Entering a Forest Wielding Axes?" *Svensk Exegetisk Årsbok* 54 (1989): 178-187.

Stoebe, H. J. "Die Bedeutung des Wortes häsäd im Alten Testament." *Vetus Testamentum* 2 (1952): 244-254.

Tate, M. E. *Psalms 51-100*. Word Biblical Commentary. Dallas, TX: Word, 1990.

_____. "Psalm 88." *Review and Expositor* 87 (1990): 91-95

Terrien, S. *The Elusive Presence: The Heart of Biblical Theology*. San Francisco: Harper & Row, 1978.

Thomas, D. W. "צַלְמָוֶת in the Old Testament." *Journal of Semitic Studies* 7 (1962): 191-200.

_____. "A Note on זְרַמְתָּם שֵׁנָה יִהְיוּ in Psalm XC 5." *Vetus Testamentum* 18 (1968): 267-268.

Tournay, R. J. "Notes sur les Psaumes." *Revue Biblique* 79 (1972): 39-58.

Tsevat, M. "Psalm XC 5-6." *Vetus Testamentum* 35 (1985): 115-116.

Vawter, B. "Postexilic Prayer and Hope." *Catholic Biblical Quarterly* 37 (1975): 460-467.

Virolleau, C. *Le Palais Royal d'Ugarit V*. Mission de Ras Shamra XI. Paris: Imprimerie Nationale and Librairie C. Klincksieck, 1965.

Von Rad, G. *Old Testament Theology*. 2 vols. London: SCM, 1962-1965.

_____. "Psalm 90." Chapter 19 in *God at Work in Israel*, translated by J. H. Marks. Nashville: Abingdon, 1980.

_____. "Statements of Faith in the Old Testament about Life and about Death." Chapter 18 in *God at Work in Israel*, translated by J. H. Marks. Nashville: Abingdon, 1980 = *Allgemeine Evangelisch-Lutherische Kirchenzeitung* 71 (1938): 826-834.

Wahl, Th. P. "Strophic Structure of individual lamnets in Psalms Books I and II." Th.D. diss., Union Theological Seminary, New York, 1977.

Weber, F. *Vom Zorne Gottes: Ein biblisch-theologischer Versuch.* Erlangen: Andreas Deichert, 1862.

Weiser, A. *The Psalms.* Translated by H. Hartwell. Philadelphia: Westminster Press, 1962.

Weiss, M. *The Bible From Within: The Method of Total Interpretation.* Jerusalem: The Magnes Press, The Hebrew University, 1984.

_____. "Die Methode der 'Total-Interpretation': Von der Notwendigkeit der Struktur-Analyse für das Verständnis der biblischen Dichtung." *Supplement to Vetus Testamentum* 22 (1972): 88-112.

Westermann, C. "Boten des Zorns: Der Begriff des Zornes Gottes in der Prophetie." In *Die Botschaft und die Boten: Festschrift für Hans Walter Wolff,* eds. J. Jeremias and L. Perlitt, 147-156. Neukirchen-Vluyn: Neukirchener Verlag, 1981. The article is reprinted in *Erträge der Forschung am Alten Testament: Gesammelte Studien III.* Munich: Chr. Kaiser Verlag, 1984.

_____. "Der 90. Psalm: Zusammenhang und Aufbau." Pp. 344-350 in *Forschung am Alten Testament: Gesammelte Studien.* Theologische Bücherei. Munich: Chr. Kaiser Verlag, 1964.

_____. *The Living Psalms.* Translated by J. R. Porter. Grand Rapids: William B. Eerdmans, 1989 = *Ausgewählte Psalmen.* Göttingen: Vandenhoeck & Ruprecht, 1984.

_____. *Praise and Lament in the Psalms.* Translated by K. R. Crim and R. N. Soulen, Atlanta: John Knox Press, 1981.

_____. *What Does the Old Testament Say About God.* Edited by F. W. Golka. Atlanta: John Knox Press, 1979.

Whitley, C. "The Text of Psalm 90:5." *Biblica* 63 (1982): 555-557.

Widengren, G. "Konungens vistelse i dödsriket: En studie till Psalm 88," *Svensk Exegetisk Årsbok* 10 (1945): 66-81.

Willesen, F. "The Cultic Situation of Psalm LXXIV." *Vetus Testamentum* 2 (1952): 289-306.

Willis, J. T. "Alternating (ABA'B') Parallelism in the Old Testament psalms and prophetic Literature." In *Directions in Biblical Hebrew Poetry,* ed. E. R. Follis, 49-76. Journal for the Study of the Old Testament Supplement Series 40. Sheffield: JSOT Press, 1987.

Yaron, R. "The Meaning of ZANACH." *Vetus Testamentum* 13 (1963): 237-239.

Young, W. A. "Psalm 74: A Methodological and Exegetical Study."
   Ph.D. dissertation, The University of Iowa, Iowa City, 1974.
Ziegler, J. "Die Hilfe Gottes 'am Morgen.'" *Bonner Biblische Beitrage*
   1 (1950):281-288.

Author Index

Ackroyd, P. R., 71
Aejmelaeus, A., 41, 50, 54, 116
Airoldi, N., 37, 41, 44
Alter, R., 22
Andersen, F. I., 122, 156, 164,
165, 166
Anderson, A. A., 77, 79
Anderson, G. W., 36,
Auffret, P., 124, 125, 126

Balentine, S. E., 57, 103–4,
147, 148, 154, 155, 158
Baloian, B. E., 142, 143, 144,
152, 154, 164
Barr, J., 55, 70
Barth, C., 100, 140, 160
Baumgartner, W., 96
Beaucamp, 49, 51, 54, 72, 77,
79
Begrich, J., 18, 43
Bentzen, A., 20, 62 63, 96,
176
Berlin, A., 22
Bertholet, A., 96
Birkeland, H., 35, 40
Booij, Th., 117, 118
Boyce, R. N., 173
Branson, R. D. 30
Briggs, C. A. & E. G., 30, 37,
38, 39, 40, 60, 73, 79, 81,
104, 107, 119

Broyles, C. C., 17, 19, 20, 21,
40, 60, 85, 89, 107, 127, 138
Brug, J. F., 29, 70
Bryn, E., 89
Buss, M. J., 49, 70
Buttenwieser, M., 29, 40, 70

Calès, J., 28, 29, 38, 40, 49,
51, 72, 96, 97
Caquot, A., 104, 105,
Castellino, G., 14, 20, 84, 96,
104, 105, 106, 107, 115, 116,
117, 119, 120, 121, 126, 127,
129, 135, 138
Childs, B. S., 151
Clark, G. R., 165, 166, 168
Coppens, J., 29
Craigie, P. C., 35, 37, 38, 39,
41 52, 53, 55, 60, 61, 135,
138
Cunchillos, J. L., 105

Dahood, M., 35, 37, 50, 51,
54, 58, 77, 81, 82, 95–96,
97, 100, 101, 104, 106, 119,
123, 158
Delekat, L., 34, 94–5
Delitzsch, F., 28, 32, 39, 49,
52, 53, 58, 63, 72, 76, 79, 81,
97, 104, 106, 107, 114, 119,
122

Donald, T., 82
Donner, H., 70, 72, 78

Eberlein, K., 80, 89
Eichrodt, W., 143
Eising, H., 33, 81
Emerton, J. A., 80

Fenton, T. L., 34
Follis, E. R., 38
Freedmann, D. N., 31, 38, 122,
  144, 156
Fretheim, T. E., 143, 154–5,
  156, 158, 164, 166
Fuhs, H. F., 121

Gelston, A., 74
Gerstenberger, E. S.,19, 21,
  138
Gibson, J. C. L., 35, 88, 97,
  104, 173
Girard, M., 39, 49, 50, 54,
  64
Glueck, N., 163, 165, 166
Goulder, M. D., 49, 107
Grelot, P., 97–8
Gruber, M. I., 57-8, 71, 102,
  144, 145
Gunkel, H., 18, 19, 32, 33, 35,
  36, 37, 38, 39, 40, 54, 60, 72,
  76, 77, 80, 81, 82, 89, 96, 98,
  99, 100, 101, 104, 106, 107,
  116, 119, 120, 121, 130, 141

Haddix, J. L., 98, 100, 101,
  104, 105
Hallesby, O., 157

Harrelson, W., 127
Heintz, J.G., 96
Herdner, A., 100,
Holladay, W. L., 31, 32, 79
Hummel, H. D., 78, 99

Jacquet, L., 28, 29, 49, 56, 64,
  77, 79, 81, 98, 118
Jepsen, A., 70, 168
Johnsen, E., 144
Johnson, A. R., 163

Keel, O., 35, 99
Kessler, M., 85
Kim, E. K., 44
Knight, G. A. F., 143
Koch, K. 74
Kraus, H. J., 28, 29, 32, 49, 64,
  72, 78, 77, 79, 81, 97, 100,
  101, 115, 117, 118, 119, 120,
  121, 122, 124, 140
Krispin, G. S., 169
Kugel, J. L., 22, 98, 123, 124,
  130

Lelièvre, A., 20, 28, 33, 77, 79,
  81, 121, 122
Leupold, H. C., 40, 50
Lohfink, N., 144
Ludwig, A. G., 33
Lund, N. W., 38
Lundblom, J., 31, 144
Lunde, 89
Luther, M, 14, 89

Maass, F., 70
Macintosh, A. A., 119

Maillot, A., 20, 28, 33, 121, 122
Marböck, J., 82
Mayer, G., 30
Merrill, A. L., 127
Michel, W. L., 55
Miller, P. D., 154
Mirsky, A., 38
Mowinckel, S., 17, 18, 19, 21, 28, 29, 35, 36, 49, 61, 70, 94, 107, 124
Müller, H. P., 114, 116, 120, 123, 126, 137
Myhre, K., 89

Nagel, N., 169
Niehr, H., 55
Nötscher, F., 52, 53, 79, 81, 96, 97, 105, 116, 118, 120, 121, 122

O'Brien, P. T., 164
Oesterley, W. O. E., 64
Overholt, T. W., 127

Parker Jr. H. M., 49
Perlitt, L. 57
Peterson, D. G., 1648
Pritchard, J. B., 13, 88

Raabe, P. R., 18, 23, 108, 135, 140, 141, 160, 169
Ridderbos, J., 39, 40, 42, 60, 77, 79, 81, 106, 115, 118
Rieterer, F., 53
Ringer, H., 147
Ringgren, H., 16-17, 56, 130

Rylaarsdam, J. C., 127

Sabourin, L., 40, 50
Sakenfeld, K., 163, 164
Schmidt, H., 35
Schreiner, J., 70
Schreiner, S., 126
Schunck, K. D., 144
Seebaß, H. 36
Seybold, K., 43, 107, 138
Sibinga, S., 38, 39
Simian-Yofre, H., 122
Sollamo, R., 72
Stoebe, H. J., 163, 164, 165
Sznycer, M., 104

Tarragin, J. M. de, 105
Tate, M. E. 76, 77, 79, 81, 82, 83, 95, 96, 97, 98, 99, 100, 104, 105, 106, 114, 117, 119, 120, 122, 135
Terrien, S., 153–4
Thomas, D. W., 54
Tournay, R. J., 117
Tsevat, M., 117

Vawter, B., 114, 121
Vieker, J. D., 169
Virolleau, C., 104–5
von Rad, G., 57, 126, 139

Wahl, T. P., 38, 39
Weber, F., 143, 144
Weiser, A., 43, 49, 50, 51, 77, 115
Weiss, M., 21, 22, 43, 47, 84, 85, 135, 137

Westermann, C., 19, 21, 126,
170, 171, 172
Whitley, C., 117
Widengren, G., 97, 98, 107
Wiklander, B., 144
Willesen, F., 85
Willis, J. T., 38
Wolf, H. W., 57

Yaron, R., 56, 57, 145
Young, W. A., 70, 71, 74, 76,
77, 79, 80, 81, 82, 83, 84, 85

Ziegler, J., 70 110, 118, 123
Zobel, H. J., 165

Scripture Index

Genesis

1:14—81
1:21—78
1:26—121
1:26–27—154
3:19—127, 150
3:27—30
7:11—80
12:1—52
12:18—70
18:28—118
18:30—41
18:32—41
20:11—121
21:25—30
25:7—119
25:8—104
27:37—100
31:30—70
34:7—82
35:18—116
40:15—54
41:21—73
47:29—30

Exodus

2:13—70
2:23–25—173
3:7–12—173
3:12—171

3:15—33, 171
6:2–8—173
6:6—86
7:9—78
7:10—78
7:12—78
9:33—102
12:29—96
13:12–13—58
14—79
15:13—86
17:6—79
18:18—31
19:4–6—86
20:2–5—175
20:5–6—159, 164, 169
21:2—97, 108
21:5—97
21:34—96
22:20–23—173
28:3—122
29:10—100
31:6—122
32:12—32, 156, 173
32:14—123
34:6—30
34:6–7—159, 164, 166, 173
34:7—169
35:26—122
35:35—122
36:2—122

Leviticus

1:4—100
16:29—95
17:15—95
23:4–8—74
26:15–16—147

Numbers

2:2—72
3:45—58
3:46–48—58
6:25—51
8:12—100
11:31—121
11:32—102
14:18—166
14:18–19—164
15:31—77
16:21—37
20—79
20:8—79
30:9—77
30:14—77

Deuteronomy

6:5—58
6:11—96
7:9–10—164
8:2–3—123
8:10—171
8:16—123
13:6—58
21:18—30
22:21—82

28—151, 159
30—151
30:15–19—139
31:17—57
32—114
32:4—123
32:6—82
32:7—123
32:8—81
32:15—82
32:33—78
32:36—122, 123
33—114
33:1—114

Joshua

2:12—163
7:6—57, 65
7:7—65
14:6—114

Judges

1:8—73
2:1—77
2:12—147
2:18—122
5:26—75
7:19—117
9:26—52
14:5—87
20:6—82
20:48—73
21—122
21:6—122
21:15—122

Ruth

2:2—30
2:10—30
2:13—30

1 Samuel

2:5—31
6:10—101
9:10—114
11:11—117
13:14—121
14:45—58

2 Samuel

1:17-27—29
3:33—82
3:33-34—29
7:23—58
8:5-14—49
9:10—122
13:12—82
13:13—82
17:19—102
22:5—100
22:6—32
24:1—145

1 Kings

5:11—95
8:31-32—35
8:38—102
13:4-11—114
15:19—77

2 Kings

8:1-3—173
8:12—73
10:11—101
17:15—147
19:21—53
23:16—156
23:26—32, 124

1 Chronicles

2:6—95
9:17-24—49
15:17—95
15:19—69, 95
15:21—28
16:5—69
17:21—58
25:1—95
25:5—95
25:6—95
26:1-19—49

2 Chronicles

18:4—114
26:21—99
29:14—95
32:21—53

Ezra

9:7—53
9:14—77

Nehemiah

2:6—38
9:17—166
12:24—114
12:36—114

Esther

2:17—30
5:2—30
9:28—33

Job

2:10—82
2:11—53
3:5—55
3:8—78
3:11—104
3:19—97, 98
7:12—78
10:21–22—55
12:14—101
12:23—102
13:3—30
13:10—30
14:18—34
18:4—34
19:14—101
21:7—34
21:13—37
24:17—54
26:5—102
26:6—103
28:3—55
28:22—32, 103
28:28—121, 129

30:9—29
30:23—32
31:12—103
34:11—123
34:20—37
37:2—119
38:4—115
38:4–11—115
38:17—55
38:28—116
40:25—78
41—78

Psalms

2:9—50
2:11—121
3:1—29
3:5—49
4:1—28
4:2—30
4:7—51
5:6—36
5:8—121
5:10—32
6—14, 21, 27, 34, 35, 38, 135,
    136, 138, 140, 152, 155, 156,
    159, 174
6:1, 28
6:2—29–30, 41, 45, 144, 149,
    151, 155
6:2–11—38
6:3—30, 31, 37, 41, 107, 149,
    157, 159–60
6:3–4—42, 44, 45, 128, 136,
    151
6:3–11—39
6:4—31, 37, 41, 42, 168

6:4–6—141
6:5—31–32, 37, 44, 122, 155,
  156, 167
6:6—32–33, 41, 45, 141, 149,
  160, 171, 172
6:6–9—43
6:7—34, 118
6:7–8—42, 44, 45, 136, 141,
  172
6:8—34–35, 102, 109, 135,
  145
6:9—36, 174
6:9–11—159
6:11—31, 36–37, 151
6:12—153
6:13—153
7:1—29
7:16—96
8:5—54
9—14, 20, 21, 135, 138, 144,
  148
9:1–11—138
9:12–21—138
9:13—148
9:14—30
9:18—37
10—14, 20, 135, 138, 144,
  148, 173
10:1—70, 104, 147, 147, 155,
  174
10:1–18—138
10:3–11—139
10:6—115
10:11—57, 147, 148 173
10:12—148
10:13—139, 173, 174
10:15—139, 160
11:6—116

12:1—28
13—18, 21, 135, 138, 140, 171
13:2—57, 147, 148, 155, 158,
  168
13:2–3—141, 1768
13:3—139
13:3–4—138
13:4—171
13:5—139
13:6—167
14:1—82
14:4—36
16:6–7—119
16:7—70
17:1—96
18:6—32
18:46—31
19:13—118
19:33—119
21:4—103
22—14, 21, 35, 134, 138, 141,
  147, 150, 153, 154, 169, 171
22:2—70, 148, 147, 174
22:2–3—141, 158, 171
22:3–6—147
22:4—160
22:5–6—141, 169
22:6—36, 160
22:7–11—172
22:7–12—169
22:8—43, 53
22:8–9—141
22:9—43
22:10–11—141, 160, 171
22:11—171
22:12—107, 141, 148, 158,
  171
22:13–14—139

22:15–16—138
22:16—150
22:17—139
22:18—138
22:19—43, 139
22:20—142, 148
22:20–21—160
22:23–29—160
25:7—167
25:9—116
25:20—36
25:22—58
27:7—49
27:9—130
28:1—96
28:3—36
28:12—119
30:4—96
30:5—33
30:6—169
30:8—57, 128
31—34
31:2—36
31:3—114–15
31:10—30, 34
31:11—34
31:12—101
31:17—51, 130
31:18—36, 37
32:2—32
32:3—31
34:12—122
34:17—33
35—21, 135, 138
35:1—139
35:1–8—171
35:4—139
35:7—139

35:9—172
35:11–12—139
35:11–16—172
35:15—153
35:15–16—139
35:17—141, 149, 168, 172
35:18—172
35:19–21—139
35:23—149, 171
35:24—171
36:6—103
36:10—140
37:31—54
38:2—29, 30,
39—14, 21, 135, 139, 150, 153
39:5–7—142
39:6—139, 150
39:9—152
39:10—150, 159
39:11—118, 151
39:12—151
41:5—30
41:11—30
42—14, 18, 21, 49, 135, 138,
    141, 144
42:2—141
42:2–3—160
42:3—139
42:4—160
42:4–5—160
42:5—141
42:7—171
42:7–8—160
42:8—100, 105, 108, 141, 150
42:9—139, 141, 160
42:10—139, 148, 160, 174
42:12—171

43—14, 18, 21, 49, 135, 138, 144
43:2—174
43:3–4—172
43:4–5—171
44—14, 15, 20, 47-48, 49, 136, 137, 139, 146, 150, 153, 154, 157, 161, 169, 173, 176
44:1—49, 94
44:2—61, 123
44:2–4—67
44:2–9—66
44:2–27—59, 60
44:3—49, 50, 63, 99, 139
44:3–4—140
44:4—50, 51, 54, 61, 169
44:4–8—62
44:5—50, 61, 64, 67
44:5–9—67, 161
44:6—136
44:6–9—66
44:7—61, 64
44:8—54, 63, 67
44:8–9—136
44:9—52, 63, 64, 65
44:10—52, 148, 149
44:10–12—140
44:10–13—66
44:10–15—62
44:10–17—67, 136
44:10–23—169
44:11—70, 150
44:11–13—142
44:11-15—52, 64
44:12—64, 67, 150, 151, 171
44:13—52, 67, 150, 151, 171
44:14—151
44:14–11,150

44:14–17—63, 66
44:15—53
44:16—53, 65
44:17—53
44:17–23—64, 136
44:18—64, 65, 67, 148, 153, 170, 173
44:18–22—67, 176
44:18–23—66, 159, 173, 174
44:19—53–54
44:19–23—153
44:20—54–55, 65, 151
44:21—54, 56, 171
44:21–22—159
44:22—54, 56
44:23—54, 65, 154
44:24—56, 66, 70, 104, 146, 147, 149, 155, 168
44:24–25—136, 151, 174
44:24–27—147
44:25—57, 66, 104, 147, 148, 158, 172
44:25–26—67
44:26—57
44:27—58, 65, 66, 67, 149, 157, 160, 167, 173
45—49
46—49
46:6—110, 123
47—49
48—49
49—49
49:15—32
49:16—58
50—67
51:3—31, 167
51:8—122
53:2—82

54:1—28
55:1—28
55:14—101
57—20
58:3—52
58:5—145
59:14—76
60—14, 20, 135, 139, 150
60:3—144, 145, 146
60:4—139, 140, 150
60:5—150, 171
60:7—49
60:12—139, 149
61:1—28
61:2—96
63:8—58
64:10—123
67:1—28
67:2—51
69:2-3—99, 108
69:4—34
69:13—28
69:16—99
69:17-18—57
69:18—130
71:3—114, 115
71:13—118
71:23—58
73—69
73:19—37
73:24—161
74—14, 15, 20, 21, 68–69, 70
  71, 77, 80, 136, 137, 139,
  141 155, 157, 159, 169, 170,
  173, 174
74:1—65, 69, 70, 84, 86, 91,
  92, 103, 144, 146, 154, 168,
  171, 174

74:1-2—137
74:1-3—84, 85, 88
74:2—71, 84, 85, 86, 87, 88,
  91, 92, 139, 171
74:2-3—149
74:3—71, 84, 86 87, 91
74:4—72, 75, 84, 87, 91
74:4-8—84, 86, 87, 91, 92
74:4-11—84
74:5—72, 73, 86
74:5-6—84, 87
74:6—73
74:7—73, 87, 92
74:8—73-74, 84, 87
74:9—72, 75, 84, 86, 87, 91,
  137, 149, 168
74:9-10—141
74:10—71, 85, 90, 91, 92, 122,
  138, 154, 168
74:10-11—84-85
74:11—75, 91,99, 141-42,
  149, 155, 174
74:12—78, 85, 86, 92, 137
  140
74:12-17—79, 84, 85, 89, 173
74:13—76, 77, 86
74:13-14—89, 99, 170
74:14—77, 78, 88
74:15—71, 80, 89
74:15-17—89, 170
74:16—81
74:16-18—172
74:17—81, 157
74:18—81, 82, 85, 90, 91, 92,
  172 174
74:18-23—84, 85, 137, 148
74:19—71, 82, 83, 85, 90, 91,
  92, 148, 172

74:19–21—136
74:20—83, 90, 91, 92, 139, 148, 170, 173
74:21—83, 85, 92, 147, 172
74:22—85, 90, 92, 147
74:23—84, 85, 92, 148
75—69
76—69
76:1—28
76:6—117
77—20, 69, 135, 167, 169
77:7—28
77:8—146, 168
77:8–10—162, 167
77:9—168
77:10—119, 148
77:12—102
77:12–21—162, 170
77:15—102
77:16—139, 171
77:17–20–170
77:17–21—89
77:18—117
77:21—171
78—69
78:11—148
78:57—53
79—14, 20, 69, 135, 139
79:5—141, 144, 145–46, 153, 168
79:6—145, 153, 174
79:8—153
79:9—153
79:10—174
79:13—115, 171, 172
80—14, 20, 69, 135, 139, 150, 169

80:2—171
80:4—51, 161
80:5—141, 157, 168, 171
80:6—150
80:7—150
80:8—51, 157, 161
80:9—139, 169
80:9–10—140
80:9–11—139
80:10–12—169
80:12—50
80:13—150, 169, 174
80:13–14—139, 140
80:14—157, 170
80:15—155
80:17 139
80:18–19—161
80:20—51, 161
81—69
82—69
83—69
84—49
85—20, 49, 135
85:2—171
85:3—153, 171
85:4—144, 145
85:4–5—145
85:6—144, 168
85:7—171
85:8—167
85:11—167
86:15—166, 167
87—49, 95
88—14, 15, 21, 49, 93–94, 136, 138, 140, 141, 147, 147, 153, 154, 155, 158, 160, 172, 1784

88:1—94–95
88:2—95, 106, 109, 111, 112, 136, 141, 158, 171
88:2–3—106, 111
88:2–9—106
88:3—96, 103, 110, 111, 112, 160
88:4—107
88:4–6—111
88:4–7—106
88:5—96-97
88:6—97-99, 108, 111, 112, 136, 161
88:6–7—141
88:7—99, 109, 111
88:7–9—158
88:8—100, 106, 108, 109, 110, 111, 112, 136, 145, 150
88:9—101, 106, 109, 111, 136, 150
88:10—102, 106, 111, 141
88:10–13—106
88:11—102
88:11–13—111, 112, 141, 158, 167, 171
88:12—982, 103, 109, 111, 112
88:13—102, 103, 109, 112
88:14—111, 112, 136, 141
88:14–15—57, 103
88:14–19—106
88:15—65, 70, 104, 107, 111, 146, 147
88:16—104-5, 111, 147
88:16–18—111, 112
88:17—105, 110, 111, 145
88:17–18—106, 150
88:18—111

88:19—105, 106, 111, 141, 150
89—14, 20, 95, 135, 139, 142, 146–47, 150, 151, 154, 161, 167, 168, 171, 173
89:2—103, 168
89:3—168
89:6—102, 168
89:15—103, 168
89:16—51
89:25—103, 168
89:27—171
89:29—168
89:34—103, 168
89:36—56
89:39—145, 148, 151
89:39–43—142
89:39–46—139
89:40—171
89:41—150, 151
89:41–42—140
89:43—150, 151
89:43–44—140
89:44—150
89:45–47—150
89:46—154
89:47—145, 147, 151, 168
89:48—139
89:48–49—174
89:50—167, 168
89:51—171
90—14, 20, 113–14, 127, 131, 136, 138, 139, 142, 143, 150, 152, 153, 156
90:1—114, 115, 125, 126, 127, 130, 131, 132, 137, 138, 162, 171

90:1–2—124, 126, 127, 140,
  173
90:2—115, 116, 129, 139
90:3—116, 125, 150
90:3–4—124, 125
90:3–12—126, 128
90:3–15—125
90:4—116, 117, 118, 129, 143
90:5—117, 118, 128, 130, 150
90:5–6—128
90:5–10—124, 125
90:6—118,
90:7—118, 119, 128, 129, 131,
  144, 150
90:7–10—142
90:8—118, 128, 151, 152
90:9—118, 119, 128, 129, 130,
  145, 151
90:10—119, 120, 121, 128,
  129, 131
90:11—121, 129, 144, 145,
  162
90:11–12—124, 124, 125, 137
90:12—122, 129, 131, 152,
  156, 162
90:13—31, 32, 38, 122, 126,
  129, 130, 131, 132, 137, 155,
  156, 162, 168, 171
90:13–15—124, 125
90:13–17—126
90:14—110, 123, 130, 131,
  167
90:14–15—132
90:15—123, 130, 151
90:16—123, 126, 130, 132,
  171
90:16–17—124, 126, 162

90:17—124, 126, 131, 132,
  171
91:9—114, 115
94:10—29, 30
94:17—58
97—33
98:3—103
100:3—89
102—21, 28, 135, 138, 139,
  150
102:2–3—57
102:4–12—138
102:9—139
102:11—146, 150
102:24—150
102:24–25—138
102:25—171
103:1–2—104
103:6—109
103:8—166, 167
103:9—169
104—78
104:8—71
104:26—78
104:29—57
105:43—96
106:13—148
106:19–20—148
106:21—148
106:43—98-99
107:22—96
108—20, 135
109:26—167
111:3—124
111:4—33
111:10—121
121:4—149

124:4–5—101
129:5—36
132:3—56
132:4—56
135:1–14—33
135:14—122, 123
136—168
137:1—83
138:3—120
139:10—75, 99
140:4—145
143:5—123
143:6–7—57
143:8—123
145:7—33
145:8—166, 167

Proverbs

1:7—121, 129
1:22–13—38
2:1–4—122
2:5—122
2:6—122
2:11–12—122
2:13–22—122
3:12—26
5:5—32
6:1–5—120
6:3—120
7:27—32
8:13—121
8:24—116
9:7—30
9:10—121
11:15—50
14:27—121
15:11—103

15:12—30
15:16—51
15:33—121
16:6—121
19:18—30
19:23—121
23:15—122
27:19—30
30:25–26—79
31:20—56

Ecclesiastes

12:1—81

Song of Songs (Canticles)

6:5—120
8:6—32

Isaiah

1:13–14—74
1:29—36
2:4—29
3:5—120
5:25—145
8:9—50
9:1—55
10:13—81
10:25—169
11:2–3—121
11:4—29
14:15—96
14:19—98
20:5—36
22:14—56
25:9—71

26:14—33, 102
26:19—102
27:1—78
32:6—82
33:9—31
34:12–15—54
38:18—96
38:20—28
43:1—89
47:7—81
47:9—37
51:9—78
51:9–10—89
51:10—78
53:8—99
54:7–8—169
54:8—169
57:6—123
57:16—169
59:13—53
59:16—100
63:17—31, 89
64:8—30

Jeremiah

2:6—55–56
2:13—140
2:19—30
3:12—169
4:14—54
4:20—37
5:22—81
7:19—53
8:2—102
8:6—123
10:16—86
10:22—54

10:24—30, 40
11:20—76
14:21—77
15:6—122
15:15—30
16:5—53
17:8—50
17:11—82
17:13—140
22:10—53
31:1—98-99
31:12—102
31:21—38
31:25—102
31:33—98-9
32:2–3—101
32:40—121
37:16—96
38:22—53
41:5—74
44:7—70
45:3—34
46:13—72
46:22–23—72–73
49:33—54
51:19—86
51:38—104
51:39—117

Lamentations

2:7—56
2:8—31
2:10—83
2:19—117, 118
2:22—52
3:7—101
3:14—28

3:22–23—110
3:31–33—169
3:54—99
5:14—28

Ezekiel

2:10—119
9:8—57
10:18–19—86
11:13—57
11:22–23—86
16:63—36
17:6—50
19:2—52
23:43—73
24:2—100, 108
29:3—54
32:2—54
32:19–27—108
32:20–32—98
32:23—96
32:24—98
37:11—99

Daniel

9:7–8—53

Hosea

4:3—31
8:3—56
8:5—56
10:11—87

12:6—33

Joel

2:13—123, 166, 167
4:3—52

Amos

2:6—52
3:6—152
3:8—87
5:8—55
5:23—94
6:5—94

Jonah

2:4—100
3:9—32, 122, 156
4:2—167

Micah

3:4—57
4:3—29
6:4—58
7:18–20—169

Nahum

1:3—166
1:4—31
3:18—117

Habakkuk

2:5—32
2:17—72
3:2—123
3:15—49
3:19—28

Haggai

1:6—122

Zechariah

1:8—99
10:11—99

1 Maccabees

3:46—74

Mark

10:45—58

Romans

8:36—64